Whatever It Is, I'm Against It

An Encyclopedia of Classical and Contemporary Abhorrence, Abnegation, Abomination, Abuse, Acrimony, Anger, Animosity, Annoyance, Antipathy, Aversion, Bitchery, Bitterness, Calumny, Cynicism, Derogation, Detestation, Disaffection, Disgust, Disparagement, Distemper, Execration, Hatred, Hostility, Insolence, Insult, Invective, Irony, Loathing, Malevolence, Malice, Malignity, Odium, Perversity, Pique, Rancor, Resentment, Revulsion, Sarcasm, Spite, Spleen, Umbrage, Venom, Vilification, Vituperation and Downright Nastiness

Compiled and Edited by

Nat Shapiro

Simon and Schuster   New York

Published by Simon and Schuster
A Division of Simon & Schuster, Inc.
Simon & Schuster Building
Rockefeller Center
1230 Avenue of the Americas
New York, New York 10020
SIMON AND SCHUSTER and colophon are registered
trademarks of Simon & Schuster, Inc.

Designed by Levavi & Levavi

Manufactured in the United States of America

10 9 8 7 6 5 4 3 2 1

Library of Congress Cataloging in Publication Data
Main entry under title:
Whatever it is, I'm against it.
    1.Quotations, English.   I.Shapiro, Nat.
PN6081.W39   1984   082   84-5432
ISBN 0-671-49748-0
ISBN 0-671-50837-7 (pbk.)

"Whatever It Is, I'm Against It" is the title of a song written by
Harry Ruby and Bert Kalmar, introduced by Groucho Marx in
the 1932 film *Horsefeathers.*

This book is dedicated to the proposition that "There is no fate that cannot be surmounted by scorn."[1] Chosen with reckless impartiality, the quotations that follow assiduously lay waste to art, automobiles, and astrology; besmirch the fair names of beauty, Beethoven, and James Bond; calumniate children, Christmas, and civilization . . . well, you get the idea.

A vast abundance of diverse and widely scattered sources—literary and otherwise—was meticulously mined to produce this collection of invective and insult. It is a distillation of venom from the pens of great misanthropes throughout history and in our time.

For those who are hostile, perverse, frustrated, disenchanted, or disillusioned, this book is offered as a purgative for pique, a cathartic celebration. The hopelessly optimistic, the incorrigibly romantic, and anyone who holds *anything* sacred are advised to proceed with caution through these spleen-filled pages.

So let the reader, amply forewarned, revel in rancor and luxuriate in loathing:

> Now Hatred is by far the longest pleasure;
> Men love in haste, but they detest at leisure.[2]

[1] Albert Camus, *The Myth of Sisyphus* (1955)
[2] Lord Byron, *Don Juan* (1819–24)

THERE IS NO FATE THAT CANNOT
BE SURMOUNTED BY SCORN.

ALBERT CAMUS
THE MYTH OF SISYPHUS, 1955

ABSOLUTE

Objection, evasion, distrust and irony are signs of health. Everything absolute belongs to pathology.

FRIEDRICH WILHELM NIETZSCHE
Beyond Good and Evil, 1886

ABSTRACT ART

Abstract art? A product of the untalented, sold by the unprincipled to the utterly bewildered.

AL CAPP
Quoted in the *National Observer*,
July 1, 1963

ACADEMY AWARD

Nothing would disgust me more, morally, than receiving an Oscar.

LUIS BUÑUEL
Quoted in *Films and Filming*,
June 1971

ACCORDION

Accordion, n. An instrument in harmony with the sentiments of an assassin.

AMBROSE BIERCE
The Devil's Dictionary,
1906, 1911

ACHIEVEMENT

Achievement, n. The death of endeavor and the birth of disgust.

> AMBROSE BIERCE
> *The Devil's Dictionary,*
> 1906, 1911

ACQUAINTANCE

The art of life is to keep down acquaintances. One's friends one can manage, but one's acquaintances can be the devil.

> EDWARD VERRALL LUCAS
> *Over Bremerton's,* 1923

ACTORS AND ACTING

Every actor has a natural animosity toward every other actor, present or absent, living or dead.

> LOUISE BROOKS
> *Lulu in Hollywood,* 1982

The most important thing in acting is honesty. If you can fake that, you've got it made.

> Attributed to GEORGE BURNS

I've known some actors who were intelligent, but the better the actor, the more stupid he is.

> TRUMAN CAPOTE
> Quoted in *Popcorn in Paradise,*
> edited by John Robert Colombo, 1979

The strolling tribe; a despicable race.

> CHARLES CHURCHILL
> *Apology,* 1761

What a set of barren asses are actors.

> JOHN KEATS
> Letter to his sister, 1819

They come for you in the morning in a limousine; they take you to the studio; they stick a pretty girl in your arms. . . . They call that a profession? Come on!

> MARCELLO MASTROIANNI
> In an interview, 1970s

Some of the greatest love affairs I've known have involved one actor—unassisted.

> Attributed to WILSON MIZNER

Acting is a masochistic form of exhibitionism. It is not quite the occupation of an adult.

> SIR LAURENCE OLIVIER
> *Time,* July 3, 1978

I made the mistake early in my career, when I moved to Hollywood, of being attracted to actresses. I used to go out exclusively with actresses and all other female impersonators.

> MORT SAHL
> *Heartland,* 1976

ADAMS, JOHN

It has been the political career of this man to begin with hypocrisy, proceed with arrogance, and finish in contempt.

> THOMAS PAINE
> *Open letter to the Citizens of*
> *the United States,* November 22, 1802

ADJECTIVE

As to the adjective; when in doubt, strike it out.

> Attributed to MARK TWAIN

ADMIRATION

Ignorance is the mother of admiration.

> GEORGE CHAPMAN
> *The Widow's Tears,* 1612

ADOLESCENT

The adolescent, though given to aggression and lust, is emotionally cold, and ratiocination can be a substitute for feeling.

> ANTHONY BURGESS
> *Urgent Copy,* 1968

ADULTS

Grown-ups never understand anything for themselves, and it is tiresome for children to be always and forever explaining things to them.

> ANTOINE DE SAINT-EXUPÉRY
> *The Little Prince,* 1943

ADVANCEMENT

The path of social advancement is, and must be, strewn with broken friendships.

H. G. WELLS
Kipps, 1905

ADVERSARY

I respect only those who resist me, but I cannot tolerate them.

CHARLES DE GAULLE
The New York Times Magazine,
May 12, 1968

ADVERTISING

Advertising is a racket . . . its constructive contribution to humanity is exactly minus zero.

F. SCOTT FITZGERALD
The Crack-Up, serialized in *Esquire*,
1936

Advertising may be described as the science of arresting the human intelligence long enough to get money from it.

STEPHEN LEACOCK
The Garden of Folly, 1924

Advertising is the rattling of a stick inside a swill bucket.

Attributed to GEORGE ORWELL

Freedom! to spit in the eye and in the soul of the passerby and the passenger with advertising.

Attributed to
ALEXANDER I. SOLZHENITSYN

Advertising is legalized lying.
Attributed to H. G. WELLS

ADVICE

All people are offensive when they give advice.

JOHN GALSWORTHY
The Roof, 1929

Please give me some good advice in your next letter. I promise not to follow it.

EDNA ST. VINCENT MILLAY
Letters, 1952

I always pass on good advice. It is the only thing to do with it. It is never any use to oneself.

OSCAR WILDE
An Ideal Husband, 1899

It is always a silly thing to give advice, but to give good advice is absolutely fatal.

OSCAR WILDE
The Portrait of Mr. W.H., 1889

AFFECTION

Most affections are habits or duties we lack the courage to end.

HENRY DE MONTHERLANT
Queen After Death, 1942

AFRICA

Africa has no future.

V. S. NAIPAUL
The New York Times Book Review,
May 13, 1979

AGENT

I dreamed the devil appeared the other night and wanted to make a bargain for my soul and the William Morris Agency handled the deal. They got me damned to hell for eternity—with options.

WOODY ALLEN
Show Business Illustrated,
October 17, 1961

AGES OF MAN

Youth is a blunder; manhood a struggle; old age a regret.

BENJAMIN DISRAELI
Coningsby, 1844

When a man is young he is so wild he is insufferable. When he is old he plays the saint and becomes insufferable again.

NIKOLAI GOGOL
Gamblers, 1842

He that is not handsome at 20, nor strong at 30, nor rich at 40, nor wise at 50, will never be handsome, strong, rich or wise.

GEORGE HERBERT
Outlandish Proverbs, 1640

Next to the very young, I suppose the very old are the most selfish.
WILLIAM MAKEPEACE THACKERAY
The Virginians, 1857–59

AGING

The only good thing about it [aging] is you're not dead.
Attributed to LILLIAN HELLMAN

AGREEMENT

It is by universal misunderstanding that all agree. For if, by ill luck, people understood each other, they would never agree.
CHARLES BAUDELAIRE
Intimate Journals, 1887

AIR

Air, n. A nutritious substance supplied by a bountiful Providence for the fattening of the poor.
AMBROSE BIERCE
The Devil's Dictionary, 1906, 1911

AIRPLANES

If God had intended us to fly he would never have given us railways.
MICHAEL FLANDERS
Quoted in his obituary,
The New York Times, April 16, 1975

The conquest of the air, so jubilantly hailed by general opinion, may turn out the most sinister event that ever befell us.
JOHN GALSWORTHY
The Observer, London, 1923

Thank God, men cannot as yet fly, and lay waste the sky as well as the earth!
HENRY DAVID THOREAU
Journal, January 3, 1861

ALLEGORY

I would rather see the portrait of a dog that I know, than all the allegorical paintings they can show me in the world.
SAMUEL JOHNSON
Quoted in Birkbeck Hill's
Johnsonian Miscellanies, 1897

ALMS

There is no one on earth more disgusting and repulsive than he who gives alms. Even as there is no one so miserable as he who accepts them.

MAXIM GORKY
Foma Gordyieff, 1899

ALPS

Such uncouth rocks and such uncomely inhabitants! . . . I hope I shall never see them again.

HORACE WALPOLE
Letter to Richard West,
November 11, 1739

ALTRUISM

No good deed goes unpunished.
CLARE BOOTHE LUCE
quoted in *Clare Boothe Luce,* by
Wilfrid Sheed, 1982

Every major horror of history was committed in the name of an altruistic motive. Has any act of selfishness ever equalled the carnage perpetrated by disciples of altruism?

AYN RAND
The Fountainhead, 1943

AMBASSADOR

An Ambassador is an honest man sent abroad to lie for the commonwealth.

SIR HENRY WOOTON, 1604

AMBITION

. . . the excrement of glory.
PIETRO ARETINO
Letter to Lionardo Parpaglioni,
December 2, 1537

Ambition, n. An overmastering desire to be vilified by enemies while living and made ridiculous by friends when dead.

AMBROSE BIERCE
The Devil's Dictionary, 1906, 1911

AMERICA AND AMERICANS

America has a new delicacy, a coarse, rank refinement.
GILBERT KEITH CHESTERTON
Charles Dickens, 1906

America is the only nation in history which miraculously has gone directly from barbarism to degeneration without the usual interval of civilization.
Attributed to GEORGES CLEMENCEAU

The discovery of America was the occasion of the greatest outburst of cruelty and reckless greed known in history.
JOSEPH CONRAD
"Geography and Some Explorers,"
Last Essays, 1926

There are no second acts in American lives.
F. SCOTT FITZGERALD
The Last Tycoon, 1941

The organization of American society is an interlocking system of semi-monopolies. Notoriously venal, an electorate notoriously unenlightened, misled by a mass media notoriously phony.
PAUL GOODMAN
The Community of Scholars, 1962

I am willing to love all mankind, except an American.
SAMUEL JOHNSON
In James Boswell's
Life of Samuel Johnson, 1791

The last word of obscene rottenness contained within an entity of mechanized egotistic will—that is what Uncle Sam is to me.
D. H. LAWRENCE
Unpublished letter, c. 1922

. . . churchly hooligans and flag-waving corporations and the rest of the small but bloody despots . . . have made the word Americanism a synonym for coercion and legal crime.
ARCHIBALD MACLEISH
In *The Nation,* December 4, 1973

The American people, taking one with another, constitute the most timorous, sniveling, poltroonish, ignominious mob of serfs and goose-steppers ever gathered under one flag in Christendom since the end of the Middle Ages.

H. L. MENCKEN
Prejudices, Third Series, 1922

The American way is to seduce a man by bribery and make a prostitute of him. Or else to ignore him, starve him into submission and make a hack out of him.

HENRY MILLER
The Air-Conditioned Nightmare, 1945

Americans can eat garbage, provided you sprinkle it liberally with ketchup, mustard, chili sauce, tabasco sauce, cayenne pepper, or any other condiment which destroys the original flavor of the dish.

HENRY MILLER
Remember to Remember, 1947

An American is either a Jew or an anti-Semite, unless he is both at the same time.

JEAN-PAUL SARTRE
Les Séquestrés d'Altona, 1959

The United States has thirty-two religions and only one dish.

Attributed to CHARLES-MAURICE
DE TALLEYRAND-PÉRIGORD

I have seen the future [America] and it does not work.

PHILIP TOYNBEE
The Observer, London,
January 27, 1974

I would certainly go to the barricades for any movement that wants to sweep away the Pentagon, *Time* magazine, and frozen French fried potatoes.

GORE VIDAL
Playboy magazine, June 1969

... there is no such thing as an American. They are all exiles uprooted, transplanted and doomed to sterility.

EVELYN WAUGH
Letter to Cyril Connolly,
January 2, 1948

In America, life is one long expectoration.

OSCAR WILDE
In conversation, 1882

ANALOGY

There is no worse enemy of thought than the demon of analogy . . .
What is more tiresome than the mania of certain writers who cannot
see an object without thinking at once of another.

ANDRÉ GIDE
Pretexts, 1903

ANCESTORS

My father was a Creole, his father a Negro, and his father a monkey; my
family, it seems, begins where yours left off.

Attributed to
ALEXANDRE DUMAS PÈRE

Our ancestors are very good kinds of folks; but they are the last people I
should choose to have a visiting acquaintance with.

RICHARD BRINSLEY SHERIDAN
The Rivals, 1775

ANNE, QUEEN OF ENGLAND

Anne . . . , when in good humor, was meekly stupid and, when in bad
humor, was sulkily stupid.

THOMAS BABINGTON MACAULAY
History of England, 1848

APHORISM

The aphorism is a personal observation inflated into a universal truth, a
private posing as a general.

STEFAN KANFER
Time, July 11, 1983

APOTHECARY

Apothecary, n. The physician's accomplice, undertaker's benefactor
and grave worm's provider.

AMBROSE BIERCE
The Devil's Dictionary, 1906, 1911

APPETITE

Nothing in the world is so incontinent as a man's accursed appetite.

HOMER
Odyssey, c. 8th century B.C.

APPLAUSE

Applause is but a fart, the crude blast of the fickle multitude.

ANONYMOUS
Wit and Drollery, 1645

A hundred hisses outweigh a thousand claps. The former come more directly from the heart.

CHARLES LAMB
Letter to William Wordsworth,
December 11, 1806

This strange beating together of hands has no meaning. To me it is very disturbing. We try to make sounds like music, and then in between comes this strange sound you make.

LEOPOLD STOKOWSKI
To an audience in 1929

APRIL

April is the cruellest month, breeding
Lilacs out of the dead land, mixing
Memory and desire, stirring
Dull roots with spring rain.

T. S. ELIOT
The Waste Land, 1922

AQUARIUM

There is something about a home aquarium which sets my teeth on edge the moment I see it. Why anyone should want to live with a small container of stagnant water populated by a half-dead guppy is beyond me.

S. J. PERELMAN
The Most of S. J. Perelman, 1958

ARCHITECTURE

. . . the art of how to waste space.

PHILIP JOHNSON
The New York Times,
December 27, 1964

ARGUMENTS

I dislike arguments of any kind. They are always vulgar, and often convincing.

OSCAR WILDE
The Importance of Being Earnest,
1895

ARISTOPHANES

The language of Aristophanes reeks of his miserable quackery: it is made up of the lowest and most miserable puns; he doesn't even please the people, and to men of judgment and honor he is intolerable; his arrogance is insufferable, and all honest men detest his malice.

PLUTARCH
Quoted by Voltaire in
Dictionnaire philosophique, 1764

ART

All the arts in America are a gigantic racket run by unscrupulous men for unhealthy women.

SIR THOMAS BEECHAM
The Observer, London, 1946

A taste of sculpture and painting is in my mind as becoming as a taste of fiddling and piping is unbecoming a man of fashion. The former is connected with history and poetry, the latter, with nothing that I know of but bad company.

LORD CHESTERFIELD
To his son, June 22, 1749

Art is too long and life is too short.
Attributed to GRACE PALEY

ASCETICISM

I believe all manner of asceticism to be the vilest blasphemy—blasphemy towards the whole of the human race.

RICHARD JEFFRIES
The Story of My Heart, 1883

ASTROLOGY

Astrology is a disease, not a science.
MOSES MAIMONIDES
Hilboth Tshuvah
(*Laws of Repentance*), c. 1195

ASTRONAUTS

The astronaughts . . . Rotarians in outer space.

GORE VIDAL
Two Sisters, 1970

ATLANTIC OCEAN

Disappointing.

OSCAR WILDE
Letter to George Alexander,
September 1894

ATLEE, CLEMENT

He is a sheep in sheep's clothing.
Attributed to WINSTON S. CHURCHILL

ATTAINMENT

Is there anything in life so disenchanting as attainment?

Attributed to
ROBERT LOUIS STEVENSON

AUDIENCES

If my film makes one more person miserable, I'll feel I've done my job.

WOODY ALLEN
Time, April 30, 1979

There is not a more mean, stupid, dastardly, pitiful, selfish, spiteful, envious, ungrateful animal than the public.

WILLIAM HAZLITT
Views of the English Stage, 1818

Damn 'em, how they hissed! . . . like a congregation of mad geese . . . like apes, sometimes snakes, that hiss'd me into madness. 'Twas like St. Anthony's temptations. Mercy on us, that God should give his favourite children, men, mouths to speak with, to discourse rationally, to promise smoothly, to flatter agreeably, to encourage warmly, to counsel wisely: to sing with, to drink with, and to kiss with: and that they should turn them into mouths of adders, bears, wolves, hyenas, and whistle like tempests, and emit breath through them like distillations of aspic poison, to asperse and vilify the innocent labours of their fellow creatures who are desirous to please them! God be pleased to make the breath stink and the teeth rot out of them all therefore!

CHARLES LAMB
Letter to Thomas Manning,
October 11, 1805

Those bastards are just sucking us to death . . . about all we can do is do it like circus animals. I resent being an artist in that respect; I resent performing for fucking idiots who don't know anything.

JOHN LENNON
Quoted in *Loose Talk*, edited by
Linda Botts, 1981

AUSTRIANS

No Italian can hate an Austrian more than I do; unless it be the English, the Austrians seem to me the most obnoxious race under the sky.

LORD BYRON
Letter to John Murray,
April 16, 1820

AUTEUR

Themes, plots, characters and dialogue are created by writers and realized by actors; sets, costumes, music, cinematography, lighting, sound effects and editing are executed by a corps of skilled craftsmen and artists; the producer provides funds, studios, organization and, often, the original idea. It follows, then, with the mad logic so characteristic of the film industry, that the director, a vastly overpaid, nebulously talented and almost always inefficient traffic manager, becomes the *"auteur"* of the film and gets his name above the title.

JEAN-MICHEL CHAPEREAU
Un Hiver américain, 1975

AUTHORITY

But who guards the guardians?

JUVENAL
Satires, VI, c. 112–128

Big brother is watching you.

GEORGE ORWELL
1984, 1948

AUTOBIOGRAPHY

Autobiography is now as common as adultery, and hardly less reprehensible.

LORD ALTRINCHAM
The Sunday Times, London,
February 28, 1962

Autobiography is probably the most respectable form of lying.
HUMPHREY CARPENTER
The New York Times Book Review
February 7, 1982

Autobiography is an unrivaled vehicle for telling the truth about other people.
PHILIP GUEDALLA
Quoted by Hugh Leonard,
The New York Times,
November 23, 1980

Next to the writer of real estate advertisements, the autobiographer is the most suspect of prose artists.
DONAL HENAHAN
The New York Times,
February 11, 1977

There ain't nothing that breaks up homes, country and nations like somebody publishing their memoirs.
WILL ROGERS
The Autobiography of Will Rogers,
1949

AUTOMOBILE

I have always considered that the substitution of the internal combustion machine for the horse marked a very gloomy milestone in the progress of mankind.
WINSTON S. CHURCHILL
A Churchill Reader, 1954

The automobile has not merely taken over the street, it has dissolved the living tissue of the city. Its appetite for space is absolutely insatiable; moving and parked, it devours urban land, leaving the buildings as mere islands of habitable space in a sea of dangerous and ugly traffic. . . . Gas-filled, noisy and hazardous, our streets have become the most inhumane landscape in the world.
JAMES MARSTON FITCH,
Professor of Architecture,
Columbia University
The New York Times, May 1, 1960

The Insolent Chariots
JOHN KEATS
Title of book on automobiles, 1958

CALUMNIATE, CALUMNIATE;
THERE WILL ALWAYS BE SOME-
THING THAT WILL STICK.

BEAUMARCHAIS
(PIERRE-AUGUSTIN CHARON)
THE BARBER OF SEVILLE, 1775

BALDNESS

Of ten bald men nine are deceitful and the tenth is stupid.

Chinese proverb

There is nothing more contemptible than a bald man who pretends to have hair.

MARTIAL
Epigrams, c. A.D. 95

BALDWIN, STANLEY

One could not even dignify him with the name of stuffed shirt. He was simply a hole in the air.

GEORGE ORWELL
The Lion and the Unicorn, 1941

BALL

A ball is man's most disastrous invention, not excluding the wheel.

Attributed to ROBERT MORLEY

BALLROOM DANCING

... that hybrid known as ballroom dancing, an art which is compounded equally of the lithe, sensuous panther, the lissom, supple gigolo, and the light-shod, look-slippy waiter who can steer a tray and twenty-four glasses through a crowd without slipping.

JAMES AGATE
Review of Fred Astaire in
The Gay Divorcee
The Sunday Times, London, 1933

BALZAC, HONORÉ DE

A fat little flabby person with the face of a baker, the clothes of a cobbler, the size of a barrelmaker, the manners of a stocking salesman, and the dress of an innkeeper.

VICTOR DE BALABIN
Diary, July 1843

BANKHEAD, TALLULAH

A day away from Tallulah is like a month in the country.

Attributed to HOWARD DIETZ

BANKRUPTS

It has been long my deliberate judgement that all bankrupts, of whatsoever denomination, civil or religious, ought to be hanged.

CHARLES LAMB
Letter to Bernard Barton,
December 8, 1829

BANKS

Banking establishments are more dangerous than standing armies.

THOMAS JEFFERSON
Letter to Elbridge Gerry,
January 26, 1799

BARBER

Probably passed on, these many years, of an overdose of garlic, the way all New York barbers eventually go.

J. D. SALINGER
Seymour: An Introduction, 1963

BARITONE

Hark to the red-faced beeritone—
Gargling, gorgling, gurgling.

ANONYMOUS

BARIUM

. . . purée of tombstone.

JONATHAN MILLER
In a television interview, 1982

BARTÓK, BÉLA

If the reader were so rash as to purchase any of Béla Bartók's compositions, he would find that they each and all consist of unmeaning
bunches of notes, apparently representing the composer promenading
the keyboard in his boots. Some can be played better with the elbows,
others with the flat of the hand. None require fingers to perform nor
ears to listen to. . . . the productions of Bartók [are] mere ordure.

FREDERICK CORDER
"On the Cult of Wrong Notes,"
Musical Quarterly, July 1915

BASKETBALL

Nothing there but basketball, a game which won't be fit for people until
they set the basket umbilicus-high and return the giraffes to the zoo.

OGDEN NASH
The Old Dog Barks Backwards, 1972

BAUDELAIRE, CHARLES

All that is worst in Mr. Swinburne belongs to Baudelaire. The offensive
choice of subject, the obtrusion of unnatural passion, the blasphemy,
the wretched animalism, are all taken intact out of the *Fleurs de Mal*.
Pitiful! that any sane man, least of all any English poet, should think
this dunghill worthy of importation.

ROBERT BUCHANAN
The Fleshly School of Poetry, 1872

BEARD

That ornamental excrement which groweth beneath the chin.

THOMAS FULLER
*The History of the Worthies
of England*, 1662

BEATLES

The Beatles are not merely awful, I would consider it sacrilegious to say
anything less than that they are godawful. . . . They are so unbelievably

horrible, so appallingly unmusical, so dogmatically insensitive to the magic of the art, that they qualify as crowned heads of anti-music . . .

WILLIAM F. BUCKLEY, JR.
In his syndicated column,
On the Right,
September 8, 1964

BEAUTY

Oh, what a vileness human beauty is, corroding, corrupting everything it touches!

EURIPIDES
Orestes, 408 B.C.

Too much has been written about beauty . . . Beauty is that which satisfies the aesthetic instinct. But who wants to be satisfied? It is only to the dullard that enough is as good as a feast. Let us face it: beauty is a bit of a bore.

W. SOMERSET MAUGHAM
Cakes and Ale, 1930

Remember that the most beautiful things in the world are the most useless; peacocks and lilies for instance.

JOHN RUSKIN
The Stones of Venice, 1851–53

Beauty, more than bitterness
Makes the heart break.

SARA TEASDALE
Rivers to the Sea, 1915

What a strange illusion it is to suppose that beauty is goodness.

LEO TOLSTOY
The Kreutzer Sonata, 1889

BEERBOHM, MAX

It always makes me cross when Max is called "The Incomparable Max." He is not incomparable at all. . . . He is a shallow, affected, self-conscious fribble—so there!

VITA SACKVILLE-WEST
Letter to Harold Nicolson,
December 9, 1959

BEETHOVEN, LUDWIG VAN

Beethoven always sounds to me like the upsetting of bags of nails, with here and there an also dropped hammer.

JOHN RUSKIN
Letter to John Brown,
February 6, 1881

BEGGARS

Beggars should be abolished. It annoys one to give to them and it annoys one not to give to them.

Attributed to
FRIEDRICH WILHELM NIETZSCHE

BELGIUM

They ask me for an epitaph for dead Belgium. In vain I rack my brains: I can find only one phrase: "At Last!"

CHARLES BAUDELAIRE
Épitaphe pour la Belgique,
c. 1864

BELLY

It's this damned belly that gives a man his worst troubles.

HOMER
Odyssey, c. 8th century B.C.,
translated by W. H. D. Rouse

BENEVOLENCE

Those who are fond of setting things to rights have no great objection to seeing them wrong. There is often a great deal of spleen at the bottom of benevolence.

WILLIAM HAZLITT
Characteristics, 1823

BERLIOZ, HECTOR

Berlioz, musically speaking, is a lunatic; a classical composer only in Paris, the great city of quacks. His music is simply and undisguisedly nonsense.

Dramatic and Musical Review,
London, January 7, 1843

BERNHARDT, SARAH

A great actress, from the waist down.
DAME MARGARET "MADGE" KENDAL
Quoted by Brooks Atkinson in
The New York Times Book Review,
May 25, 1969

BEST-SELLER

A best-seller is the gilded tomb of a mediocre talent.
LOGAN PEARSALL SMITH
Afterthoughts, 1931

BIBLE

The Old Testament is responsible for more atheism, agnosticism, disbelief—call it what you will—than any book ever written; it has emptied more churches than all the counter-attractions of cinema, motorbicycle and golf course.
Attributed to A. A. MILNE

One had better put on gloves before reading the New Testament. The presence of so much filth makes it very advisable.
FRIEDRICH WILHELM NIETZSCHE
The Antichrist, 1888

Whenever we read the obscene stories, the voluptuous debaucheries, the cruel and tortuous executions, the unrelenting vindictiveness, with which more than half the Bible is filled, it would be more consistent that we called it the word of a demon than the word of God. It is a history of wickedness that has served to corrupt and brutalize mankind.
THOMAS PAINE
The Age of Reason, 1794

BICYCLE

Some time since I put myself on record as an antagonist of the devil's own toy, the bicycle. . . . Any contrivance or invention intended to supersede the use of human feet on God's own ground is damnable. Walking, running, leaping, and dancing are legitimate and natural joys of the body, and every attempt to stride on stilts, dangle on ropes, or wiggle on wheels is an affront to the Almighty.
JOHN RUSKIN
Quoted in *Facts and Fancies for
the Curious,* edited by
Charles C. Bombaugh, 1905

BIERCE, AMBROSE

Bierce would bury his best friend with a sigh of relief, and express satisfaction that he was done with him.

JACK LONDON
Quoted in *Ambrose Bierce,*
The Devil's Lexicographer,
by Paul Fatout, 1951

BIOGRAPHY

Biography is one of the new terrors of death.

DR. JOHN ARBUTHNOT
Quoted in *Life of Pope,*
by Robert Carruthers, 1853

One of the most arrogant undertakings, to my mind, is to write the biography of a man which pretends to go beyond external facts, and give the inmost motives. One of the most mendacious is autobiography.

THEODOR HAECKER
Journal in the Night, 1950

BIRTH

Birth, n. The first and direst of all disasters.

AMBROSE BIERCE
The Devil's Dictionary, 1906, 1911

No one recovers from the disease of being born, a deadly wound if there ever was one.

E. M. CIORAN
The Fall into Time, 1971

Thou know'st, the first time that we smell the air
We wawl and cry . . .
When we are born, we cry that we are come
To this great stage of fools.

WILLIAM SHAKESPEARE
King Lear, 1605–6

BLUE

Deep, dismal blue
Becomes alone the melancholy crew;
Emblem of plagues, the worst which Heaven hath sent,
Of cankered care, and gloomy discontent.

CHARLES STEARNS
The Ladies' Philosophy of Love, 1797

BODY

This body of ours consists of four elements; viz., of what is warm, that is, of blood; of what is dry, that is, of yellow bile; of what is moist, that is, of phlegm; of what is cold, that is, of black bile.

SAINT JOHN CHRYSOSTOM
Homily, c. 388

BOND, JAMES

... the really interesting thing about Bond is that he would be what I call the ideal defector. Because if the money was better, the booze freer and women easier over there in Moscow, he'd be off like a shot. Bond, you see, is the ultimate prostitute.

JOHN LE CARRÉ
Quoted in *Who's Who in Spy Fiction*,
by Donald McCormick, 1977

BONNEY, WILLIAM H. "BILLY THE KID"

A nondescript, adenoidal, weasel-eyed, narrow-chested, stoop-shouldered, repulsive-looking creature with all the outward appearance of a cretin.

BURTON RASCOE
Belle Starr, 1941

BOOKS

Books are fatal: they are the curse of the human race. Nine-tenths of existing books are nonsense, and the clever books are the refutation of that nonsense. The greatest misfortune that ever befell man was the invention of printing.

BENJAMIN DISRAELI
Lothair, 1870

Of making many books there is no end; and much study is a weariness of the flesh.

Ecclesiastes 12:12,
c. 200 B.C.

Never read any book that is not a year old.

RALPH WALDO EMERSON
The Conduct of Life, 1860

Borrowers of books—those mutilators of collections, spoilers of the symmetry of shelves, and creators of odd volumes.

CHARLES LAMB
"The Two Races of Men,"
Essays of Elia, 1823

Books, nowadays, are printed by people who do not understand them, sold by people who do not understand them, read and reviewed by people who do not understand them, and even written by people who do not understand them.

G. C. LICHTENBERG
Reflections, 1799

The multitude of books is a great evil.
MARTIN LUTHER
Table Talk, 1569

Books for general reading always smell badly; the odor of common people hangs about them.

FRIEDRICH WILHELM NIETZSCHE
Beyond Good and Evil, 1886

I hate books, for they only teach people to talk about what they do not understand.

JEAN-JACQUES ROUSSEAU
Émile, 1762

BOOKSELLERS

Printers and booksellers are born to be the most dilatory and tedious of all creatures.

WILLIAM COWPER
To William Unwin, May 23, 1781

Booksellers are all cohorts of the devil; there must be a special hell for them somewhere.

JOHANN WOLFGANG VON GOETHE
According to Siegfried Unseld in
The Author and His Publisher, 1980

BORN AGAIN

The trouble with born-again Christians is that they are an even bigger pain the second time around.

HERB CAEN
San Francisco Chronicle,
July 20, 1981

BOSTON

I have just returned from Boston. It is the only thing to do if you find yourself up there.

FRED ALLEN
Letter to Groucho Marx,
June 12, 1953

Clear out eight hundred thousand people and preserve it as a museum piece.

> FRANK LLOYD WRIGHT
> *The New York Times,*
> November 27, 1955

BOSWELL, JAMES

That he was a coxcomb and a bore, weak, vain, pushing, curious, garrulous, was obvious to all who were acquainted with him. That he could not reason, that he had no wit, no humor, no eloquence, is apparent from his writings. . . . Nature had made him a slave and an idolater. His mind resembled those creepers which the botanists call parasites and which can subsist only by clinging round the stems and imbibing the juices of stronger plants.

> THOMAS BABINGTON MACAULAY
> *Life of Samuel Johnson,* 1856

BOURGEOISIE

Axiom: hatred of the bourgeois is the beginning of wisdom.

> GUSTAVE FLAUBERT
> Letter to George Sand, May 10, 1867

BOXING

This is the only sport in the world where two guys get paid for doing something they'd be arrested for if they got drunk and did it for nothing.

> CARL FOREMAN
> Screenplay, *Champion,* 1949

BOYS

Boys are capital fellows in their own way, among their mates; but they are unwholesome companions for grown people.

> CHARLES LAMB
> "The Old and the
> New Schoolmaster,"
> *Essays of Elia,* 1823

BRAHMS, JOHANNES

To me it seems quite obvious that the real Brahms is nothing more than a sentimental voluptuary . . . He is the most wanton of composers. . . . Only his wantonness is not vicious; it is that of a great baby . . . rather tiresomely addicted to dressing himself up as Handel or Beethoven and making a prolonged and intolerable noise.

GEORGE BERNARD SHAW
The World, June 21, 1893

I have played over the music of that scoundrel Brahms. What a giftless bastard!

PETER ILYICH TCHAIKOVSKY
Diary, October 9, 1886

BRANDY

Brandy, n. A cordial composed of one part thunder-and-lightning, one part remorse, two parts bloody murder, one part death-hell-and-the-grave and four parts clarified Satan. Dose, a headful all the time. Brandy is said by Dr. Johnson to be the drink of heroes. Only a hero will venture to drink it.

AMBROSE BIERCE
The Devil's Dictionary, 1906, 1911

Brandy and water spoils two good things.

Attributed to CHARLES LAMB

BREAD

Bread made only of the branny part of the meal, which the poorest sort of people use, especially in time of dearth and necessity, giveth a very bad and excremental nourishment to the body: it is well called *panis canicarius*, because it is more fit for dogs than for men.

TOBIAS VENNER
Via recta, 1620

BREASTS

A full bosom is actually a millstone around a woman's neck ... [Breasts] are not parts of a person but lures slung around her neck, to be kneaded and twisted like magic putty, or mumbled and mouthed like lolly ices.

GERMAINE GREER
The Female Eunuch, 1971

BROADWAY

What a glorious garden of wonders the lights of Broadway would be to anyone lucky enough to be unable to read.

GILBERT KEITH CHESTERTON
What I Saw in America, 1923

BROTHERHOOD

The lion and the calf shall lie down together, but the calf won't get much sleep.

WOODY ALLEN
Without Feathers, 1975

When you deal with your brother, be pleasant, but get a witness.

HESIOD
Works and Days, 8th century B.C.

BROWNING, ROBERT

His muse is as much invalid as his wife was invalide.

OLIVER ST. JOHN GOGARTY
*As I Was Going Down Sackville
Street*, 1937

BRYAN, WILLIAM JENNINGS

A mouthing, slobbering demagogue whose patriotism is all in his jaw-bone.

THOMAS DIXON, 1896
Quoted by Mark Sullivan,
Our Times, Vol. I, 1926

He was, in fact, a charlatan, a mountebank, a zany without sense or dignity. . . . He seemed only a poor clod like those around him, deluded by a childish theology, full of an almost pathological hatred of all learning, all human dignity, all beauty, all fine and noble things. . . . What animated him from end to end of his grotesque career was simply ambition.

H. L. MENCKEN
The American Mercury, October 1925

BURKE, EDMUND

The execrable cantmonger and sycophant who, in the pay of the English oligarchy, played the romantic laudator temporis acti against the French Revolution, just as, in the pay of the North American colonies, . . . he had played the liberal against the English oligarchy, was an out and out vulgar bourgeois.

KARL MARX
Das Kapital, 1867

BUTCHER

The cutthroat butchers, wanting throats to cut,
At Lent's approach their bloody shambles shut;
For forty days their tyranny doth cease,
And men and beasts take truce and live at peace.
JOHN TAYLOR
Jack-a-Lent, 1630

BYRON, GEORGE GORDON, LORD

Mad, bad and dangerous to know.
LADY CAROLINE LAMB
Journal, March 1812

From the poetry of Lord Byron they drew a system of ethics compounded of misanthropy and voluptuousness—a system in which the two greatest commandments were to hate your neighbor and to love your neighbor's wife.

THOMAS BABINGTON MACAULAY
Quoted in Moore's *Life of Byron,*
1831

CALIFORNIA

All the artistic words have changed their meaning in California. Book means magazine, music means jazz, act means behaving, picture means a snapshot. They haven't even a place to keep books.

STELLA BENSON
The Poor Man, 1922

California is the biggest collection of losers who ever met on one piece of real estate.

DAVID KARP
The New York Times,
August 17, 1968

... nothing wrong with Southern California that a rise in the ocean level wouldn't cure.

ROSS MACDONALD
The Drowning Pool, 1950

It is the land of perpetual pubescence, where cultural lag is mistaken for renaissance.

ASHLEY MONTAGU
The American Way of Life, 1967

CAMPBELL, MRS. PATRICK

It is greatly to Mrs. Patrick Campbell's credit that, bad as the play was, her acting was worse. It was a masterpiece of failure.

GEORGE BERNARD SHAW
Review of *Fedora* at the Haymarket
Theatre, London, May 1895

CAPITALISM

There is a good deal of solemn cant about the common interests of capital and labor. As matters stand, their only common interest is that of cutting each other's throat.

BROOKS ATKINSON
Once Around the Sun, 1951

We will bury you.

NIKITA S. KHRUSHCHEV
Quoted in
the *New York Herald Tribune*,
September 17, 1959

You show me a capitalist, I'll show you a bloodsucker.

MALCOLM X
Malcolm X Speaks, 1965

CAPOTE, TRUMAN

Truman Capote has made lying an art. A *minor* art.

GORE VIDAL
Viva, October 1977

CARLYLE, THOMAS

It was very good of God to let Carlyle and Mrs. Carlyle marry one another and so make only two people miserable instead of four.

SAMUEL BUTLER
Letter to Miss Savage,
November 21, 1884

Carlyle is the same old sausage, fizzing and sputtering in his own grease.

HENRY JAMES, SR.
Letter, 1856,
quoted by Van Wyck Brooks,
New England Indian Summer, 1940

CATS

They smell and they snarl and they scratch; they have a singular aptitude for shredding rugs, drapes and upholstery; they're sneaky, selfish and not particularly smart; they are disloyal, condescending and totally useless in any rodent-free environment.

JEAN-MICHEL CHAPEREAU
Un Hiver américain, 1975

CELIBACY

. . . the worst form of self-abuse . . .
PETER DE VRIES
Quoted in *The New York Times*,
June 12, 1983

CHAMPAGNE

I hate champagne more than anything in the world next to Seven-Up.
ELAINE DUNDY
The Dud Avocado, 1958

CHAPLIN, CHARLES

The son of a bitch is a ballet dancer.
Attributed to W. C. FIELDS

CHARITY

. . . one of the serious obstacles to the improvement of our race is indiscriminate charity.

ANDREW CARNEGIE
The Gospel of Wealth, 1889

Never look a gift horse in the mouth.
SAINT JEROME
On the Epistle to the Ephesians,
c. 420

The man who leaves money to charity in his will is only giving away what no longer belongs to him.

VOLTAIRE
Letter, 1769

CHASTITY

We may eventually come to realize that chastity is no more a virtue than malnutrition.

ALEX COMFORT
Quoted in *The New York Times*,
February 18, 1968

Chastity is an insult to the Creator and an abomination to man and beast.

NORMAN DOUGLAS
An Almanac, 1945

Chastity is a monkish and evangelical superstition, a greater foe to natural temperance even than unintellectual sensuality; it strikes at the root of all domestic happiness, and consigns more than half of the human race to misery.

PERCY BYSSHE SHELLEY
Queen Mab, notes, 1813

CHATEAUBRIAND, VICOMTE FRANÇOIS-RENÉ DE

Chateaubriand is a miserable boaster without character, with a groveling soul and an itch for writing.

NAPOLEON I
To Barry E. O'Meara at St. Helena,
January 28, 1818

CHESS

It is a game too troublesome for some men's braines, too testy full of anxiety, all out as bad as study; besides, it is a cholericke game, and very offensive to him that looseth the Mate. William the Conqueror in his younger years, playing at chesse with the Prince of France . . . , losing a Mate, knocked the Chessboard about his pate, which was a cause afterward of much enmity between them.

ROBERT BURTON
The Anatomy of Melancholy, 1621

Life's too short for chess.
HENRY JAMES BYRON
Our Boys, 1874

CHICAGO

Most cities have a smell of their own. Chicago smells like it's not sure.
Attributed to ALAN KING

. . . this vicious, stinking zoo, this mean-grinning, mace-smelling bone-yard of a city: an elegant rockpile monument to everything cruel and stupid and corrupt in the human spirit.

HUNTER S. THOMPSON
The Great Shark Hunt, 1979

CHILDHOOD

Childhood, n. The period of human life intermediate between the idi-ocy of infancy and the folly of youth—two removes from the sin of manhood and three from the remorse of age.

AMBROSE BIERCE
The Devil's Dictionary, 1906, 1911

A happy childhood is poor preparation for human contacts.

COLETTE
Quoted in *Colette*,
by Michèle Sarde, 1978

The days of childhood are but days of woe.

ROBERT SOUTHEY
"The Retrospect,"
The Poetical Works, 1845

CHILDREN

Beat your child once a day. If you don't know why, the child does.

CHINESE PROVERB

How inimitably graceful children are in general—before they learn to dance.

SAMUEL TAYLOR COLERIDGE
Table-Talk, January 1, 1832

Desire not a multitude of unprofitable children.

Ecclesiasticus 16:1, c. 180 B.C.

All children are by nature children of wrath, and are in danger of eternal damnation in Hell.

JONATHAN EDWARDS
Sermon to Children, 1740

A child is a curly, dimpled lunatic.

RALPH WALDO EMERSON
Nature, 1841

The childless escape much misery.
EURIPIDES
Medea, 431 B.C.

Children should neither be seen nor heard from—ever again.
Attributed to W. C. FIELDS

A loud noise at one end and no sense of responsibility at the other.
Attributed to RONALD ARBUTHNOTT
KNOX

Insanity is hereditary; you can get it from your children.
Attributed to SAM LEVENSON

If a child shows himself incorrigible, he should be decently and quietly beheaded at the age of twelve, lest he grow to maturity, marry, and perpetuate his kind.

DON MARQUIS
The Almost Perfect State, 1927

I love children—especially when they cry, for then someone takes them away.
Attributed to NANCY MITFORD

Children are never too tender to be whipped:—like tough beefsteaks, the more you beat them the more tender they become.
EDGAR ALLAN POE
Graham's Magazine,
May–June 1850

Any man who hates small dogs and children can't be all bad.
LEO ROSTEN
Referring to W. C. Fields
at a banquet in Los Angeles,
February 16, 1939

Children, after being limbs of Satan in traditional theology and mystically illuminated angels in the minds of educational reformers, have reverted to being little devils—not theological demons inspired by the Evil One, but scientific Freudian abominations inspired by the Unconscious.

BERTRAND RUSSELL
"The Virtue of the Oppressed,"
Unpopular Essays, 1950

All children have wicked hearts when they are born: and that makes them so wicked when they grow up into life. Even little infants, that appear so innocent and pretty, are God's little enemies at heart.

SAMUEL SPRING
Three Sermons to Little Children,
1819

Children are a torment, and nothing else.

LEO TOLSTOY
The Kreutzer Sonata, 1890

I don't like the size of them; the scale is all wrong. The heads tend to be too big for the bodies and the hands and feet are a disaster and they keep falling into things . . . they should be neither seen nor heard. And no one must make another one.

GORE VIDAL
Interview, April 1975

Of children as of procreation—the pleasure momentary, the posture ridiculous, the expense damnable.

EVELYN WAUGH
Letter to Nancy Mitford,
May 5, 1954

My children weary me. I can only see them as defective adults; feckless, destructive, frivolous, sensual, humorless.

EVELYN WAUGH
Time, October 17, 1977

Children begin by loving their parents. After a time they judge them. Rarely, if ever, do they forgive them.

OSCAR WILDE
A Woman of No Importance, 1894

CHIVALRY

Chivalry is the most delicate form of contempt.

ALBERT GUÉRARD
Bottle in the Sea, 1954

CHOCOLATE

The Marquise de Poëtlogon took too much chocolate, being pregnant last year, that she was brought to bed of a little boy who was as black as the devil.

MARQUISE DE SÉVIGNÉ
Letters, 1725

CHOIR

Choristers bellow the tenor, as it were oxen; bark a counterpart, as it were a kennel of dogs; roar out a treble, as it were a sort of bulls; and grunt out a bass, as it were a number of hogs.

WILLIAM PRYNNE
Histriomastix, 1632

CHOP

Chop, n. A piece of leather skillfully attached to a bone and administered to the patients at restaurants.

AMBROSE BIERCE
The Devil's Dictionary, 1906, 1911

CHRIST, JESUS

... A parish demagogue.
PERCY BYSSHE SHELLEY
Queen Mab, 1813

CHRISTIANS AND CHRISTIANITY

Christianity is the bastard progeny of Judaism. It is the basest of all national religions.

CELSUS
True Discourse,
c. 178

I decline Christianity because it is Jewish, because it is international, and because, in cowardly fashion, it preaches Peace on Earth.

Attributed to
GENERAL ERICH VON LUDENDORFF

I call Christianity the one great curse, the one great intrinsic depravity, the one great instinct of revenge, for which no means are venomous enough, or secret, subterranean and small enough—I call it the one immortal blemish upon the human race.

FRIEDRICH WILHELM NIETZSCHE
The Antichrist, 1888

How like a fawning publican he looks!
I hate him for he is a Christian.
WILLIAM SHAKESPEARE
The Merchant of Venice, c. 1597

CHRISTMAS

Bah, Humbug!
> CHARLES DICKENS
> *A Christmas Carol,* 1843

This holiday which reminds me only of the birth of a Jew who gave the world debilitating and devitalizing theories . . .
> BENITO MUSSOLINI
> Quoted in *Ciano's Hidden Diary,*
> 1953

. . . something in me resists the calendar expectation of happiness. *Merry Christmas yourself!* it mutters as it shapes a ghostly grin.
> J. B. PRIESTLEY
> *Outcries and Asides,* 1974

I am sorry to have to introduce the subject of Christmas . . . It is an indecent subject; a cruel, gluttonous subject; a drunken, disorderly subject; a wasteful disastrous subject; a wicked, cadging, lying, filthy, blasphemous, and demoralizing subject. Christmas is forced on a reluctant and disgusted nation by the shopkeepers and the press: on its own merits it would wither and shrivel in the fiery breath of universal hatred; and anyone who looked back to it would be turned into a pillar of greasy sausages.
> GEORGE BERNARD SHAW
> *Our Theatres in the Nineties,*
> Volume 3,
> January 1, 1898

Or consider Christmas—could Satan in his most malignant mood have devised a worse combination of graft plus buncombe than the system whereby several hundred million people get a billion or so gifts for which they have no use, and some thousands of shop-clerks die of exhaustion while selling them and every other child in the western world is made ill from overeating—all in the name of the lowly Jesus?
> UPTON SINCLAIR
> *Money Writes!,* 1927

CHURCH, CATHOLIC

Abhor that arrant Whore of Rome,
And all her blasphemies;
And drink not of her cursed cup,
Obey not her decrees.
> NEW ENGLAND PRIMER, c. 1688

CHURCHILL, WINSTON S.

He is a man suffering from petrified adolescence.

ANEURIN BEVAN
Quoted in *Aneurin Bevan*,
by Vincent Brome, 1953

He is not a man for whom I ever had esteem. Always in the wrong, always surrounded by crooks, a most unsuccessful father—simply a "Radio Personality" who outlived his prime. "Rallied the nation" indeed! I was a serving soldier in 1940. How we despised his oration.

EVELYN WAUGH
Letter to Ann Fleming,
January 27, 1965

CIRCUS

I still abstain from circuses . . . because I cannot endure seeing animals performing unnatural tricks at the command of trainers whom I would shoot at sight if I could be sure of a verdict of justifiable homicide.

GEORGE BERNARD SHAW
Everybody's Political What's What?,
1944

CITIES

Great cities must be obliterated from the earth.

OTTO VON BISMARCK
Speech in the Prussian Lower House,
March 20, 1852

Cities are built to kill people.

CHARLES BUKOWSKI
Notes of a Dirty Old Man, 1969

God the first garden made, and the first city Cain.

ABRAHAM COWLEY
"The Garden," *Essays on
Verse and Prose*, 1668

I view great cities as pestilential to the morals, the health and the liberties of man.

Attributed to THOMAS JEFFERSON

The city is squalid and sinister,
With the silver-barred street in the midst,

Slow-moving,
A river leading nowhere.
AMY LOWELL
Sword Blades and Poppy Seeds, 1914

Clearly, then, the city is not a concrete jungle, it is a human zoo.
DESMOND MORRIS
The Human Zoo, 1970

The city . . . a natural territory for the psychopath with histrionic gifts.
JONATHON RABAN
Soft City, 1974

Cities are the abyss of the human species. At the end of a few generations in them races perish or degenerate, and it is necessary to renew them. This renewal always comes from the country.
JEAN-JACQUES ROUSSEAU
Émile, 1762

CIVILIZATION

The crimes of extreme civilization are probably worse than those of extreme barbarism, because of their refinement, the corruption they presuppose, and their superior degree of intellectuality.
JULES BARBEY D'AUREVILLY
Les Diaboliques, 1874

Our civilization is still in a middle stage, scarcely beast, in that it is no longer wholly guided by instinct; scarcely human, in that it is not yet wholly guided by reason.
THEODORE DREISER
Sister Carrie, 1900

Imagine the great ship from a far galaxy which inspects a thousand green planets and then comes to ours and, from on high, looks down at all the scabs, the buzzings, the electronic jabberings, the poisoned air and water, the fetid night glow. A little cave-dwelling virus mutated, slew the things which balanced the ecology, and turned the fair planet sick. . . . I think they would be concerned. They would be glad to have caught it in time.
JOHN D. MACDONALD
A Deadly Shade of Gold, 1965

You can't say civilization don't advance . . . for in every war they kill you a new way.
WILL ROGERS
The Autobiography of Will Rogers,
1949

Civilized man is born, lives, and dies in slavery; at his birth he is confined in swaddling clothes; at death, he is nailed in a coffin. So long as he retains the human form he is fettered by our institutions.

> JEAN-JACQUES ROUSSEAU
> *Émile*, 1962

Soap and education are not as sudden as a massacre, but they are more deadly in the long run.

> MARK TWAIN
> *Sketches New and Old*, 1900

CIVIL SERVANTS

I see the woman with a scarf twisted round her hair and a cigarette in her mouth. She has put a tea tray down upon the file on which my future depends.

> JOHN BETJEMAN
> *First and Last Loves*, 1952

CLASSICS

Every man with a bellyful of the classics is an enemy to the human race.

> HENRY MILLER
> *Tropic of Cancer*, 1934

"Classic." A book which people praise and don't read.

> MARK TWAIN
> *Following the Equator*, 1897

CLERGY

As a career, the business of an orthodox preacher is about as successful as that of a celluloid dog chasing an asbestos cat through Hell.

> ELBERT HUBBARD
> *Roycroft Dictionary and Book*
> *of Epigrams*, 1923

The Presbyterian clergy are the loudest, the most intolerant of all sects; the most tyrannical and ambitious, ready at the word of the law-giver, if such a word could not be obtained, to put their torch to the pile, and to rekindle in this virgin hemisphere the flame in which their oracle, Calvin, consumed poor Servetus.

> THOMAS JEFFERSON
> Letter to William Short,
> April 13, 1820

Pope, cardinals, bishops, are a pack of guzzling, stuffing wretches, rich, wallowing in wealth and laziness, resting secure in their power, and never, for a moment, thinking of accomplishing God's will.

MARTIN LUTHER
Table Talk, 1569

There are three sexes—men, women and clergymen.

SYDNEY SMITH
Quoted in Lady Holland's
*Memoir of the Reverend Sydney
Smith*, 1855

Who within the realm are more corrupt in life and manners than are they that are called the clergy, living in whoredom and adultery, deflowering virgins, corrupting matrons, and doing all abomination without fear of punishment?

Supplication to the Scottish
Parliament, 1560

He has the canonical smirk and the filthy clammy palm of a chaplain.

WILLIAM WYCHERLEY
The Country Wife, c. 1673

CLOSET

The last place people want to hang clothes is their clothes closet. Closets are mean, inconvenient, often dark and always overcrowded. If a person's closet isn't overcrowded, you can bet that person needs a psychiatrist.

ANDREW A. ROONEY
And More by Andy Rooney, 1982

CLOTHES

The woman shall not wear that which pertaineth unto a man, neither shall a man put on a woman's garment: for all that do so are abomination unto the Lord thy God.

Deuteronomy 22:5, c. 650 B.C.

In a world of moral nudism, wearing clothes doesn't just mean that you're prudish; it suggests that you may have something to hide.

LOUIS KRONENBERGER
Company Manners, 1954

If God intended for women to wear slacks, He would have constructed them differently.

Attributed to EMILY POST

CLUBS

Those mausoleums of inactive masculinity are places for men who prefer armchairs to women.

Attributed to V. S. PRITCHETT

COCKTAIL

A cocktail is to a glass of wine as rape is to love.

Attributed to PAUL CLAUDEL

Cocktails have all the disagreeability without the utility of a disinfectant.

SHANE LESLIE
The Observer, London, 1939

COCKTAIL PARTIES

The cocktail party has the form of friendship without the warmth and devotion. It is a device either for getting rid of social obligations hurriedly en masse, or for making overtures towards more serious social relationships, as in the etiquette of whoring.

BROOKS ATKINSON
Once Around the Sun, 1951

COCOA

Tea, although an Oriental,
Is a gentleman at least;
Cocoa is a cad and coward,
Cocoa is a vulgar beast.

GILBERT KEITH CHESTERTON
"The Song of Right and Wrong,"
Collected Poems, 1927

"Cocoa," she said. "Cocoa. Damn miserable puny stuff, fit for kittens and unwashed boys. Did Shakespeare drink cocoa?"

SHIRLEY JACKSON
The Bird's Nest, 1954

COFFEE

Trifle away their time, scald their chops, and spend their money, all for a little base, black, thick, nasty, bitter, stinking, nauseous puddle water.

ANONYMOUS
The Women's Petition Against
Coffee, 1674

Coffee in England is just toasted milk.
> CHRISTOPHER FRY
> Quoted in the *New York Post*,
> November 29, 1962

COHN, HARRY

You had to stay in line to hate him.
> HEDDA HOPPER
> After Cohn's death, 1958

Well, it only proved what they always say—give the public something they want to see, and they'll come out for it.
> Attributed to RED SKELTON
> On the large crowd that turned out
> for Cohn's funeral, 1958

COLD DUCK

A carbonated wine foisted upon Americans (who else would drink it) by winery ad agencies as a way of getting rid of inferior champagne by mixing it with inferior sparkling burgundy.
> JOHN CIARDI
> *A Second Browser's Dictionary*, 1983

COLLABORATION

Two or more people getting together to write something is like three people getting together to make a baby.
> Attributed to EVELYN WAUGH

COLLECTOR

The collector walks with blinders on; he sees nothing but the prize. In fact, the acquisitive instinct is incompatible with true appreciation of beauty.
> ANNE MORROW LINDBERGH
> "A Few Shells,"
> *Gift from the Sea*, 1955

COLOGNE

In Köln, a town of monks and bones,
And pavements, fang'd with murderous stones,
And rags, and hags, and hideous wenches;
I counted two and seventy stenches,

All well defined, and several stinks!
Ye nymphs that reign o'er sewers and sinks,
The river Rhine, it is well known,
Doth wash your city of Cologne;
But tell me, nymphs! what power divine
Shall henceforth wash the river Rhine?
SAMUEL TAYLOR COLERIDGE
Cologne, 1817

COMEDY AND COMEDIANS

What a sad business is being funny!
CHARLES CHAPLIN
Limelight, film, 1952

Comedy like sodomy is an unnatural act.
MARTY FELDMAN
The Times, London, June 9, 1969

. . . a comedian is not an actor. His work bears the same relation to acting . . . as that of a hangman, a midwife or a divorce lawyer bears to poetry, or that of a bishop to religion.

H. L. MENCKEN
Baltimore Evening Sun,
November 18, 1929

COMIC BOOKS

The marijuana of the nursery, the bane of the bassinet, the horror of the home, the curse of the kids, and a threat to the future.
Attributed to JOHN MASON BROWN

COMMITTEE

What is a committee? A group of the unwilling, picked from the unfit, to do the unnecessary.
RICHARD HARKNESS
New York Herald Tribune,
June 15, 1960

I hate being placed on committees. They are always having meetings at which half are absent and the rest late.
OLIVER WENDELL HOLMES
*The Life and Letters of Oliver
Wendell Holmes,* 1892

COMMON MAN

God must hate the common people, because he made them so common.

Attributed to PHILIP WYLIE

COMMUNICATIONS

Don't pin much hope on the mail and when the phone rings don't expect anyone wonderful to be calling.

ANDREW A. ROONEY
Letter, August 23, 1983

COMPARISONS

Comparisons are odious.

JOHN FORTESCUE
De Landibus Legum Anglial, 1471

COMPETITION

The more modern nations detest each other the more meekly they follow each other; for all competition is in its nature only a furious plagiarism.

GILBERT KEITH CHESTERTON
Charles Dickens, 1906

COMPOSER

Composers shouldn't think too much—it interferes with their plagiarism.

HOWARD DIETZ
To Goddard Lieberson,
November 1974

A good composer does not imitate; he steals.

IGOR STRAVINSKY
To Peter Yates, *Twentieth
Century Music*, 1967

CONCERTS

Yet I detest
   These scented rooms, where to a gaudy throng,
Heaves the proud harlot her distended breast
   In intricacies of laborious song.
SAMUEL TAYLOR COLERIDGE
"Lines Composed in a Concert-Room,"
1799

CONDOLENCE

Of all cruelties those are the most intolerable that come under the name of condolence and consolation.

WALTER SAVAGE LANDOR
Letter to Robert Southey, 1816

CONGRESS

Congress—these, for the most part, illiterate hacks whose fancy vests are spotted with gravy, and whose speeches, hypocritical, unctuous, and slovenly, are spotted also with the gravy of political patronage.

MARY MCCARTHY
On the Contrary, 1961

Congress consists of one-third, more or less, scoundrels; two-thirds, more or less, idiots; and three-thirds, more or less, poltroons.

H. L. MENCKEN
A Book of Burlesques, 1920

It could probably be shown by facts and figures that there is no distinctly native American criminal class except Congress.

MARK TWAIN
Following the Equator, 1897

CONNOLLY, CYRIL

I have always disliked myself at any given moment; the total of such moments is my life.

CYRIL CONNOLLY
Enemies of Promise, 1938

CONSCIENCE

Conscience is the inner voice which warns us that someone may be looking.

H. L. MENCKEN
A Mencken Chrestomanthy, 1949

CONSERVATIVE

Conservative, n. A statesman who is enamored of existing evils, as distinguished from the Liberal, who wishes to replace them with others.

AMBROSE BIERCE
The Devil's Dictionary, 1906, 1911

A conservative is a man too cowardly to fight and too fat to run.
> ELBERT HUBBARD
> *A Thousand and One Epigrams*, 1911

CONSISTENCY

Consistency requires you to be as ignorant today as you were a year ago.
> BERNARD BERENSON
> Notebook, 1892

The man who never alters his opinion is like standing water, and breeds reptiles of the mind.
> WILLIAM BLAKE
> *The Marriage of Heaven and Hell*,
> 1790–93

A foolish consistency is the hobgoblin of little minds adored by little statesmen and philosophers and divines.
> RALPH WALDO EMERSON
> "Self-Reliance," *Essays*,
> First Series, 1841

Too much consistency is as bad for the mind as for the body. Consistency is contrary to nature, contrary to life. The only completely consistent people are the dead.
> ALDOUS HUXLEY
> *Do What You Will*, 1929

The foolish and the dead alone never change their opinion.
> JAMES RUSSELL LOWELL
> *My Study Windows*, 1871

Consistency is the last refuge of the unimaginative.
> Attributed to OSCAR WILDE

CONSUL

Consul, n. In American politics, a person who having failed to secure an office from the people is given one by the Administration on condition that he leave the country.
> AMBROSE BIERCE
> *The Devil's Dictionary*, 1906, 1911

CONSUMER

Let the buyer beware.
(*Caveat emptor.*)
ROMAN MAXIM

In a consumer society there are inevitably two kinds of slaves: the prisoners of addiction and the prisoners of envy.

> IVAN ILLICH
> *Tools for Conviviality*, 1973

CONTINENCE

Mr. Mercaptan went on to preach a brilliant sermon on that melancholy sexual perversion known as continence.

> ALDOUS HUXLEY
> *Antic Hay*, 1925

CONTRACEPTION

I once read in a medical book this unconsciously sardonic sentence: "Precautionary measures are never infallible and one should not be cocksure about any contraceptive."

> JAMES THURBER
> Letter to his daughter,
> December 6, 1954

CONVENT

The convent is supreme egotism resulting in supreme self-denial.

> VICTOR HUGO
> *Les Misérables*, 1862

CONVERSATION

Conversation is the enemy of good wine and food.

> ALFRED HITCHCOCK
> Quoted in *Time*,
> October 9, 1978

COOK

God sends meat, but the Devil sends cooks.

> English proverb, traced to 1542

You think I am cruel and gluttonous when I beat my cook for sending in a bad dinner. But if that is too trivial a cause, what other can there be for beating a cook?

> MARTIAL
> *Epigrams*, c. 95

It is no wonder that diseases are innumerable: count the cooks.

> SENECA
> *Epistulae morales ad Lucilium*,
> c. 63

COOKING

Cooking is a minor art. I can't imagine a hilarious soufflé, or a deeply moving stew.

KENNETH TYNAN
The Sound of Two Hands Clapping,
1975

COOKING, GERMAN

German cooking, above all!—how much it has upon its conscience! Soup before the meal, meats cooked to death, fat and mealy vegetables!

FRIEDRICH WILHELM NIETZSCHE
Ecce Homo, 1888

COOLIDGE, CALVIN

How can they tell?

DOROTHY PARKER
On being told that ex-President
Coolidge had died, 1933

CORN LICKER

It smells like gangrene starting in a mildewed silo, it tastes like the wrath to come, and when you absorb a deep swig of it you have all the sensations of having swallowed a lighted kerosene lamp. A sudden, violent jolt of it has been known to stop the victim's watch, snap his suspenders and crack his glass eye right across.

IRVIN S. COBB
Addressed to the Distillers Code
Authority, NRA, early 1930s

CORPORATION

Corporation, n. An ingenious device for obtaining individual profit without individual responsibility.

AMBROSE BIERCE
The Devil's Dictionary, 1906, 1911

COSELL, HOWARD

If Howard Cosell were a sport, he'd be a roller derby.

JIMMY CANNON
Nobody Asked Me, but . . . , 1978

COUNTRY

The country has charms only for those not obliged to stay there.

Attributed to
ÉDOUARD MANET

... They can have the good old smell of the earth. Nine times out of ten it isn't the good old smell of the earth that they smell so much as the good old smell of chicken feathers, stagnant pools of water, outhouse perfumes, cooking odors from badly designed kitchens and damp wall plaster.

GEORGE JEAN NATHAN
The Bachelor Life, 1941

O Lord! I don't know which is the worst of the country, the walking or the sitting at home with nothing to do.

GEORGE BERNARD SHAW
Mrs. Warren's Profession, 1893

I have no relish for the country; it is a kind of healthy grave.

SYDNEY SMITH
Letter to Miss Harcourt, 1838

COURAGE

The horse does abominate the camel; the mighty elephant is afraid of a mouse; and they say that the lion, which scorneth to turn his back upon the stoutest animal, will tremble at the crowing of a cock.

INCREASE MATHER
Remarkable Providences, 1684

COURTESY

In courteous towns it is impossible to acquire knowledge of the world; every one is so courteously honest, so courteously rude, so courteously deceitful.

GEORG CHRISTOPH LICHTENBERG
Quoted in *The Last Word,* by
Louis Kronenberger, 1972

CRAWFORD, JOAN

The best time I ever had with Joan Crawford was when I pushed her down the stairs in *Whatever Happened to Baby Jane.*

BETTE DAVIS
Quoted in *Popcorn in Paradise,* by
John Robert Colombo, 1979

Closing these two books, a reader senses that Joan Crawford, idol of an age, would have made an exemplary prison matron, possibly at Buchenwald. She had the requisite sadism, paranoia and taste for violence.

HARRIET VAN HORNE
Reviewing books on Joan Crawford
by Christina Crawford and
Bob Thomas, *New York Post*,
October 29, 1978

CREAM

Cream . . . is the very head and flower of milk: but it is somewhat of a gross nourishment, and by reason of the unctuosity of it, quickly cloyeth the stomach, relaxeth and weakeneth the retentive faculty thereof, and is easily converted into phlegm, and vaporous fumes.

TOBIAS VENNER
Via recta, 1620

CREDULITY

There's a sucker born every minute.

Attributed to
PHINEAS TAYLOR BARNUM

CREED

A creed is an ossified metaphor.

ELBERT HUBBARD
The Notebook, 1927

CRITICS AND CRITICISM

. . . Drooling, driveling, doleful, depressing, dropsical drips.

SIR THOMAS BEECHAM
On critics, May 21, 1955

Poor devils! Where do they come from? At what age are they sent to the slaughterhouse? What is done with their bones? Where do such animals pasture in the daytime? Do they have females, and young? How many of them handled the brush before being reduced to the broom?

HECTOR BERLIOZ
Les Grotesques de la musique, 1859

Critics!—appalled I venture on the name,
Those cut-throat bandits in the paths of fame.

ROBERT BURNS
Third Epistle to Mr. Graham of Fintry,
1791

Seek roses in December—ice in June,
Hope, constancy in wind, or corn in chaff;
Believe a woman or an epitaph,
Or any other thing that's false, before
You trust in critics.

LORD BYRON
English Bards and Scotch Reviewers,
1809

For critics I care the five hundredth thousandth part of the tythe of a half-farthing.

CHARLES LAMB
Letter to Bernard Barton, 1830

Critics are a dissembling, dishonest, contemptible race of men. Asking a working writer what he thinks about critics is like asking a lamppost what it feels about dogs.

JOHN OSBORNE
Time, October 31, 1977

I am sitting in the smallest room in the house. I have your review in front of me. Soon it will be behind me.

MAX REGER
To a music critic, quoted by
Eliot Fremont-Smith, *New York*
magazine, July 8, 1974

They [the critics] are without intellect, perception, sensitivity or background. They pander to the tastes of the empty-headed, the bored, the insensitive and the complacent.

ELMER RICE
Advertisement in *The New York
Times,* November 11, 1934

Of all the cants which are canted in this canting world—though the cant of hypocrites may be the worst—the cant of criticism is the most tormenting.

LAURENCE STERNE
Tristram Shandy, 1762

I had another dream the other day about music critics. They were small and rodent-like with padlocked ears, as if they had stepped out of a painting by Goya.

IGOR STRAVINSKY
Evening Standard, London,
October 29, 1969

I have just read your lousy review. You sound like a frustrated old man who never made a success, an eight-ulcer man on a four-ulcer job. . . . I have never met you but if I do, you'll need a new nose, a lot of beefsteak for black eyes, and a supporter below.

> HARRY S. TRUMAN
> Letter to critic Paul Hume,
> December 1950, in response to an
> unflattering review of the President's
> daughter Margaret's singing recital

The trade of critic, in literature, music, and the drama, is the most degraded of all trades.

> MARK TWAIN
> *Autobiography*, 1924

They search for ages for the wrong word, which, to give them credit, they eventually find.

> PETER USTINOV
> On BBC radio, February 1952

Has anybody ever seen a dramatic critic in the daytime? Of course not. They come out after dark, up to no good.

> P. G. WODEHOUSE
> *New York Mirror*, May 27, 1955

CROMWELL, OLIVER

That grand imposter, that loathsome hypocrite, that detestable traitor, that prodigy of nature, that opprobrium of mankind, that landscape of iniquity, that sink of sin, that compendium of baseness, who now calls himself our Protector.

> Address of the Anabaptists to
> Charles II, c. 1658

CROQUET

. . . the ineffably insipid diversion they call croquet.

> MARK TWAIN
> *The Innocents at Home*, 1872

CUCUMBER

A cucumber should be well sliced and dressed with pepper and vinegar, and then thrown out, as good for nothing.

> SAMUEL JOHNSON
> October 5, 1773,
> quoted in James Boswell's *Tour to the
> Hebrides*, 1786

CULTURE

Launch your boat, blest youth, and flee at full speed from every form of culture.

EPICURUS
Letter to Pythocles, c. 300 B.C.

Culture is an instrument wielded by professors to manufacture professors, who when their turn comes, will manufacture professors.

SIMONE WEIL
The Need for Roots, 1952

CUPID

Cupid, n. The so-called god of love. This bastard creation of a barbarous fancy was no doubt inflicted upon mythology for the sins of its deities. Of all the unbeautiful and inappropriate conceptions this is the most reasonless and offensive. The notion of symbolizing sexual love by a semi-sexless babe and comparing the pains of passion to the wounds of an arrow—of introducing this pudgy homunculus into art grossly to materialize the subtle spirit and suggestion of the work—this is eminently worthy of the age that, giving it birth, laid it on the doorstep of posterity.

AMBROSE BIERCE
The Devil's Dictionary, 1906, 1911

CURIOSITY

Shun the inquisitive man, for thou wilt find him leaky; open ears do not keep what has been entrusted to them.

HORACE
Epistles, c. 5 B.C.

CUSTARD

Custard, n. A detestable substance produced by a malevolent conspiracy of the hen, the cow and the cook.

AMBROSE BIERCE
The Devil's Dictionary, 1906, 1911

CUSTOM

Custom is the plague of wise Men, and the Idol of Fools.

THOMAS FULLER
Gnomologia, 1732

Custom makes monsters of us all.

NGAIO MARSH
Death in Ecstasy, 1941

The despotism of custom is everywhere the standing hindrance to human advancement.

JOHN STUART MILL
On Liberty, 1859

"CYMBELINE"

"Cymbeline" . . . is for the most part stagey trash of the lowest melodramatic order, in parts abominably written, throughout intellectually vulgar, foolish, offensive, indecent, and exasperating beyond all tolerance.

GEORGE BERNARD SHAW
Saturday Review, September 1896

CYNIC

A cynic is a man who knows the price of everything, and the value of nothing.

OSCAR WILDE
Lady Windermere's Fan, 1892

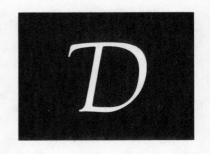

THE FIRST HUMAN BEING WHO
HURLED A CURSE INSTEAD OF A
WEAPON . . . WAS THE FOUNDER
OF CIVILIZATION.

Attributed to

SIGMUND FREUD

DANCING

Dancing? Oh, dreadful. How it was ever adopted in a civilized country I cannot find out; 'tis certainly a barbarian exercise, and of savage origin.

FANNY BURNEY
Cecilia, 1782

DANTE ALIGHIERI

All right, then I'll say it. Dante makes me sick.

Attributed to LOPE DE VEGA
When assured that he was dying, 1635

DARTMOUTH, WILLIAM, EARL OF

Lord Dartmouth only stayed long enough [in the cabinet] to prostitute his character and authenticate his hypocrisy.

HORACE WALPOLE
"Lord North," *Memoirs and Portraits,*
published posthumously in
sections, starting in 1820.

DAUGHTER

Daughters and dead fish do not keep well.

English proverb

A daughter is an embarrassing and ticklish possession.

MENANDER
Perinthas, c. 300 B.C.

If a daughter you have, she's the plague of your life,
No peace shall you know, tho' you've buried your wife,
At twenty she mocks at the duty you taught her,
Oh, what a plague is an obstinate daughter.

RICHARD BRINSLEY SHERIDAN
The Duenna, 1775

They're a mess no matter how you look at 'em, a headache till they get married—*if* they get married—and, after that, they get worse. . . . Either they leave their husbands and come back with four children and move into your guest room or their husband loses his job and the whole *caboodle* comes back. Or else they're so homely you can't get rid of them at all and they hang around the house like Spanish Moss and shame you into an early grave.

PRESTON STURGES
Screenplay, *The Miracle of Morgan's Creek*, 1944

DAY, DORIS

The only real talent Miss Day possesses is that of being absolutely sanitary: her personality untouched by human emotions, her brow unclouded by human thought, her form unsmudged by the slightest evidence of femininity.

JOHN SIMON
Private Screenings, 1967

DAYDREAMS

How many of our daydreams would darken into nightmares, were there a danger of their coming true!

LOGAN PEARSALL SMITH
Afterthoughts, 1934

DECENT

Respectable means rich, and decent means poor. I should die if I heard my family called decent.

THOMAS LOVE PEACOCK
Crotchet Castle, 1831

DEFINITION

Every definition is dangerous.
> DESIDERIUS ERASMUS
> *Adagia,* 1500

It is one of the maxims of the civil law that definitions are hazardous.
> SAMUEL JOHNSON
> *The Rambler,* May 28, 1751

To define is to exclude and negate.
> JOSÉ ORTEGA Y GASSET
> *The Modern Theme,* 1923

DEMAGOGUE

The qualities necessary to a demagogue are these: to be foul-mouthed, base-born, a low, mean fellow.
> ARISTOPHANES
> *The Knights,* 424 B.C.

DEMOCRACY

A democracy is a government in the hands of men of low birth, no property, and vulgar employments.
> ARISTOTLE
> *Politics,* 4th century B.C.

The tendency of democracies is, in all things, to mediocrity.
> JAMES FENIMORE COOPER
> *The American Democrat,* 1838

Democracy is also a form of religion. It is the worship of jackals by jackasses.
> H. L. MENCKEN
> *A Little Book in C Major,* 1916

Under democracy one party always devotes its chief energies to trying to prove that the other party is unfit to rule—and both commonly succeed, and are right.
> H. L. MENCKEN
> *Minority Report:*
> *H. L. Mencken's Notebooks,* 1956

Democracy substitutes election by the incompetent many for appointment by the corrupt few.
> GEORGE BERNARD SHAW
> *Maxims for Revolutionists,* 1903

Democracy means simply the bludgeoning of the people by the people for the people.

OSCAR WILDE
The Soul of Man Under Socialism,
1891

DEMOCRATIC PARTY

The Democratic Party is like a mule. It has neither pride of ancestry nor hope of posterity.

IGNATIUS DONNELLY
Speech to the Minnesota legislature,
September 13, 1863

DENNIS, SANDY

Pauline Kael has aptly observed that Miss Dennis "has made an acting style out of postnasal drip." It should be added that she balanced her postnasal condition with something like prefrontal lobotomy, so that when she is not a walking catarrh she is a blithering imbecile.

JOHN SIMON
Review of *The Fox,* March 1968

DEPARTMENT STORES

Fearsome hordes of wild-eyed harpies career headlong through the aisles—jostling, pushing and sweeping everything and everyone aside in their fiendish quest. Their ravenous appetites are not sated with simple sales. They lust for the maximum mark-down, the quintessential clearance and the ultimate, absolute and final reduction.

JEAN-MICHEL CHAPEREAU
Un Hiver américain, 1975

DESIRE

Desire is poison at lunch and wormwood at dinner; your bed is a stone, friendship is hateful and your fancy is always fixed on one thing.

PIETRO ARETINO
Letter to Conte di San Secondo,
June 24, 1537

There are two tragedies in life. One is not to get your heart's desire. The other is to get it.

GEORGE BERNARD SHAW
Man and Superman, 1903

DESTINY

Destiny, n. A tyrant's authority for crime and a fool's excuse for failure.
AMBROSE BIERCE
The Devil's Dictionary, 1906, 1911

Destiny is the invention of the cowardly and the resigned.
Attributed to
IGNAZIO SILONE

DETAILS

Details are always vulgar.
Attributed to OSCAR WILDE

DETECTIVE STORIES

. . . the art-for-art's sake of yawning Philistinism.
V. S. PRITCHETT
Books in General, 1953

DEWEY, THOMAS E.

You have to know Mr. Dewey very well in order to dislike him.
WOLCOTT GIBBS AND
JOHN BAINBRIDGE
The New Yorker, May 25, 1940

DICE

Dice-playing . . . is a door and window into all theft, murder, whoredom, swearing, blasphemy, banqueting, dancing, rioting, drunkenness, pride, covetousness, craft, deceit, lying, brawling, fighting, prodigality, night-watchings, idleness, beggary, poverty, bankrupting, misery, prisonment, hanging, etc.
JOHN NORTHBROOKE
Against Dicing, 1577

DICKENS, CHARLES

Dickens was the incarnation of cockneydom, a caricaturist who aped the moralist; he should have kept to short stories. If his novels are read at all in the future people will wonder what we saw in him.
GEORGE MEREDITH
To Edward Clodd,
Fortnightly Review, July 1909

DICTIONARY

Dictionary, n. A malevolent literary device for cramping the growth of a language and making it hard and inelastic.

AMBROSE BIERCE
The Devil's Dictionary, 1906, 1911

The trouble with dictionaries is, they tell you more about words than you want to know without answering the question you have.

ANDREW A. ROONEY
And More by Andy Rooney, 1982

DIET

What some call health, if purchased by perpetual anxiety about diet, isn't much better than tedious disease.

GEORGE DENNISON PRENTICE
Prenticeana, 1860

The allegory of Adam and Eve eating of the tree of evil, and entailing upon their posterity the wrath of God and the loss of everlasting life, admits of no other explanation than the disease and crime that have flowed from unnatural diet.

PERCY BYSSHE SHELLEY
Queen Mab, notes, 1813

DIGNITY

Dignity is the quality that enables a man who says nothing, does nothing and knows nothing to command a great deal of respect.

JOHN W. RAPER
What This World Needs, 1954

DINNER PARTIES

The best number for a dinner party is two—myself and a dam' good head waiter.

NUBAR SARKIS GULBENKIAN
Interviewed in the *Daily Telegraph*,
London, January 14, 1965

Dinner at the Huntercombes' possessed only two dramatic features—the wine was a farce and the food a tragedy.

ANTHONY POWELL
The Acceptance World, 1955

DIPLOMACY

Diplomacy, n. The patriotic art of lying for one's country.

AMBROSE BIERCE
The Devil's Dictionary, 1906, 1911

Diplomacy is to do and say the nastiest thing in the nicest way.

ISAAC GOLDBERG
The Reflex, 1930

Diplomacy is the lowest form of politeness because it misquotes the greatest number of people. A nation, like an individual, if it has anything to say, should simply say it.

E. B. WHITE
One Man's Meat, 1944

DIRECTORS

Every director bites the hand that lays the golden egg.

Attributed to
SAMUEL GOLDWYN

The theater got along very nicely without directors for approximately two thousand five hundred and thirty-five years.

WALTER KERR
Pieces at Eight, 1957

The director is the most overrated artist in the world. He is the only artist who, with no talent whatsoever, can be a success for 50 years without his lack of talent ever being discovered.

ORSON WELLES
Time, March 3, 1982

DISCIPLES

No new sect ever had humor; no disciples either, even the disciples of Christ.

ANNE MORROW LINDBERGH
Dearly Beloved, 1962

DISCO DANCING

Disco dancing is really dancing for people who hate dancing, since the beat is so monotonous that only champions can find interesting ways of reacting to it. There is no syncopation, just the steady thump of a giant moron knocking in an endless nail.

CLIVE JAMES
The Sunday Observer, London,
December 17, 1978

DISRAELI, BENJAMIN

He is a liar in action and words. . . . His life is a living lie. He is a disgrace to his species. . . . England is degraded in tolerating or having upon the face of her society a miscreant of his abominable, foul and atrocious nature. If there be harsher terms in the British language I should use them.

DANIEL O'CONNELL
Speech, Dublin, 1835

DOCTORS

. . . we may lay it down as a Maxim, that when a Nation abounds in Physicians it grows thin of people.

JOSEPH ADDISON
The Spectator, March 24, 1711

I die by the help of too many physicians.

ALEXANDER THE GREAT
When on his deathbed, 323 B.C.

In all times, in the opinion of the multitude, witches and old women and imposters have had a competition with physicians.

SIR FRANCIS BACON
The Advancement of Learning, 1605

Cure the disease, and kill the patient.

SIR FRANCIS BACON
"Of Friendship," *Essays*, 1612

Keep away from physicians. It is all probing and guessing and pretending with them. They leave it to Nature to cure in her own time, but they take the credit. As well as very fat fees.

ANTHONY BURGESS
Nothing Like the Sun, 1964

Doctors are just the same as lawyers; the only difference is that lawyers merely rob you, whereas doctors rob you and kill you, too.

ANTON CHEKHOV
Ivanov, 1887

God heals and the doctor takes the fee.

BENJAMIN FRANKLIN
Poor Richard's Almanack, 1732–57

Doctors cut, burn, and torture the sick, and then demand of them an undeserved fee for such services.

HERACLITUS
Fragments, c. 500 B.C.

Physicians are many in title but very few in reality.

HIPPOCRATES
The Law, c. 400 B.C.

Physicians think they do a lot for a patient when they give his disease a name.

Attributed to
IMMANUEL KANT

I often say a great doctor kills more people than a great general.

Attributed to
GOTTFRIED WILHELM VON LEIBNIZ

Diaulus, once a doctor, is now an undertaker; what he does as an undertaker he used to do also as a doctor.

MARTIAL
Epigrams, c. 95

There's a sort of decency among the dead, a remarkable discretion: you never find them making any complaint against the doctor who killed them!

MOLIÈRE
A Doctor in Spite of Himself, 1666

No doctor takes pleasure in the health even of his friends.

MICHEL DE MONTAIGNE
Essays, 1580

Physicians acquire their knowledge from our dangers, making experiments at the cost of our lives. Only a physician can commit homicide with impunity.

PLINY THE ELDER
Natural History, 1st century

If your friend is a doctor, send him to the house of your enemy.

PORTUGUESE PROVERB

. . . when we summon the wisest of them to our aid, the chances are that we may be relying on a scientific truth the error of which will be recognized in a few years' time.

MARCEL PROUST
Remembrance of Things Past,
1913–27

[Pantagruel] thought of studying medicine here but decided the profession was too troublesome and morbid. Besides, physicians smelled hellishly of enemas.

> FRANÇOIS RABELAIS
> *Gargantua and Pantagruel,* 1534

Doctors should never talk to patients about anything but medicine. When doctors talk politics, economics or sports, they reveal themselves to be ordinary mortals, idiots like the rest of us.

> ANDREW A. ROONEY
> Letter, August 23, 1983

The patient dies while the physician sleeps.

> WILLIAM SHAKESPEARE
> *The Rape of Lucrece,* 1594

. . . send the doctors out of the house. They live on the fear of death.

> GEORGE BERNARD SHAW
> Letter to Erica Cotterill
> November 27, 1907

Doctors is all swabs.

> ROBERT LOUIS STEVENSON
> *Treasure Island,* 1883

Doctors are men who prescribe medicines of which they know little, to cure diseases of which they know less, in human beings of whom they know nothing.

> Attributed to VOLTAIRE

DOG

Americans devote hundreds of millions of dollars each year to the care and worship of useless and dependent four-pawed canine parasites. They desex these creatures and then proudly teach them to beg and preen. As a reward, they buy them designer garments, stuff them with vitamin-enriched foods and then, at least once a day, take them out-of-doors and lovingly exhort them to defile the public streets and parks.

> JEAN-MICHEL CHAPEREAU
> *Un Hiver américain,* 1975

Has he bit any of the children yet? If he has, have them shot, and keep him for curiosity, to see if it was the hydrophobia.

> CHARLES LAMB
> Letter to P. G. Patmore,
> September 1827

Beware of the dog. (*Cave canem.*)
ROMAN INSCRIPTION

DOG OWNERS

I loathe people who keep dogs. They are cowards who haven't got the guts to bite people themselves.

AUGUST STRINDBERG
A Madman's Diary, 1895

DOUGHNUT

Anyhow, the hole in the doughnut is at least digestible.

H. L. MENCKEN
A Mencken Chrestomathy, 1949

DRACULA

Dracula sucks.

GRAFFITO

DREAMS

Dreams are the children of the idle brain,
Begot of nothing but vain fantasy,
Which is as thin of substance as the air
And more inconstant than the wind.

WILLIAM SHAKESPEARE
Romeo and Juliet, c. 1596

DREAMS, INTERPRETATION OF

One of the greatest pieces of charlatanic, and satanic, nonsense imposed on a gullible public is the Freudian interpretation of dreams.

VLADIMIR NABOKOV
Speaking Frankly, 1973

DRINK

Drink, sir, is a great provoker of three things . . . nose-painting, sleep, and urine. Lechery, sir, it provokes, and unprovokes; it provokes the desire, but it takes away the performance.

WILLIAM SHAKESPEARE
Macbeth, 1606

O God, that men should put an enemy in their mouths to steal away their brains! that we should with joy, pleasancy, revel, and applause transform ourselves into beasts!

WILLIAM SHAKESPEARE
Othello, 1604–5

DUTY

Duty largely consists of pretending that the trivial is critical.

JOHN FOWLES
The Magus, 1965

That dull, leaden, soul-depressing sensation known as the sense of duty.

O. HENRY
"No Story," *Options*, 1909

LATENT IN EVERY MAN IS A VENOM OF AMAZING BITTER-
NESS, A BLACK RESENTMENT; SOMETHING THAT CURSES
AND LOATHES LIFE, A FEELING OF BEING TRAPPED, OF
HAVING TRUSTED AND BEEN FOOLED, OF BEING THE
HELPLESS PREY OF IMPOTENT RAGE, BLIND SURRENDER,
THE VICTIM OF A SAVAGE, RUTHLESS POWER THAT GIVES
AND TAKES AWAY, ENLISTS A MAN, DROPS HIM, PROMISES
AND BETRAYS, AND—CROWNING INJURY—INFLICTS ON
HIM THE HUMILIATION OF FEELING SORRY FOR HIM-
SELF . . .

PAUL VALÉRY
MAUVAISES PENSÉES ET AUTRES, 1942

EAGLE

I wish the bald eagle had not been chosen as the representative of our Country: he is a bird of bad moral Character . . . he is generally poor, and often very lousy.

BENJAMIN FRANKLIN
Letter to Sarah Bache,
January 26, 1784

EARLY RISING

Early risers, as a rule, are a notably arrogant set.

WALTER DWIGHT
The Saving Sense, 1947

Early morning cheerfulness can be extremely obnoxious.

WILLIAM FEATHER
The Business of Life, 1949

Early to bed, and you'll wish you were dead.
Bed before eleven, nuts before seven.

DOROTHY PARKER
"The Little Hours,"
Not So Deep as a Well, 1936

The horror of getting up is unparalleled, and I am filled with amazement every morning when I find that I have done it.

LYTTON STRACHEY
Virginia Woolf and Lytton Strachey
Letters, 1956

Early to rise and to bed makes a male healthy and wealthy and dead.

JAMES THURBER
Fables for Our Time, 1970

ECONOMICS

What we might call, by way of eminence, the dismal science.

THOMAS CARLYLE
The Nigger Question, 1849

ECONOMIST

If all economists were laid end to end, they would not reach a conclusion.

Attributed to
GEORGE BERNARD SHAW

EDDY, MARY BAKER

To be a moral thief, an unblushing liar, a supreme dictator, and a cruel, self-satisfied monster, and attain, in the minds of millions, the status of a deity, is not only remarkable but a dismal reflection on the human race. She had much in common with Hitler, only no moustache.

NOËL COWARD
Diary, July 29, 1962

. . . a brass god with clay legs.

MARK TWAIN
Christian Science, 1907

EDINBURGH

That most picturesque (at a distance) and nastiest (when near) of all capital cities.

THOMAS GRAY
Letter to Dr. Wharton, September
1765

EDITOR

An editor—a person employed on a newspaper whose business it is to separate the wheat from the chaff, and to see that the chaff is printed.

ELBERT HUBBARD
A Thousand and One Epigrams, 1911

An editor is one who separates the wheat from the chaff and prints the chaff.

ADLAI E. STEVENSON
The Stevenson Wit, 1966

EDUCATION

Much learning doth make thee mad.

Acts 26:24

Nothing in education is so astonishing as the amount of ignorance it accumulates in the form of inert facts.

HENRY ADAMS
The Education of Henry Adams, 1907

I thank God there are no free schools nor printing, and I hope we shall not have these hundred years; for learning has brought disobedience and heresy and sects into the world, and printing has divulged them, and libels against the best government. God keep us from both!

WILLIAM BERKELEY,
Governor of Virginia
Report to the English Committee for
the Colonies, 1671

The effects of infantile instruction are, like those of syphilis, never completely cured.

ROBERT BRIFFAULT
Sin and Sex, 1931

How is it that little children are so intelligent and men so stupid? It must be education that does it.

ALEXANDRE DUMAS, FILS
Quoted in L. Treich's
L'Esprit français, 1947

Education is the process of casting false pearls before real swine.

Attributed to
IRWIN EDMAN

Colleges hate geniuses, just as convents hate saints.

Attributed to
RALPH WALDO EMERSON

We are shut up in schools and college recitation rooms for ten or fifteen years, and come out at last with a bellyful of words and do not know a thing.

RALPH WALDO EMERSON
Journal, 1839

Universities are fit for nothing but to debauch the principles of young men, to poison their minds with romantic notions of knowledge and virtue.

HENRY FIELDING
The Temple Beau, 1730

A learned blockhead is a greater blockhead than an ignorant one.
BENJAMIN FRANKLIN
Poor Richard's Almanack, 1732–57

Education makes us more stupid than the brutes. A thousand voices call to us on every hand, but our ears are stopped with wisdom.
JEAN GIRAUDOUX
The Enchanted, 1933

Universal education is the most corroding and disintegrating poison that liberalism has ever invented for its own destruction.
ADOLF HITLER
Quoted by Dr. Hermann Rauschning

Colleges are places where pebbles are polished and diamonds are dimmed.
ROBERT G. INGERSOLL
Prose-Poems and Selections, 1884

Education: the inculcation of the incomprehensible into the indifferent by the incompetent.
Attributed to
JOHN MAYNARD KEYNES

It is tiresome to hear education discussed, tiresome to educate, and tiresome to be educated.
Attributed to
WILLIAM LAMB,
second Viscount Melbourne

You can't expect a boy to be depraved until he has been to a good school.
SAKI (H. H. MUNRO)
"A Baker's Dozen," *Reginald in Russia*, 1910

For every person wishing to teach there are thirty not wishing to be taught.

W. C. SELLAR AND R. J. YEATMAN
And Now All This, 1932

Education has produced a vast population able to read but unable to distinguish what is worth reading.

GEORGE MACAULAY TREVELYAN
English Social History, 1942

In the first place God made idiots. This was for practice. Then he made school boards.

MARK TWAIN
Following the Equator, 1897

EDWARD VII

Bertie seemed to display a deepseated repugnance to every form of mental exertion.

LYTTON STRACHEY
Queen Victoria, 1921

EDWARDS, JONATHAN

He believed in the worst God, preached the worst sermons, and had the worst religion of any human being who ever lived on this continent.

M. M. RICHTER
Jonathan Edwards, 1920

EGGS

And then I'm frightened of eggs, worse than frightened; they revolt me. That white round thing without any holes ... Brr! Have you ever seen anything more revolting than an egg yolk breaking and spilling its yellow liquid? Blood is jolly, red. But egg yolk is yellow, revolting. I've never tasted it.

ALFRED HITCHCOCK
In an interview with Oriana Fallaci,
Cannes, 1963

EIGHTEENTH CENTURY

The putrid Eighteenth Century: such an ocean of sordid nothingness, shams and scandalous hypocrisies as never weltered in the world before.

THOMAS CARLYLE
Letter to Ralph Waldo Emerson,
April 8, 1854

EINSTEIN, ALBERT

What does all this worked-up enthusiasm about Einstein mean? I have never met a man yet who understands in the least what Einstein is driving at . . . I very seriously doubt that Einstein himself really knows what he is driving at. . . . In a word, the outcome of this doubt and befogged speculation about time and space is a cloak which hides the ghastly apparition of atheism.

WILLIAM HENRY
CARDINAL O'CONNELL
Time, May 13, 1929

ELECTIONS

An election is a moral horror, as bad as a battle except for the blood: a mud bath for every soul concerned in it.

GEORGE BERNARD SHAW
Back to Methuselah, 1921

ELIOT, GEORGE

George Eliot had the heart of Sappho; but the face, with the long proboscis, the protruding teeth of the Apocalyptic horse, betrayed animality.

GEORGE MEREDITH
Fortnightly Review, July 1909

ELIZABETH I

As just and merciful as Nero and as good a Christian as Mahomet.

JOHN WESLEY
Journal, April 29, 1768

EMERSON, RALPH WALDO

A foul mouth is so ill-matched with a white beard that I would gladly believe the newspaper scribes alone responsible for the bestial utterances which they declare to have dropped from a teacher whom such disciples as these exhibit to our disgust and compassion as performing on their obscene platform to a gap-toothed and hoary-headed ape, carried at first into notice on the shoulder of Carlyle, and who now in his dotage spits and chatters from a dirtier perch of his own finding and fouling: coryphaeus or choragus of his Bulgarian tribe of autocoprophagous baboons, who make the filth they feed on.

ALGERNON C. SWINBURNE
Letter to Ralph Waldo Emerson,
January 30, 1874

EMPIRE

The English sent all their bores abroad, and acquired the empire as a punishment.

EDWARD BOND
Narrow Road to the Deep North,
1968

ENGLAND AND THE ENGLISH

For 'tis a low, newspaper, humdrum, law-suit Country.

LORD BYRON
Don Juan, 1819–24

Mad Dogs and Englishmen Go Out in the Noonday Sun

NOËL COWARD
Song title, 1931

I curse their head and all hairs of their head. I curse their face, their eyes, their mouth, their nose, their tongue, their teeth, their shoulders, their back, and their heart, their arms, their legs, their hands, their feet, and every part of their body from the top of their head to the soles of their feet, before and behind, within and without. . . . I curse them walking, and I curse them riding. I curse them eating, and I curse them drinking. I curse them within the house, and I curse them without the house. I curse their wives, their bairns and their servants. . . . I curse their cattle, their wool, their sheep, their horses, their swine, their geese, and their hens. I curse their halls, their chambers, their stables, and their barns . . .

Curse on the English read by Scottish
priests on the closing of the religious
houses, c. 1530

It is not that the Englishman can't feel—it is that he is afraid to feel. He has been taught at his public school that feeling is bad form. He must not express great joy or sorrow, or even open his mouth too wide when he talks—his pipe might fall out if he did.

E. M. FORSTER
Abinger Harvest, 1936

England is a prison for men, a paradise for women, a purgatory for servants, a hell for horses.

THOMAS FULLER
The Holy State and the Profane
State, 1642

The English (it must be owned) are rather a foul-mouthed nation.

WILLIAM HAZLITT
"On Criticism," *Table-Talk*,
1821–22

The most repulsive race which God in His wrath ever created.

HEINRICH HEINE
Shakespeare's Maidens, 1839

I consider the government of England as totally without morality, insolent beyond bearing, inflated with vanity and ambition, aiming at the exclusive dominion of the sea, lost in corruption, of deep-rooted hatred toward us, hostile to liberty wherever it endeavors to show its head, and the eternal disturber of the peace of the world.

THOMAS JEFFERSON
Letter to Thomas Leiper,
June 1815

Of all nations on earth, the British require to be treated with the most *hauteur*. They require to be kicked into common manners.

THOMAS JEFFERSON
Letter to Colonel W. S. Smith, 1787

Curse the blasted jelly-boned swines, the slimy belly-wriggling invertebrates, the miserable sodding rotters, the flaming sods, the snivelling, dribbling, dithering, palsied pulseless lot that make up England today. They've got white of egg in their veins, and their spunk is that watery it's a marvel they can breed. . . . Why, why, why, was I born an Englishman!

D. H. LAWRENCE
Letter to Edward Garnett,
July 3, 1912

England is a nation of shopkeepers.

Attributed to NAPOLEON I
(An earlier reference to the phrase
"nation of shopkeepers" appears in
Adam Smith's *An Enquiry into the Nature and Causes of the Wealth of Nations*, 1776.)

The English have no exalted sentiments. They can all be bought.

NAPOLEON I
To Gaspard Gourgaud at St. Helena,
September 26, 1817

There lives not three good men in England, and one of them is fat and grows old.

WILLIAM SHAKESPEARE
Henry IV, Part I, c. 1605

It must be acknowledged that the English are the most disagreeable of all the nations of Europe—more surly and morose, with less disposition to please, to exert themselves for the good of society, to make small sacrifices, and to put themselves out of their way.

SYDNEY SMITH
In the *Edinburgh Review*, 1818

What a pity it is that we have no amusements in England but vice and religion.

SYDNEY SMITH
Quoted in *The Smith of Smiths*,
by Hesketh Pearson, 1934

Whenever he met a great man he grovelled before him, and my-lorded him as only a free-born Briton can do.

WILLIAM MAKEPEACE THACKERAY
Vanity Fair, 1847–48

England has forty-two religions and only two sauces.

Attributed to VOLTAIRE

There is something utterly nauseating about a system of society which pays a harlot twenty-five times as much as it pays its Prime Minister, two hundred and fifty times as much as it pays its Members of Parliament, and five hundred times as much as it pays some of its ministers of religion.

HAROLD WILSON
Speech in the House of Commons,
1963, on the case of Christine Keeler

EPISCOPALIANS

The three kinds of services you generally find in the Episcopal churches. I call them either low-and-lazy, broad-and-hazy, or high-and-crazy.

WILLA GIBBS
The Dean, 1957

EQUALITY

Equality may perhaps be a right, but no power on earth can ever turn it into a fact.

HONORÉ DE BALZAC
La Duchesse de Langeais, 1834

Nature has never read the Declaration of Independence. It continues to make us unequal.

WILL DURANT
Quoted in the *New York Daily News,*
May 3, 1970

That all men are equal is a proposition to which, at ordinary times, no sane individual has ever given his assent.

ALDOUS HUXLEY
Proper Studies, 1927

ETERNITY

Eternity is a terrible thought. I mean, where's it going to end?

TOM STOPPARD
*Rosencrantz and Guildenstern Are
Dead,* 1967

EUCHARIST

Neither antiquity nor any other sect of the present day has imagined a more atrocious and blasphemous absurdity than that of eating God. It is a most revolting dogma, insulting to the Supreme Being, the height of madness and folly.

FREDERICK THE GREAT
Letter to Voltaire,
March 19, 1776

EUROPE

Goddamn the continent of Europe. It is merely of antiquarian interest. Rome is only a few years behind Tyre and Babylon. The negroid streak creeps northward to defile the Nordic race. Already the Italians have the souls of blackamoors. . . . France made me sick. . . . I think it's a shame that England and America didn't let Germany conquer Europe.

F. SCOTT FITZGERALD
Letter to Edmund Wilson,
May 1921

EVERYBODY

We hate everybody, regardless of race, creed or color.

GRAFFITO

EVERYONE

Everyone is as God made him, and often a great deal worse.

MIGUEL DE CERVANTES
Don Quixote, 1605–15

On this earth, there is one thing which is terrible, and that is that everyone has his own good reasons.

JEAN RENOIR
The Rules of the Game, film, 1939

EVERYTHING

Almost all human affairs are tedious. Everything is too long. Visits, dinners, concerts, plays, speeches, pleadings, essays, sermons, are too long. Pleasure and business labour equally under this defect, or, as I should rather say, this fatal superabundance.

SIR ARTHUR HELPS
Friends in Council, 1847–59

EVOLUTION

If a minister believes and teaches evolution, he is a stinking skunk, a hypocrite, and a liar.

WILLIAM A. "BILLY" SUNDAY
Interview, 1925

EXAMPLE

Few things are harder to put up with than the annoyance of a good example.

MARK TWAIN
Pudd'nhead Wilson, 1894

EXECUTIVE

Damn the great executives, the men of measured merriment, damn the men with careful smiles, damn the men that run the shops, oh, damn their measured merriment.

SINCLAIR LEWIS
Arrowsmith, 1925

EXERCISE

Faddists are continually proclaiming the value of exercise; four people out of five are more in need of rest than exercise.

LOGAN CLENDENING
Modern Methods of Treatment, 1924

I get my exercise acting as a pallbearer to my friends who exercise.

Attributed to
CHAUNCEY DEPEW

Whenever I feel the urge to exercise I lie down until it passes.
                                                    ROBERT HUTCHINS
                                        Quoted by Helen Lawrenson in
                                              Whistling Girl, 1978

To preserve one's health by too strict a regimen is in itself a tedious malady.

                                                            FRANÇOIS,
                                        DUC DE LA ROCHEFOUCAULD
                                                    Maxims, c. 1675

Bodily exercise profiteth little.
                                                    I Timothy 4:8

I have never taken any exercise, except for sleeping and resting, and I never intend to take any. Exercise is loathsome.
                                                        MARK TWAIN
                                        Mark Twain's Speeches, 1923

EXPERIENCE

Experience is the name everyone gives to their mistakes.
                                                    OSCAR WILDE
                                        Lady Windermere's Fan, 1892

EXPERT

An expert is a man who avoids the small errors as he sweeps on to the grand fallacy.

                                                BENJAMIN STOLBERG
                                        Quoted in *Reader's Digest,*
                                                    September 1936

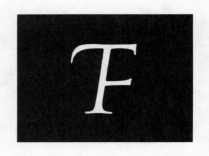

EVERY NORMAL MAN MUST BE
TEMPTED AT TIMES TO SPIT ON HIS
HANDS, HOIST THE BLACK FLAG,
AND BEGIN SLITTING THROATS.

H. L. MENCKEN

PREJUDICES, FIRST SERIES, 1919

FACT

I hate facts. I always say the chief end of man is to form general proposi-
tions—adding that no general proposition is worth a damn.

OLIVER WENDELL HOLMES, JR.
*The Mind and Faith of Justice
Holmes*, 1943

. . . the fatal futility of fact.

HENRY JAMES
The Spoils of Poynton, 1907

FAITH

The most costly of all follies is to believe passionately in the palpably
not true. It is the chief occupation of mankind.

H. L. MENCKEN
A Mencken Chrestomathy, 1949

Faith may be defined briefly as an illogical belief in the occurrence of
the improbable.

H. L. MENCKEN
Prejudices, Third Series, 1922

Never believe in mirrors or newspapers.

JOHN OSBORNE
The Hotel in Amsterdam, 1968

86

Faith is believing what you know ain't so.
MARK TWAIN
Following the Equator, 1897

To believe is very dull. To doubt is intensely engrossing. To be on the alert is to live; to be lulled into security is to die.
OSCAR WILDE
The Epigrams of Oscar Wilde, 1952

FAITH, HOPE AND CHARITY

I have no faith, very little hope and as much charity as I can afford.
Attributed to
THOMAS HENRY HUXLEY

FALSTAFF, SIR JOHN

Why dost thou converse with that trunk of humours, that bolting-hutch of beastliness, that swoln parcel of dropsies, that huge bombard of sack, that stuffed cloakbag of guts, that roasted Manning tree ox with the pudding in his belly, that reverend vice, that grey iniquity, that vanity in years?
WILLIAM SHAKESPEARE
King Henry IV, Part II, 1597–98

FAME

Fame is the stepmother of death and ambition the excrement of glory.
PIETRO ARETINO
Letter to Lionardo Parpaglioni,
December 2, 1537

We cannot put the face of a person on a stamp unless said person is deceased. My suggestion, therefore, is that you drop dead.
JAMES EDWARD DAY,
Postmaster General
Letter written but not mailed to
a petitioner who wanted himself
portrayed on a postage stamp
Quoted in *The New York Times*,
March 7, 1962

How dreary to be somebody!
How public, like a frog
To tell your name the livelong day
To an admiring bog!
EMILY DICKINSON
Poems, 1, 1890 (posthumous)

How vain, without the merit, is the name.

HOMER
Iliad, c. 8th century B.C.

Reputation is an idle and most false imposition; oft got without merit, and lost without deserving.

WILLIAM SHAKESPEARE
Othello, 1604–5

A plague on eminence! I hardly dare cross the street any more without a convoy, and I am stared at wherever I go like an idiot member of a royal family or an animal in a zoo; and zoo animals have been known to die from stares.

IGOR STRAVINSKY
"Stravinsky on the Musical Scene
and Other Matters," *The New York
Review of Books,* May 12, 1966

Fame is a vapor, popularity an accident; the only earthly certainty is oblivion.

MARK TWAIN
Mark Twain's Notebook, 1935

FAMILIARITY

Familiarity breeds contempt.
PUBLILIUS SYRUS
Sententiae, c. 50 B.C.

Familiarity breeds contempt—and children.

MARK TWAIN
Mark Twain's Notebook, 1935

FAMILY

I believe that more unhappiness comes from this source [the family] than from any other—I mean from the attempt to prolong family connections unduly and to make people hang together artificially who would never naturally do so.

SAMUEL BUTLER
Note-Books, 1912

I can trace my ancestry back to a protoplasmal primordial atomic globule. Consequently, my family pride is something in-conceivable. I can't help it. I was born sneering.

W. S. GILBERT
The Mikado, 1885

The family is the ultimate American fascism.

> Attributed to
> PAUL GOODMAN

Far from being the basis of the good society, the family, with its narrow privacy and tawdry secrets, is the source of all our discontents.

> EDMUND LEACH
> BBC Reith Lectures, 1967

The son dishonoreth the father, the daughter riseth up against her mother, the daughter-in-law against her mother-in-law; a man's enemies are the men of his own house.

> Micah 7:6, c. 700 B.C.

A family is but too often a commonwealth of malignants.

> ALEXANDER POPE
> *Thoughts on Various Subjects*, 1717

As a rule there is only one person an English girl hates more than she hates her eldest sister; and that's her mother.

> GEORGE BERNARD SHAW
> *Man and Superman*, 1903

Sacred family! . . . The supposed home of all the virtues, where innocent children are tortured into their first falsehoods, where wills are broken by parental tyranny, and self-respect is smothered by crowded, jostling egos.

> AUGUST STRINDBERG
> *The Son of a Servant*, 1886

FARM

A farm is a hunk of land on which, if you get up early enough mornings and work late enough nights, you'll make a fortune—if you strike oil on it.

> FIBBER MCGEE
> Quoted in *Reader's Digest*,
> November 1949

A farm is an irregular patch of nettles bounded by short term notes, containing a fool and his wife who didn't know enough to stay in the city.

> S. J. PERELMAN
> *Acres and Pains*, 1947

It makes but little difference whether you are committed to a farm or a county jail.

> HENRY DAVID THOREAU
> *Walden*, 1854

FARMERS

No more grasping, selfish and dishonest mammal . . . is known to students of Anthropoidea. When the going is good for him he robs the rest of us to the extreme limit of our endurance; when the going is bad he comes bawling for help out of the public till. . . . Yet we are asked to venerate this prehensile moron as the *Ur*-burgher, the citizen *par excellence*, the foundation-stone of the state! And why? Because he produces something that all of us must have . . .

H. L. MENCKEN
Prejudices, Second Series, 1920

FASHION

Fashion is the abortive issue of vain ostentation and exclusive egotism: it is haughty, trifling, affected, servile, despotic, mean and ambitious, precise and fantastical, all in a breath—tied to no rule, and bound to conform to every whim of the minute.

WILLIAM HAZLITT
"On Fashion," *Sketches and Essays*,
1839

Fashions exist for women with no taste, etiquette for people with no breeding.

QUEEN MARIE OF RUMANIA
Reader's Digest, April 1938

Fashion is something barbarous, for it produces innovation without reason and imitation without benefit.

GEORGE SANTAYANA
Reason in Religion, 1905

Fashions, after all, are only induced epidemics.

GEORGE BERNARD SHAW
The Doctor's Dilemma, 1913

Fashion is a form of ugliness so intolerable that we have to alter it every six months.

Attributed to
OSCAR WILDE

FAST-FOOD HAMBURGERS

We were taken to a fast-food café where our order was fed into a computer. Our hamburgers, made from the flesh of chemically impregnated cattle, had been broiled over counterfeit charcoal, placed between slices of artificially flavored cardboard and served to us by recycled juvenile delinquents.

JEAN-MICHEL CHAPEREAU
Un Hiver américain, 1975

FASTING

The popish fasting is murder, whereby many people have been destroyed, observing the fasts strictly, and chiefly, by eating one sort of food, so that nature's strength is thereby weakened.

MARTIN LUTHER
Table Talk, 1569

FAT

Nobody loves a fat man.

EDMUND DAY
The Round-Up, 1907

FATHER

Don't fathers know that they may only be revered when they are far away?

RICHARD CONDON
A Trembling upon Rome, 1983

FESTIVALS

All festivals are bunk. . . . Festivals are for the purpose of attracting trade to the town. What that has to do with music I don't know.

SIR THOMAS BEECHAM
Quoted in *Jazz Journal,* October 1956

FICTION

[Fiction is] a confidence trick, trying to make believe something is true that isn't.

ANGUS WILSON
Interview, *Paris Review,*
in *Writers at Work,* 1958

FIELDS, W. C.

Bill never really wanted to hurt anybody. He just felt an obligation.

GREGORY LA CAVA
Quoted in *W. C. Fields,*
by Robert L. Taylor, 1949

FILMS

American motion pictures are written by the half-educated for the half-witted.

ST. JOHN ERVINE
Quoted in the *New York Mirror*,
June 6, 1963

It is my indignant opinion that ninety per cent of the moving pictures exhibited in America are so vulgar, witless and dull that it is preposterous to write about them in any publication not intended to be read while chewing gum.

WOLCOTT GIBBS
Quoted in *Popcorn Paradise*,
edited by John Robert Colombo, 1979

Movies are one of the bad habits that have corrupted our century. . . .
They have slipped into the American mind more misinformation in one evening than the Dark Ages could muster in a decade.

BEN HECHT
Child of the Century, 1954

There is only one thing that can kill the movies, and that is education.

WILL ROGERS
The Autobiography of Will Rogers,
1949

Film, called the Seventh Lively Art, all too often usurps its title after the fashion of the Holy Roman Empire: it is generally not in the least lively, not seventh but seventh-rate, and decidedly not art.

JOHN SIMON
Acid Test, 1963

FIRST NIGHT

The typical first night is a cross between a witch's sabbath, a dowdy fashion show and a minor horse race. It brings no credit on the theater and the idea of it being glamorous is on a par with the idea of whores being good-hearted.

CLIVE BARNES
Plays and Players, December 1972

FISHING

A fishing-rod is a stick with a hook at one end and a fool at the other.
SAMUEL JOHNSON
Quoted by William Hazlitt in
On Egotism, 1825

Fishing is a delusion entirely surrounded by liars in old clothes.
Attributed to DON MARQUIS

FLAG

Have not I myself known five hundred living soldiers sabred into crows' meat for a piece of glazed cotton which they called their flag; which, had you sold it in any market-cross, would not have brought above three groschen?
THOMAS CARLYLE
Sartor Resartus, 1836

FLATTERY

Flattery is alright, if you don't inhale.
ADLAI E. STEVENSON
Speech, February 1, 1961

FLORIDA

In none of the forty-eight states does life leap so suddenly, in an hour's motor drive, from the suburban snooze to the primeval ooze.
ALISTAIR COOKE
One Man's America, 1952

FLOWERS

They are for prima donnas or corpses; I am neither.
Attributed to ARTURO TOSCANINI
Refusing a floral tribute
after a performance

FLUTE

What is worse than a flute? Two flutes.
ANONYMOUS

FOOTBALL

Football is nothyng but beastely fury and extreme violence, whereof procedeth hurte, and consequently rancour and malice do remayne with thym that be wounded, wherefore it is to be put in perpetuall silence.
SIR THOMAS ELYOT, 1531

The Football . . . as it is now commonly used, with thronging of a rude multitude, with bursting of skinnes, and breaking of legges, be neither civill, neither worthy of the name of any traine to health.

RICHARD MELCASTER, 1581

. . . rather a bloody and murdering practise than a felowley sporte or pastime . . . sometimes their necks are broken, sometimes their backs, sometimes their legs, sometimes their armes; sometime one part thrust out of joynt, sometime another; sometime their noses gush out with blood, sometime their eyes start out; and sometimes hurt in one place, sometimes in another; . . . and hereof groweth envie, malice, rancour, choler, hatred, displeasure, enmitie, and what not els: and sometimes fighting, brawling, contention, quarrel picking, murder, homicide, and great effusion of blood . . .

PHILIP STUBBES
Anatomie of Abuses, 1583

FOOTNOTES

A footnote is like running downstairs to answer the doorbell during the first night of marriage.

Attributed to
JOHN BARRYMORE

. . . scholarly barbed wire.

EDMUND WILSON
Princeton Alumni Weekly,
December 4, 1973

FOOT RACING

If God had intended man for racing, He would have given him four legs like a horse.

WALTER "RED" SMITH
The Red Smith Reader, 1982

FORD MADOX FORD

Freud Madox Fraud.

OSBERT SITWELL
Quoted in *The Literary Life,*
by R. Phelps and P. Deane, 1968

FOREST

A forest of all manner of trees is poor, if not disagreeable, in effect; a mass of one species of tree is sublime.

JOHN RUSKIN
Modern Painters, 1856

FORK

Fork, n. An instrument used chiefly for the purpose of putting dead animals into the mouth.

AMBROSE BIERCE
The Devil's Dictionary, 1906, 1911

FORTUNE

Fortune loves to give bedroom slippers to people with wooden legs, and gloves to those with no hands.

THÉOPHILE GAUTIER
Mademoiselle de Maupin, 1835

. . . that arrant whore.
WILLIAM SHAKESPEARE
King Lear, 1605–6

FORTY

Every man over forty is a scoundrel.
GEORGE BERNARD SHAW
Maxims for Revolutionists, 1903

FOX HUNTING

The English country gentleman galloping after a fox—the unspeakable in full pursuit of the uneatable.

OSCAR WILDE
A Woman of No Importance, 1893

FRANCE AND THE FRENCH

The French are irreconcilable, savage foes; and, if you strip them of the cook, the tailor and the hairdresser, you will find nothing left in them but copper-skinned Indians.

Attributed to
OTTO VON BISMARCK, c. 1880

. . . a relatively small and eternally quarrelsome country in Western Europe, fountainhead of rationalist political manias, militarily impotent, historically inglorious during the past century, democratically bankrupt, Communist-infiltrated from top to bottom.

WILLIAM F. BUCKLEY, JR.
In his syndicated column,
On the Right, April 2, 1964

France was long a despotism tempered by epigrams.

> THOMAS CARLYLE
> *The French Revolution*, 1837

I hate the hollowness of French principles; I hate the republicanism of French politics; I hate the hostility of the French people to revealed religion; I hate the artificiality of French cooking; I hate the acidity of French wines; I hate the flimsiness of the French language.

> Attributed to
> SAMUEL TAYLOR COLERIDGE
> In J. C. Young's
> *A Memoir of Charles Mayne Young*,
> 1871

Ungovern'd passion settled first in France,
Where mankind lives in haste, and thrives by chance,
A dancing nation, fickle and untrue:
Have oft undone themselves, and others too.

> DANIEL DEFOE
> *The True-Born Englishman*, 1701

How can you be expected to govern a country that has two hundred and forty-six kinds of cheese?

> CHARLES DE GAULLE
> *Newsweek*, October 1, 1962

The French!—vain, insolent, thoughtless, bloodthirsty, active and impetuous by Nature, so susceptible as to have their little reason always blinded by the bubble of Glory held before the mind's eye, a People who are brilliant without intensity, have courage without firmness, are polite without benevolence, and tender without heart; tall, fierce, and elegant in their looks; depraved, lecherous, and blasphemous in their feelings; mingling the most disgusting offices of Nature with the most elegant duties of Social Life. Good God!

> BENJAMIN ROBERT HAYDON
> *Diary*, June 25, 1815

The French are an indelicate people; they will spit upon any place.

> SAMUEL JOHNSON
> May 14, 1778, quoted in James
> Boswell's *Life of Samuel Johnson*,
> 1791

I would have loved it [France]—without the French.

> D. H. LAWRENCE
> Letter to Catherine Carswell,
> May 28, 1920

The French are the wittiest, the most charming and (up to the present, at all events) the least musical race on earth.

STENDHAL
Life of Rossini, 1824

[Menton is] a calcined, scalped, rasped, scraped, flayed, broiled, powdered, leprous, blotched, mangy, grimy, parboiled country *without* trees, water, grass, fields . . . it is infinitely liker hell than earth, and one looks for tails among the people.

ALGERNON CHARLES SWINBURNE
Letters, 1919

France has neither winter nor summer nor morals—apart from these drawbacks it is a fine country.

MARK TWAIN
Mark Twain's Notebook, 1935

France is a nation devoted to the false hypothesis on which it then builds marvelously logical structures.

GORE VIDAL
American Film, April 1977

France is the only country where the money falls apart and you can't tear the toilet paper.

Attributed to
BILLY WILDER

FREEDOM

If people have to choose between freedom and sandwiches, they will take sandwiches.

LORD BOYD-ORR
"Sayings of the Year,"
The Observer, London, 1955

Freedom is a bourgeois notion devised as a cloak for the specter of economic slavery.

Attributed to
NIKOLAI LENIN

O Freedom, what crimes are committed in thy name!

Attributed to
JEANNE MANON ROLAND

FREEDOM OF SPEECH

Why should freedom of speech and freedom of the press be allowed?
Why should a government which is doing what it believes to be right

allow itself to be criticized? It would not allow opposition by lethal weapons. Ideas are much more fatal things than guns. Why should any man be allowed to buy a printing press and disseminate pernicious opinions calculated to embarrass the government?

NIKOLAI LENIN
Speech in Moscow, 1920

FRENCH-FRIED POTATOES

The French fried potato has become an inescapable horror in almost every public eating place in the country. "French fries," say the menus, but they are not French fries any longer. They are a furry-textured substance with the taste of plastic wood.

RUSSELL BAKER
The New York Times,
February 22, 1968

FRENCH REVOLUTION

With mere political liberty we are worse off than under despotism. . . . Formerly we had half a million despots; now we have a million oppressors.

JEAN-PAUL MARAT
Letter to Camille Desmoulins,
June 24, 1790

FREUD, SIGMUND

I think he's crude, I think he's medieval, and I don't want an elderly gentleman from Vienna with an umbrella inflicting his dreams upon me.

VLADIMIR NABOKOV
In a TV interview, 1966

FRIENDS

Friendship is a very taxing and arduous form of leisure activity.

MORTIMER ADLER
Speaking on public television,
March 22, 1979

A friend is one who dislikes the same people that you dislike.

ANONYMOUS

I don't trust him. We're friends.

BERTOLT BRECHT
Mother Courage, 1938–39

The one thing your friends will never forgive you is your happiness.
ALBERT CAMUS
The Fall, 1957

Of all plagues, good Heaven, thy wrath can send,
Save, save, oh! save me from the candid friend.
GEORGE CANNING
The New Morality, 1823

To have a good enemy, choose a friend: he knows where to strike.
Attributed to
DIANE DE POITIERS

God save me from my friends; I can take care of my enemies.
ENGLISH PROVERB, c. 1477

Old friendships are like meats served up repeatedly: cold, comfortless,
and distasteful. The stomach turns against them.
WILLIAM HAZLITT
On the Pleasure of Hating, 1821

Histories are more full of examples of the fidelity of dogs than of
friends.
ALEXANDER POPE
Letter to Henry Cromwell,
October 19, 1709

I cannot forgive my friends for dying: I do not find these vanishing acts
of theirs at all amusing.
LOGAN PEARSALL SMITH
All Trivia, 1949

I am weary of friends, and friendships are all monsters.
JONATHAN SWIFT
Journal to Stella,
October 23, 1710

Everytime a friend succeeds, I die a little.
GORE VIDAL
Quoted in *The New York Times,*
February 4, 1973

New friends, like new mistresses, are got by disparaging old ones.
WILLIAM WYCHERLEY
The Plain Dealer, c. 1674

FROGS

I marvel why frogs and snails are with some people, and in some countries, in great account, and judged wholesome food, whereas indeed they have in them nothing else but a cold, gross, slimy and excremental juice.

TOBIAS VENNER
Via recta, 1620

FUGUE

A fugue is a piece of music in which the voices come in one after another and the audience goes out one after another.

ANONYMOUS

FUNERALS

The pomp of funerals has more regard to the vanity of the living than to the honor of the dead.

FRANÇOIS, DUC
DE LA ROCHEFOUCAULD
Maxims, 1665

FUTURE

Only one more indispensable massacre of Capitalists or Communists or Fascists or Christians or Heretics, and there we are in the Golden Future.

ALDOUS HUXLEY
Time Must Have a Stop, 1944

The world began without man, and it will complete itself without him.

CLAUDE LÉVI-STRAUSS
Triste Tropiques, 1955

It is bad enough to know the past; it would be intolerable to know the future.

W. SOMERSET MAUGHAM
Quoted in *Foreign Devil,*
by Richard Hughes, 1972

If you want a picture of the future, imagine a boot stomping on a human face—forever . . .

GEORGE ORWELL
1984, 1948

GANDHI, MOHANDAS K. "MAHATMA"

It is alarming and also nauseating to see Mr. Gandhi, a seditious Middle Temple lawyer, now posing as a fakir of a type well known in the East, striding half-naked up the steps of the viceregal palace . . . to parley on equal terms with the representative of the king-emperor.

WINSTON S. CHURCHILL
Speech, February 23, 1931

Gandhi has been assassinated. In my humble opinion a bloody good thing but far too late.

NOËL COWARD
Diary, January 30, 1948

GARDEN

A garden is ceaselessly fertilized, corrupted, wounded, devoured by great monsters equipped with armor, wings and claws. Its enemies mock at the artless weapons with which it blindly bristles. Its thorns give us a proof of its fears and seem to us more like permanent goose-flesh than like an arsenal.

JEAN COCTEAU
The Difficulty of Being, 1957

A garden is like those pernicious machineries which catch a man's coat-skirt or his hand, and draw in his arm, his leg, and his whole body to irresistible destruction.

RALPH WALDO EMERSON
The Conduct of Life, 1860

A garden was the primitive prison, till man, with Promethean felicity and boldness, luckily sinned himself out of it.

CHARLES LAMB
Letter to William Wordsworth,
January 22, 1830

GARFIELD, JAMES A.

Garfield has shown that he is not possessed of the backbone of an angle-worm.

ULYSSES S. GRANT
Quoted in *Garfield of Ohio: The Available Man,* by Jeremiah Black,
1885

GARLAND, JUDY

In the first of these films, Miss Garland plays herself, which is horrify-ing; in the second, someone else, which is impossible. . . . her figure re-sembles the giant economy-size tube of tooth paste in girls' bathrooms: squeezed intemperately at all points, it acquires a shape that defies defi-nition by the most resourceful solid geometrician.

JOHN SIMON
Reviewing *I Could Go On Singing*
and *A Child Is Waiting* in
Private Screenings, 1967

GARNER, JOHN NANCE

A labor-baiting, poker-playing, whiskey-drinking, evil old man.

JOHN L. LEWIS
Statement to the press, Washington,
July 27, 1939

GARRICK, DAVID

In declamation he never charmed me; nor could he be a gentleman. . . . Applause had turned his head, and yet he was never content even with that prodigality. His jealousy and envy were unbounded.

HORACE WALPOLE
Letter to the Countess of Upper
Ossory, February 1, 1779

GAUGUIN, PAUL

Don't talk to me of Gauguin. I'd like to wring the fellow's neck!
Attributed to
PAUL CÉZANNE

GAY

Show me a happy homosexual and I'll show you a gay corpse.
MATT CROWLEY
The Boys in the Band, 1968

"Gay" used to be one of the most agreeable words in the language. Its appropriation by a notably morose group is an act of piracy.
ARTHUR M. SCHLESINGER, JR.
The American Heritage Dictionary,
1976

GENERALIZATION

All generalizations are false, including this one.
ANONYMOUS

GENERALS

I didn't fire him because he was a dumb son-of-a-bitch, although he was, but that's not against the law for generals. If it was, half to three-quarters of them would be in jail.
HARRY S. TRUMAN
Quoted in Merle Miller's
*Plain Speaking: An Oral
Biography of Harry S. Truman*, 1974

GENESIS

Take away from Genesis the belief that Moses was the author, on which only the strange belief that it is the word of God has stood, and there remains nothing of Genesis but an anonymous book of stories, fables, and traditionary or invented absurdities, or of down-right lies.
THOMAS PAINE
The Age of Reason, 1794

GENITALS

The genitals themselves have not undergone the development of the rest of the human form in the direction of beauty.
SIGMUND FREUD
Quoted in *The Unfashionable Human
Body*, by Bernard Rudofsky, 1971

GENIUS

I have known no man of genius who had not to pay, in some affliction or defect either physical or spiritual, for what the gods had given him.

MAX BEERBOHM
And Even Now, 1921

In the republic of mediocrity, genius is dangerous.

Attributed to
ROBERT G. INGERSOLL

GENTILITY

[Gentility is] a more select and artificial kind of vulgarity.

WILLIAM HAZLITT
Table-Talk, 1821–22

GENTLEMAN

I am a gentleman: I live by robbing the poor.

GEORGE BERNARD SHAW
Man and Superman, 1903

GEORGE III

George the Third
Ought never to have occurred.
One can only wonder
At so grotesque a blunder.

EDMUND CLERIHEW BENTLEY
Biography for Beginners, 1925

An old, mad, blind, despised, and dying king.

PERCY BYSSHE SHELLEY
England in 1819, 1819

GEORGE IV

George the First was always reckoned
Vile, but viler George the Second;
And what mortal ever heard
Any good of George the Third?
When from earth the Fourth descended
(God be praised!) the Georges ended!

WALTER SAVAGE LANDOR
The Georges, 1855

A noble, nasty race he ran,
Superbly filthy and fastidious;
He was the world's first gentleman,
And made the appellation hideous.
W. M. PRAED
Proposed epitaph for George IV, 1825

GEORGE, HENRY

Did you ever read Henry George's book *Progress and Poverty?* It's more
damneder nonsense than poor Rousseau's blether.
THOMAS HENRY HUXLEY
Letter, December 14, 1889

GERMAN LANGUAGE

Life is too short to learn German.
Attributed to
RICHARD PORSON
(1759–1808)

GERMANS

The Germans are very seldom troubled with any extraordinary ebulli-
tions or effervescences of wit, and it is not prudent to try it upon them.
LORD CHESTERFIELD
Letter to his son, July 21, 1752

Everything German is odious to me. . . . Everything German affects me
like an emetic. The German language rends my ears. At times my own
poems nauseate me, when I see they are written in German.
HEINRICH HEINE
Letter, April 1882

The human as distinct from the German mind.
Attributed to
WILLIAM JAMES

Everything that is ponderous, viscous and pompously clumsy, all long-
winded and wearying kinds of style, are developed in great variety
among Germans.
FRIEDRICH WILHELM NIETZSCHE
The Genealogy of Morals, 1887

Where the German sets his foot the earth bleeds for a hundred years.
Where the German draws and drinks water the springs rot for a hundred years.

Where the German draws a breath the pest rages for a hundred years.
He betrays the strong and robs the weak and rules them.
If there were a direct road to Heaven he would not hesitate to dethrone
   God.
And we shall yet see that the German steals the sun from Heaven.

> Attributed to
> LUCIAN RYDLA, a Polish
> poet, by Prelate Klos in a speech at
> Posen, July 2, 1929

GIFTS

How painful to give a gift to any person of sensibility, or of equality! It
is next worst to receiving one.

> RALPH WALDO EMERSON
> Journal, 1836

Gifts are like hooks.

> MARTIAL
> *Epigrams*, 86

GIVING

We do not quite forgive a giver. The hand that feeds us is in some danger of being bitten.

> RALPH WALDO EMERSON
> "Gifts," *Essays*, Second Series, 1844

GLADSTONE, WILLIAM E.

If Gladstone fell into the Thames it would be a misfortune. But if someone dragged him out again, it would be a calamity.

> Attributed to
> BENJAMIN DISRAELI

Posterity will do justice to that unprincipled maniac Gladstone—
extraordinary mixture of envy, vindictiveness, hypocrisy, and superstition; and with one commanding characteristic—whether prime minister or leader of Opposition, whether preaching, praying, speechifying,
or scribbling—never a gentleman.

> BENJAMIN DISRAELI
> Letter, October 1876

A sophistical rhetorician, inebriated with the exuberance of his own ver-
bosity.

> BENJAMIN DISRAELI
> Speech, July 27, 1878

GLASSES

Men seldom make passes.
at girls who wear glasses.
                    DOROTHY PARKER
        "News Item," *Enough Rope*, 1927

GLORY

When we examine what glory is, we discover that it is nearly nothing.
To be judged by the ignorant and esteemed by imbeciles, to hear one's
name spoken by a rabble who approve, reject, love or hate without reason—that is nothing to be proud of.
                            FREDERICK THE GREAT
                Letter to Voltaire, January 3, 1773

GOD

For me the single word "God" suggests everything that is slippery,
shady, squalid, foul and grotesque.
                                Attributed to
                                ANDRÉ BRETON

The idea of a Supreme Being who creates a world in which one creature
is designed to eat another in order to subsist, and then passes a law saying "Thou shalt not kill," is so monstrously, immeasurably, bottom-
lessly absurd that I am at a loss to understand how mankind has
entertained or given it house room all this long.
                                PETER DE VRIES
                Slouching Towards Kalamazoo, 1983

The God that holds you over the pit of Hell, much as one holds a spider, or some loathsome insect, over the fire, abhors you, and is dread-
fully provoked; His wrath towards you burns like fire; He looks upon
you as worthy of nothing else but to be cast into the fire; He is of purer
eyes than to bear to have you in His sight; you are ten thousand times
more abominable in His eyes than the most hateful venomous serpent is
in ours.
                            JONATHAN EDWARDS
                *Sinners in the Hands of an Angry
                God*, 1741

God is the immemorial refuge of the incompetent, the helpless, the
miserable. They find not only sanctuary in His arms, but also a kind of
superiority, soothing to their macerated egos; He will set them above
their betters.
                                H. L. MENCKEN
                *Minority Report: H. L. Mencken's
                Notebooks*, 1956

God is a thought that makes crooked all that is straight.
FRIEDRICH WILHELM NIETZSCHE
Thus Spake Zarathustra, 1883–92

GOLD

Gold begets in brethren hate;
Gold in families debate;
Gold does friendship separate;
Gold does civil wars create.
ABRAHAM COWLEY
Anacreon, 1656

The lust of gold, unfeeling and remorseless!
The last corruption of degenerate man.
SAMUEL JOHNSON
Irene, 1749

Gold defiles with frequent touch;
There's nothing fouls the hand so much.
JONATHAN SWIFT
The Fable of Midas, 1712

GOOD

How hard it is for the Good to go wrong! I seem to find all the pleasant
paths of transgression barred and barricaded against me.
LOGAN PEARSALL SMITH
Afterthoughts, 1934

GOOD LOSER

Show me a good loser and I'll show you an idiot.

Attributed to
LEO DUROCHER

G.O.P.

Grand Old Platitudes
HARRY S. TRUMAN
Quoted in *Time,* April 30, 1961

GOSSIP

Gossip is the opiate of the oppressed.
ERICA JONG
Fear of Flying, 1973

GOURMET

A gourmet is just a glutton with brains.
PHILLIP W. HABERMAN, JR.
"How To Be a Calorie Chiseler,"
Vogue, January 15, 1961

GOVERNMENT

The worst thing in this world, next to anarchy, is government.
HENRY WARD BEECHER
Proverbs from Plymouth Pulpit, 1887

The world is disgracefully managed, one hardly knows to whom to complain.
RONALD FIRBANK
Vainglory, 1915

Frankly, I'd like to see the government get out of war altogether and leave the whole field to private industry.
JOSEPH HELLER
Catch-22, 1961

Society is produced by our wants and government by our wickedness.
THOMAS PAINE
Common Sense, 1776

Monarchy degenerates into tyranny, aristocracy into oligarchy, and democracy into savage violence and anarchy.
POLYBIUS
Histories, c. 125 B.C.

To be governed is to be watched, inspected, spied upon, directed, law-ridden, regulated, penned up, indoctrinated, preached at, checked, appraised, seized, censured, commanded, by beings who have neither title nor knowledge nor virtue. To be governed is to have every operation, every transaction, every movement noted, registered, counted, rated, stamped, measured, numbered, assessed, licensed, refused, authorized, endorsed, admonished, prevented, reformed, redressed, corrected.
PIERRE-JOSEPH PROUDHON
Confessions d'un révolutionnaire, 1849

Government is an association of men who do violence to the rest of us.
LEO TOLSTOY
The Kingdom of God Is Within You,
1893

In general, the art of government consists in taking as much money as possible from one class of citizens to give to the other.

VOLTAIRE
Dictionnaire philosophique, 1764

GRAMMAR

Any fool can make a rule and every fool will mind it.

HENRY DAVID THOREAU
Journal, February 3, 1860

GRAMMARIAN

Thou eunuch of language: thou butcher, imbruing thy hands in the bowels of orthography: thou arch-heretic in pronunciation: thou pitch-pipe of affected emphasis: thou carpenter, mortising the awkward joints of jarring sentences: thou squeaking dissonance of cadence; thou pimp of gender: thou scape-gallows from the land of syntax: thou scavenger of mood and tense: thou murderous accoucheur of infant learnings: thou *ignis fatuus,* misleading the steps of benighted ignorance: thou pickle-herring in the puppet-show of nonsense.

ROBERT BURNS
Memorandum on an unidentified
critic, c. 1791

GRANT, ULYSSES S.

He is a scientific Goth, resembling Alaric, destroying the country as he goes and delivering the people over to starvation. Nor does he bury his dead, but leaves them to rot on the battlefield.

JOHN TYLER
Letter to Sterling Price,
July 7, 1864

GRASS

Grass is hard and lumpy and damp, and full of dreadful black insects.

OSCAR WILDE
The Decay of Lying, 1891

GRATITUDE

Next to ingratitude, the most painful thing to bear is gratitude.

HENRY WARD BEECHER
Proverbs from Plymouth Pulpit, 1887

Gratitude is a burden upon our imperfect nature.
LORD CHESTERFIELD
Letter to his son, November 7, 1765

GREAT MEN

I have had my bellyfull of great men . . . In real life they are nasty creatures, persecutors, temperamental, despotic, bitter and suspicious.
GEORGE SAND
Correspondence, Vol. II, 1895

GREAT SALT LAKE, UTAH

The largest inland body of salt water in the world, of no use, even for suicide.
CECIL ROBERTS
And So to America, 1946

GREECE

The plain facts are that Greek science, even at its best, would be hard to distinguish from the science prevailing among Hottentots, Haitians and Mississippi Baptists today; that Greek art was chiefly only derivative and extremely narrow in range; that Greek philosophy was quite as idiotic as any other philosophy, and that the government of the Greeks, even at its best, was worse than the worst of Tammany.
H. L. MENCKEN
The American Mercury,
October 1927

GREEKS

After shaking hands with a Greek, count your fingers.
ALBANIAN PROVERB

Never trust a Greek.
EURIPIDES
Iphigenia in Aulis, c. 410 B.C.

I fear the Greeks even when they bring gifts.
VIRGIL
Aeneid, 30–19 B.C.

GREELEY, HORACE

A self-made man who worships his creator.
Attributed to
HENRY CLAPP, c. 1858

GROUSE

He gave us a very choice, very tasty dinner, a real gourmet's dinner, including some grouse whose scented flesh [Alphonse] Daudet compared to an old courtesan's flesh marinated in a bidet.

EDMOND DE GONCOURT
Diary, April 3, 1878

GROWTH

Growth for the sake of growth is the ideology of the cancer cell.

Attributed to
EDWARD ABBEY

GUESTS

One guest hates the other, and the host both.
BULGARIAN PROVERB

Fish and visitors smell in three days.
BENJAMIN FRANKLIN
Poor Richard's Almanack, 1732–57

GUGGENHEIM MUSEUM

The Solomon R. Guggenheim Museum . . . is a war between architecture and painting in which both come out badly maimed.

JOHN CANADAY
The New York Times,
October 21, 1959

GYPSY

A Gypsy tells the truth once in his life, and immediately repents.
RUSSIAN PROVERB

TO KNOCK A THING DOWN, ESPECIALLY IF IT IS COCKED AT AN ARROGANT ANGLE, IS A DEEP DELIGHT TO THE BLOOD.

GEORGE SANTAYANA

THE LIFE OF REASON: REASON IN SOCIETY, 1905–6

HABIT

Habit is a great deadener.
SAMUEL BECKETT
Waiting for Godot, 1952

HAIR

Doth not even nature itself teach you, that, if a man have long hair, it is a shame unto him?
I Corinthians 11:14, c. 57

Nature herself abhors to see a woman shorn or polled; a woman with cut hair is a filthy spectacle, and much like a monster.
WILLIAM PRYNNE
Histriomastix, 1632

HALO

What after all is a halo? It's only one more thing to keep clean.
CHRISTOPHER FRY
The Lady's Not for Burning, 1948

HAMILTON, ALEXANDER

. . . the bastard brat of a Scotch peddler.

Attributed to
JOHN ADAMS

"HAMLET"

Hamlet is a coarse and barbarous play . . . One might think the work is the product of a drunken savage's imagination.

VOLTAIRE
Dissertation sur la tragédie ancienne et moderne, 1748

HAPPINESS

Happiness, n. An agreeable sensation arising from contemplating the misery of another.

AMBROSE BIERCE
The Devil's Dictionary, 1906, 1911

I can sympathize with people's pains, but *not* with their pleasure. There is something curiously boring about somebody else's happiness.

ALDOUS HUXLEY
Limbo, 1923

Happiness Is a Warm Gun

JOHN LENNON
AND PAUL McCARTNEY
Song title, 1968

Unbroken happiness is a bore.

MOLIÈRE
Les Fourberies de Scapin, 1671

HAPSBURGS

The Hapsburgs have become powerful by plundering older families— the Hungarians, for instance. At bottom they are only a family of police spies who made their fortune by confiscations.

Attributed to
OTTO VON BISMARCK

HARDING, WARREN G.

Harding was not a bad man. He was just a slob.

Attributed to
ALICE ROOSEVELT LONGWORTH

He writes the worst English that I have ever encountered. It reminds me of a string of wet sponges; it reminds me of tattered washing on the line; it reminds me of stale bean soup, of college yells, of dogs barking idiotically through endless nights. It is so bad that a sort of grandeur creeps into it. It drags itself out of the dark abyss (I was about to write abscess!) or pish, and crawls insanely up to the topmost pinnacle of posh. It is rumble and bumble. It is flap and doodle. It is balder and dash.

H. L. MENCKEN
Baltimore Evening Sun,
March 7, 1921

No other such complete and dreadful nitwit is to be found in the pages of American history . . .

H. L. MENCKEN
Letter to Carl Van Doren,
March 4, 1921

If there ever was a he-harlot, it was this same Warren G. Harding.
WILLIAM ALLEN WHITE
Quoted in *The Shadow of Blooming
Grove: President Harding—His Life
and Times,* by Francis Russell, 1968

HARPSICHORD

The sound of a harpsichord: Two skeletons copulating on a galvanized tin roof.

SIR THOMAS BEECHAM
Beecham Stories, 1978

HARRIS, JED

When I die, I want to be cremated and have my ashes thrown in Jed Harris's face.

GEORGE S. KAUFMAN, 1929

HARTE, FRANCIS BRET

He hadn't a sincere fiber in him. I think he was incapable of emotion, for I think he had nothing to feel with. I think his heart was merely a pump and had no other function.

MARK TWAIN
Autobiography, edited by
Charles Neider, 1959

HASTE

Nothing is more vulgar than haste.
RALPH WALDO EMERSON
The Conduct of Life, 1860

HASTINGS, WARREN

His crimes are the only great thing about him, and these are contrasted by the littleness of his motives. He is at once a tyrant, a trickster, a visionary and a deceiver. . . . He reasons in bombast, prevaricates in metaphor, and quibbles in heroics.

RICHARD BRINSLEY SHERIDAN
Speech in the House of Lords,
May 30, 1799

HAYES, HELEN

Fallen Archness
FRANKLIN PIERCE ADAMS (F.P.A.)
Reviewing Miss Hayes as
Cleopatra, 1925

HAZLITT, WILLIAM

A mere ulcer; a sore from head to foot; a poor devil so completely flayed that there is not a square inch of healthy flesh on his carcass; an overgrown pimple . . .

ANONYMOUS
Quarterly Review, 1817

HEALTH

What have I gained by health? Intolerable dullness. What by early hours and moderate meals? A total blank.

CHARLES LAMB
Letter to William Wordsworth,
January 22, 1830

HEALTH FOODS

In San Francisco and Los Angeles I encountered a number of sun-baked zealots who insisted upon the ingestion of tasteless grains, gloomy greens and an astonishing variety of obscure vegetables. All of the above were viable only if diligently nurtured in excrement-flavored soil. They also enthusiastically imbibed "cocktails," the ingredients of which included the mixed juices of turnips, cucumbers and carrots. These excruciating concoctions were all self-righteously set forth on the puritanical premise that the denial of sweetness, spice and succulence leads—at the very least—to eternal life.

JEAN-MICHEL CHAPEREAU
Un Hiver américain, 1975

HEARST, WILLIAM RANDOLPH

There is not a cesspool of vice and crime which Hearst has not raked and exploited for moneymaking purposes. No person with intellectual honesty or moral integrity will touch him with a ten-foot pole for any purpose or to gain any end. Unless those who represent American scholarship, science, and the right of a free people to discuss public questions freely stand together against his insidious influence he will assassinate them individually by every method known to yellow journalism.

CHARLES BEARD
Speech, February 24, 1935

HEAVEN

Heaven, as conventionally conceived, is a place so inane, so dull, so useless, so miserable, that nobody has ever ventured to describe a whole day in heaven, though plenty of people have described a day at the seaside.

GEORGE BERNARD SHAW
Misalliance, 1910

HEINE, HEINRICH

Blackguard Heine is worth very little.
THOMAS CARLYLE
Letter to Ralph Waldo Emerson,
November 5, 1836

HEMINGWAY, ERNEST

Ernest Hemingway: when his cock wouldn't stand up, he blew his head off. He sold himself a line of bullshit and bought it.

GERMAINE GREER
Quoted in *Loose Talk*, compiled by
Linda Botts, 1981

HENRY VIII

The plain truth is, that he was a most intolerable ruffian, a disgrace to human nature, and a blot of blood and grease upon the History of England.

CHARLES DICKENS
A Child's History of England, 1853

HEPBURN, KATHARINE

She runs the gamut of emotions all the way from A to B.
DOROTHY PARKER
In a review of Hepburn's performance
in *The Lake*, 1933

HEREAFTER

Men have feverishly conceived a heaven only to find it insipid, and a hell to find it ridiculous.

GEORGE SANTAYANA
*The Life of Reason: Reason
in Art*, 1905–6

HEREDITY

I grew up to have my father's looks—my father's speech patterns—my father's posture—my father's walk—my father's opinions and my mother's contempt for my father.

JULES FEIFFER
Hold Me, 1964

HERO

Every hero becomes a bore at last.
RALPH WALDO EMERSON
Representative Men, 1850

Show me a hero and I'll write you a tragedy.

F. SCOTT FITZGERALD
The Crack-Up, 1945

HESTON, CHARLTON

Heston throws all his punches in the first ten minutes (three grimaces and two intonations) so that he has nothing left long before he stumbles to the end, four hours later, and has to react to the crucifixion. (He does make it clear, I must admit, that he quite disapproves of it.)

DWIGHT MACDONALD
On *Ben Hur* in *Esquire's World of
Humor*, 1964

HIGHWAYS

Thanks to the Interstate Highway System, it is now possible to travel across the country from coast to coast without seeing anything.

CHARLES KURALT
CBS-TV, September 7, 1971

HINDSIGHT

Don't look back. Something may be gaining on you.

Attributed to
SATCHEL PAIGE

HIPPIE

A hippie is someone who looks like Tarzan, walks like Jane and smells like Cheeta.

Attributed to
RONALD REAGAN

HISTORY AND HISTORIANS

History, n. An account mostly false, of events mostly unimportant, which are brought about by rulers mostly knaves, and soldiers mostly fools.

AMBROSE BIERCE
The Devil's Dictionary, 1906, 1911

We want a Society for the Suppression of Erudite Research and the Decent Burial of the Past. The ghosts of the dead past want quite as much laying as raising.

SAMUEL BUTLER
Note-Books, 1912

I am ashamed to see what a shallow village tale our so-called history is.
RALPH WALDO EMERSON
History, 1841

History is bunk.
HENRY FORD
In court, during a libel action
against the *Chicago Tribune*, 1919

All the historical books which contain no lies are extremely tedious.
ANATOLE FRANCE
The Crime of Sylvestre Bonnard,
The Log, December 24, 1849

History, which is, indeed, little more than the register of the crimes, follies, and misfortunes of mankind.

EDWARD GIBBON
*The Decline and Fall of the Roman
Empire*, 1776–88

History repeats itself; historians repeat each other.

Attributed to
PHILIP GUEDALLA

What experience and history teach is this—that people and governments never have learned anything from history, or acted on principles deduced from it.

GEORG WILHELM FRIEDRICH HEGEL
Philosophy of History, 1821

History is too serious to be left to the historians.

IAIN MACLEOD
The Observer, London, July 16, 1961

History is nothing but a collection of fables and useless trifles, cluttered up with a mass of unnecessary figures and proper names.

Attributed to
LEO TOLSTOY

How much charlatanry has been put into history, either by astonishing the reader with prodigies, by titillating human malignity with satire, or by flattering the families of tyrants with infamous praise!

VOLTAIRE
Dictionnaire philosophique, 1764

History is but a tableau of crimes and misfortunes.

VOLTAIRE
L'Ingénu, 1767

History, the longer it runs, contracts the more filth, and retains in it the additional ordure of every soil through which it appears.

WILLIAM WARBURTON,
Bishop of Gloucester
The Causes of Prodigies and Miracles,
1727

HOLIDAY

Holidays are often overrated disturbances of routine, costly and uncomfortable, and they usually need another holiday to correct their ravages.

EDWARD VERRALL LUCAS
365 Days and One More, 1926

HOLLAND

What wounds one's feeling in Holland is the perpetual consciousness that the country has no business being there at all. You see it all below the level of the water, soppy, hideous and artificial . . :

MATTHEW ARNOLD
Letter to Miss Arnold, June 19, 1859

HOLLYWOOD

You can take all the sincerity in Hollywood, place it in the navel of a fruit fly and still have room enough for three caraway seeds and a producer's heart.

FRED ALLEN
Quoted in *Popcorn in Paradise*,
edited by John Robert Colombo, 1979

Hollywood is like being nowhere and talking to nobody about nothing.
MICHELANGELO ANTONIONI
The Sunday Times, London,
June 20, 1971

Strip away the phony tinsel of Hollywood and you'll find the real tinsel underneath.

Attributed to
OSCAR LEVANT

A dreary industrial town controlled by hoodlums of enormous wealth.
Attributed to
S. J. PERELMAN

HOLY ROMAN EMPIRE

This thing which was called and which still calls itself the Holy Roman Empire was neither holy nor Roman nor an empire.

VOLTAIRE
Essai sur les moeurs, 1756

HOMEMADE

Who hath not met with home-made bread,
A heavy compound of putty and lead—
And home-made wines that rack the head,
And home-made liquors and waters?
Home-made pop that will not foam,
And home-made dishes that drive one from home—
Home-made by the homely daughters.

THOMAS HOOD
*Miss Kilmansegg and Her
Precious Leg*, 1841–43

HOMEOPATHY

Homeopathy [is] . . . a mingled mass of perverse ingenuity, of tinsel erudition, of imbecile credulity, and of artful misrepresentation, too often mingled in practice . . . with heartless and shameless imposition.
OLIVER WENDELL HOLMES
Medical Essays, 1883

HOMES, STATELY

Those comfortably padded lunatic asylums which are known, euphemistically, as the stately homes of England.
VIRGINIA WOOLF
The Common Reader, 1925

HOMOSEXUALITY

The love that previously dared not speak its name has now grown hoarse from screaming it.
ROBERT BRUSTEIN
The New York Times,
November 20, 1977

If homosexuality were the normal way, God would have made Adam and Bruce.
ANITA BRYANT
Rolling Stone, July 14, 1977

I thought men like that shot themselves.
KING GEORGE V
Quoted in *Maugham*,
by Ted Morgan, 1980

HONESTY

Everybody has a little bit of Watergate in him.
REVEREND BILLY GRAHAM
At a church dedication, Fort
Lauderdale, Florida, February 3, 1974

I have no idea what the mind of a low-life scoundrel is like, but I know what the mind of an honest man is like: it is terrifying.
ABEL HERMANT
Le Bourgeois, 1906

HONEYMOON

The grossness underlying the idea of the honeymoon is of an unescapable obviousness . . . at bottom . . . merely a sex orgy conducted in public, an elaborate tournament in armour. . . . Imagine a civilized and well-mannered man and woman taking as boudoir confidantes chauffeurs, baggage-men, Pullman porters, hotel clerks, bell-boys, chambermaids, and several hundred shoe-drummers, smutty old ladies, house detectives and other such hotel fauna.

GEORGE JEAN NATHAN
The World in Falseface, 1923

HOOVER, J. EDGAR

. . . J. Edgar Hoover, whom you should trust as much as you would a rattlesnake with a silencer on its rattle.

DEAN ACHESON
Letter, June 27, 1960

HOPE

Hope in reality is the worst of all evils, because it prolongs the torments of man.

FRIEDRICH WILHELM NIETZSCHE
Human, All Too Human, 1878

HOPPER, HEDDA

She was venomous, vicious, a pathological liar, and quite stupid.

RAY MILLAND
Wide-Eyed in Babylon, 1974

HORSE

Dangerous at both ends and uncomfortable in the middle.

IAN FLEMING
The Sunday Times, London,
October 9, 1966

Woe to them that . . . rely on horses.
Isaiah 31:1, 8th century B.C.

HORSERACING

Everyone knows that horse-racing is carried on mainly for the delight and profit of fools, ruffians, and thieves.

GEORGE GISSING
The Private Papers of Henry Ryecroft,
1903

HOSPITALITY

People are far more sincere and good-humored at speeding their parting guests than on meeting them.

ANTON CHEKHOV
"The Kiss," *Collected Short Stories,*
1916–22

HOT DOG

I've often wondered what goes into a hot dog. Now I know and I wish I didn't.

WILLIAM ZINSSER
The Lunacy Boom, 1970

HOUSES

Our houses are such unwieldy property that we are often imprisoned rather than housed in them.

HENRY DAVID THOREAU
Walden, 1854

HOUSTON, TEXAS

This city has been an act of real estate rather than an act of God or man.

ADA LOUISE HUXTABLE
The New York Times,
February 15, 1976

HUCKLEBERRY FINN

If Mr. Clemens cannot think of something better to tell our pure-minded lads and lasses, he had best stop writing for them.

LOUISA MAY ALCOTT
In support of the library ban of
Huckleberry Finn in Concord,
Massachusetts, 1885

HUGO, VICTOR

A glittering humbug.

THOMAS CARLYLE
To Henry B. Stanton, 1840

HUMANITY

The wickedness of the world is so great you have to run your legs off to avoid having them stolen from under you.

BERTOLT BRECHT
The Threepenny Opera, 1928

I hate humanity and all such abstracts: but I love people. Lovers of "Humanity" generally hate people and children, and keep parrots or puppy dogs.

ROY CAMPBELL
Light on a Dark Horse, 1951

Man is, and was always, a block-head and dullard; much readier to feel and digest, than to think and consider.

THOMAS CARLYLE
Sartor Resartus, 1833–34

Most men are in a coma when they are at rest and mad when they act.

EPICURUS
"Vatican Sayings," in *Letters,*
Principal Doctrines, and Vatican
Sayings, 3rd century B.C.

There are only two great currents in the history of mankind: the baseness which makes conservatives and the envy which makes revolutionaries.

EDMOND AND JULES DE GONCOURT
Journal, July 12, 1867

At least two thirds of our miseries spring from human stupidity, human malice and those great motivators and justifiers of malice and stupidity, idealism, dogmatism and proselytizing zeal on behalf of religious or political idols.

ALDOUS HUXLEY
Tomorrow and Tomorrow
and Tomorrow, 1956

He who is the friend of all humanity is not my friend.

MOLIÈRE
Le Misanthrope, 1666

Humanity is a pigsty where liars, hypocrites and the obscene in spirit congregate.

GEORGE MOORE
Confessions of a Young Man, 1888

When any man is more stupidly vain and outrageously egotistic than his fellows, he will hide his hideousness in humanitarianism.

GEORGE MOORE
Confessions of a Young Man, 1888

Whenever a massacre of Armenians is reported from Asia Minor, everyone assumes that it has been carried out "under orders" from somewhere or another; no one seems to think that there are people who might *like* to kill their neighbours now and then.

SAKI (H. H. MUNRO)
"Filboid Studge, The Story of a
Mouse That Helped," *The Chronicles
of Clovis, 1912*

Hell is—other people!

JEAN-PAUL SARTRE
No Exit, 1944

There are times when one would like to hang the whole human race, and finish the farce.

MARK TWAIN
*A Connecticut Yankee at King
Arthur's Court, 1889*

HUMAN NATURE

The nature of men and women—their *essential nature*—is so vile and despicable that if you were to portray a person as he really is, no one would believe you.

W. SOMERSET MAUGHAM
To Robin Maugham in *Conversations
with Willie, 1978*

HUMILITY

Even if you aim at humility, there is no guarantee that when you have attained the state you will not be proud of the feat.

Attributed to
BONAMY DOBRÉE

Don't be humble, you're not that great.

Attributed to
GOLDA MEIR

HUNGARIANS

If you have a Hungarian for a friend, you don't need an enemy.

ANONYMOUS

HUNTING

It is very strange, and very melancholy, that the paucity of human pleasures should persuade us ever to call hunting one of them.

SAMUEL JOHNSON
Johnsonian Miscellanies, 1897

Wild animals never kill for sport. Man is the only one to whom the torture and death of his fellow creatures is amusing in itself.

JAMES A. FROUDE
Oceana, 1886

HUSBAND

If a woman's husband gets on her nerves, she should fly at him. If she thinks him too sweet and smarmy with other people, she should let him have it to his nose, straight out. She should lead him a dog's life, and never swallow her bile.

D. H. LAWRENCE
Fantasia of the Unconscious, 1922

HYGIENE

Hygiene is the corruption of medicine by morality.

H. L. MENCKEN
Prejudices, Third Series, 1922

HYPHEN

If you take hyphens seriously you will surely go mad.

JOHN BENBOW
Manuscript and Proof, 1943

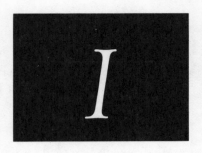

PRIDE AND HATRED INVIGORATE
THE SOUL; AND LOVE AND HUMIL-
ITY ENFEEBLE IT.

DAVID HUME

A TREATISE OF HUMAN NATURE,
1759

"I AM A CAMERA"

Me no Leica.

WALTER KERR
In his review of the John
Van Druten play, 1951

IDEA

Hang ideas! They are tramps, vagabonds, knocking at the back-door of your mind, each taking a little of your substance, each carrying away some crumb of that belief in a few simple notions you must cling to if you want to live decently and would like to die easy!

JOSEPH CONRAD
Lord Jim, 1900

IDEALISM

Whenever one comes to close grips with so-called idealism, as in war time, one is shocked by its rascality.

H. L. MENCKEN
*Minority Report: H. L. Mencken's
Notebooks,* 1956

IDEALIST

An idealist is one who, on noticing that a rose smells better than a cabbage, concludes that it will also make better soup.

H. L. MENCKEN
A Mencken Chrestomathy, 1949

The idealist is incorrigible: if be be thrown out of his Heaven he makes an ideal of his Hell.

FRIEDRICH WILHELM NIETZSCHE
Human, All Too Human, 1878

IDEALS

Positive ideals are becoming a curse, for they can seldom be achieved without someone being killed, or maimed or interned.

E. M. FORSTER
"Tolerance," *Picture Post,*
July 1939

Don't use that foreign word "ideals." We have that excellent native word "lies."

HENRIK IBSEN
The Wild Duck, 1884

ILLUSION

The most dangerous of our calculations are those we call illusions.

GEORGES BERNANOS
Dialogue des Carmélites, 1949

IMAGINATION

. . . that deceitful part in man, that mistress of error and falsity . . . the enemy of reason.

BLAISE PASCAL
Pensées, 1670

IMMORTALITY

Soon you will have forgotten the world, and the world will have forgotten you.

MARCUS AURELIUS
Meditations, 2nd century

INACCURACY

I do not mind lying, but I hate inaccuracy.

SAMUEL BUTLER
Note-Books, 1912

INANIMATE OBJECTS

The goal of all inanimate objects is to resist man and ultimately to defeat him.

RUSSELL BAKER
The New York Times,
June 18, 1968

INDEX

'Tis a pitiful piece of knowledge that can be learnt from an index, and a poor ambition to be rich in the inventory of another's treasure.

JOSEPH GLANVILL
The Vanity of Dogmatizing, 1661

INDIANA

I come from Indiana, the home of more first-rate second-class men than any state in the Union.

Attributed to
THOMAS R. MARSHALL

INDIANS

The only good Indians I ever saw were dead.

GENERAL PHILIP HENRY SHERIDAN
Reply to an Indian who said
"Me good Indian," January 1869

He is little, and scrawny, and black, and dirty; and, judged by even the most charitable of our canons of human excellence, is thoroughly pitiful and contemptible. . . . truly he is nothing but a poor, filthy, naked scurvy vagabond, whom to exterminate were a charity to the Creator's worthier insects and reptiles which he oppresses. . . . He is ignoble—base and treacherous, and hateful in every way. Not even imminent death can startle him into a spasm of virtue.

MARK TWAIN
The Noble Red Man, 1870

INDUSTRY

We have created an industrial order geared to automatism, where feeble-mindedness, native or acquired, is necessary for docile productivity in the factory; and where a pervasive neurosis is the final gift of the meaningless life that issues forth at the other end.

LEWIS MUMFORD
The Conduct of Life, 1951

Industry is the root of all ugliness.
OSCAR WILDE
*Phrases and Philosophies for the
Use of the Young*, 1891

INNOCENCE

Everybody has something to conceal.
DASHIELL HAMMETT
The Maltese Falcon, 1930

We have no choice but to be guilty.
God is unthinkable if we are innocent.
ARCHIBALD MACLEISH
J.B., 1958

INSECTS

Men should stop fighting among themselves and start fighting insects.
Attributed to
LUTHER BURBANK

INSPIRATION

[Inspiration is] a farce that poets have invented to give themselves importance.
JEAN ANOUILH
The New York Times,
October 2, 1960

INSTITUTION

The working of great institutions is mainly the result of a vast mass of routine, petty malice, self-interest, carelessness, and sheer mistake. Only a residual fraction is thought.
GEORGE SANTAYANA
The Crime of Galileo, 1967

INSURANCE AGENTS

I detest life-insurance agents; they always argue that I shall some day die, which is not so.
STEPHEN LEACOCK
Literary Lapses, 1910

INTEGRITY

Never underestimate the effectiveness of a straight cash bribe.
CLAUD COCKBURN
The Village Voice, October 4, 1976

Integrity is so perishable in the summer months of success.
VANESSA REDGRAVE
Quoted in *Goodbye Baby & Amen*,
by David Bailey, 1969

INTELLIGENCE

The voice of the intelligence . . . is drowned out by the roar of fear. It is ignored by the voice of desire. It is contradicted by the voice of shame. It is hissed away by hate, and extinguished by anger. Most of all it is silenced by ignorance.
KARL MENNINGER
The Progressive, October 1955

INTENTIONS, GOOD

Hell is paved with good intentions.
SAMUEL JOHNSON
To James Boswell, April 16, 1775

There's nothing we read of in torture's inventions
Like a well-meaning dunce with the best of intentions.
JAMES RUSSELL LOWELL
A Fable for Critics, 1848

INTERIOR DECORATOR

The interior decorator is simply an inferior desecrator of the work of an artist.
FRANK LLOYD WRIGHT
Quoted in the *Manchester Guardian*,
1959

INVALIDS

The modern sympathy with invalids is morbid. Illness of any kind is hardly a thing to be encouraged in others.
OSCAR WILDE
The Importance of Being Earnest,
1895

INVENTOR

Inventor, n. A person who makes an ingenious arrangement of wheels, levers and springs, and believes it civilization.

AMBROSE BIERCE
The Devil's Dictionary, 1906, 1911

IRELAND AND THE IRISH

The Irish people do not gladly suffer common sense.

OLIVER ST. JOHN GOGARTY
The Observer, London, 1935

The Irish are not in a conspiracy to cheat the world by false representations of the merits of their countrymen. No, Sir; the Irish are FAIR PEOPLE; they never speak well of one another.

SAMUEL JOHNSON
February 18, 1775, quoted in James
Boswell's *Life of Samuel Johnson,*
1791

Ireland is the old sow that eats her farrow.

JAMES JOYCE
*A Portrait of the Artist as a Young
Man,* 1916

Ireland has the honor of being the only country which never persecuted the Jews . . . because she never let them in.

JAMES JOYCE
Ulysses, 1922

Ireland is a fatal disease—fatal to Englishmen and doubly fatal to Irishmen.

GEORGE MOORE
Confessions of a Young Man, 1888

This book is flung in the face of the Irish—a fighting race who never won a battle, a race of politicians who cannot govern themselves, a race of writers without a great one of native strain, an island who have yet to man a fleet for war, for commerce or for the fishing banks and to learn how to build ships, a pious race excelling in blasphemy, who feel most wronged by those they have first injured, who sing of love and practise fratricide, preach freedom and enact suppression, a race of democrats who sweat the poor, have a harp for an emblem and no musicians, revelled on foreign gold and cringed without it, whose earlier history is myth and murder, whose later, murder, whose tongue is silver and whose heart is black, a race skilled in idleness, talented in hate, inventive only in slander, whose land is a breeding-ground of modern reaction and the cradle of western crime.

TOM PENHALIGON
The Impossible Irish, dedication, 1935

This savage manner of incivility amongst the Irish is bred in the bone; they have it by nature, and so I think of their inhuman cruelty, that are so apt to run into rebellion, and so ready to attempt any other kind of mischief.

BARNABE RICH
The Anathomy of Ireland, 1615

Put an Irishman on the spit and you can always get another Irishman to turn him.

GEORGE BERNARD SHAW
Preface to *John Bull's Other Island*, 1907

I reckon no man is thoroughly miserable unless he be condemned to live in Ireland.

JONATHAN SWIFT
Letter to Ambrose Philips,
October 30, 1709

A servile race in folly nursed,
Who truckle most when treated worst.
JONATHAN SWIFT
On the Death of Dr. Swift, 1731

ITALY AND THE ITALIANS

Italy is a paradise for horses, a hell for women.

ROBERT BURTON
The Anatomy of Melancholy, 1621

Ah, servile Italy, thou inn of grief, ship without pilot in a mighty storm, no longer queen of provinces, but a brothel.

DANTE
Purgatorio, c. 1320

God placed popedom in Italy not without cause, for the Italians can make out many things to be real and true which in truth are not so: they have crafty and subtle brains.

MARTIN LUTHER
Table Talk, 1569

The Italians are all thieves.

Attributed to
NAPOLEON I

The Italians have not sense or patience enough to taste a ripe peach . . .
They are sunk beneath all sympathy and have become detestable—
down to the very children.

JOHN RUSKIN
Letter to Jean Ingelow, July 19, 1869

There are two Italies . . . The one is the most sublime and lovely con-
templation than can be conceived by the imagination of man; the other
is the most degraded, disgusting and odious. What do you think?
Young women of rank actually eat—you will never guess what—garlick!

PERCY BYSSHE SHELLEY
Letter, December 22, 1818

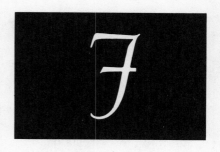

IT DOES NOT MATTER MUCH WHAT
A MAN HATES PROVIDED HE HATES
SOMETHING.

SAMUEL BUTLER

NOTE-BOOKS, c. 1890

JACKSON, ANDREW

I feel much alarmed at the prospect of seeing General Jackson President. He is one of the most unfit men I know of for such a place.

THOMAS JEFFERSON
To Daniel Webster, 1824

JAMES, HENRY

Henry James was one of the nicest old ladies I ever met.

Attributed to
WILLIAM FAULKNER

Henry James writes fiction as if it were a painful duty.

OSCAR WILDE
The Decay of Lying, 1891

JANUARY

January, month of empty pockets! . . . let us endure this evil month, anxious as a theatrical producer's forehead.

COLETTE
Journey for Myself, 1922

JAZZ

Jam sessions, jitterbugs and cannibalistic rhythmic orgies are wooing our youth along the primrose path to Hell!

THE MOST REVEREND
FRANCIS J. L. BECKMAN
Address to the National Council of
Catholic Women, Biloxi, Mississippi,
October 25, 1938

JEALOUSY

The venom clamors of a jealous woman
Poisons more deadly than a mad dog's tooth.

WILLIAM SHAKESPEARE
Othello, 1604

JEFFERSON, THOMAS

The moral character of Jefferson was repulsive. Continually puling about liberty, equality, and the degrading curse of slavery, he brought his own children to the hammer, and made money of his debaucheries.

THOMAS HAMILTON
Men and Manners in America, 1833

JEHOVAH

I have been reading the Old Testament, a most bloodthirsty and perilous book for the young. Jehovah is beyond doubt the worst character in fiction.

EDWARD ARLINGTON ROBINSON
Letter to Mrs. Henry Richards
(date unknown)

JESUITS

I do not like the reappearance of the Jesuits. If ever there was a body of men who merited damnation on earth and in Hell it is this society of Loyola's. Nevertheless, we are compelled by our system of religious toleration to offer them an asylum.

JOHN ADAMS
Letter to Thomas Jefferson, 1816

The voluminous Jesuits, those Laplanders of Peripateticism, do but subtly trifle; and their philosophic undertakings are much like his who spent his time in darting cummin seeds through the eye of a needle.

JOSEPH GLANVILL
The Vanity of Dogmatizing, 1661

No religion that I know of in all the world ever had such lewd and scandalous casuists. Their main business seems to be, not to keep men from sin, but to teach them how near they might lawfully come, without sinning.

JOHN TILLOTSON,
Archbishop of Canterbury
Sermons, 1694

JEWS

How odd
Of God
To choose
The Jews

HOWLAND SPENCER
How Odd, 1915

JOGGING

The modish mortification of the flesh.
PETER S. PRESCOTT
Newsweek, February 12, 1979

JOHNSON, SAMUEL

Pomposo, insolent and loud,
Vain idol of a scribbling crowd . . .
Whose cursory flattery is the tool
Of every fawning, flattering fool;
Who wit with jealous eye surveys,
And sickens at another's praise; . . .
Who to increase his native strength
Draws words six syllables in length,
With which, assisted with a frown,
By way of club, he knocks us down.
CHARLES CHURCHILL
The Ghost, 1763

Envy (the mother of many vices) was the bosom serpent of this literary despot.

WILLIAM HAYLEY
Letter to Anna Seward, 1785

I own I like not Johnson's turgid style,
That gives an inch the importance of a mile,
Casts of manure a wagon-load around

To raise a simple daisy from the ground;
Uplifts the club of Hercules, for what?
To crush a butterfly or brain a gnat!

JOHN WOLCOT
On Dr. Samuel Johnson, 1785

JOHNSON, SAMUEL, AND BOSWELL, JAMES

You have but two subjects, yourself and me. I am sick of both.

Attributed to
SAMUEL JOHNSON

JOLLY GREEN GIANT

I'd like to see somebody run up to the Jolly Green Giant and say, "Ho, ho, ho yourself, you big queer."

Attributed to
JOHNNY CARSON

JOURNALISM

The difference between literature and journalism is that journalism is unreadable, and literature is not read.

OSCAR WILDE
The Critic as Artist, 1891

As for modern journalism, it is not my business to defend it. It justifies its own existence by the great Darwinian principle of the survival of the vulgarest.

OSCAR WILDE
The Critic as Artist, 1891

JOURNALISTS

They are a sort of assassins who sit with loaded blunderbusses at the corner of streets and fire them off for hire or for sport at any passenger they select.

JOHN QUINCY ADAMS
Diary, September 7, 1820

A spirit of national masochism prevails, encouraged by an effete corps of impudent snobs who characterize themselves as intellectuals.

SPIRO AGNEW
Speech, 1969

A would-be satirist, a hired buffoon,
A monthly scribbler of some low lampoon,
Condemn'd to drudge, the meanest of the mean,
And furbish falsehoods for a magazine.

> LORD BYRON
> *English Bards and Scotch Reviewers*, 1809

I'll tell you briefly what I think of newspapermen: the hand of God reaching down into the mire couldn't elevate one of them to the depths of degradation—not by a million miles.

> BEN HECHT
> Screenplay, *Nothing Sacred*, 1937

Journalists! Peeking through keyholes! Running after fire engines like a lot of coach dogs! Waking people up in the middle of the night to ask them what they think of Mussolini. Stealing pictures off of old ladies of their daughters that got raped in Oak Park. A lot of lousy, daffy buttinskis, swelling around with holes in their pants, borrowing nickels from office boys! And for what? So a million hired girls and motormen's wives'll know what's going on.

> BEN HECHT
> AND CHARLES MACARTHUR
> *The Front Page*, 1928

A newswriter is a man without virtue, who writes lies at home for his own profit. To these compositions is required neither genius nor knowledge, neither industry nor sprightliness; but contempt of shame and indifference to truth are absolutely necessary.

> SAMUEL JOHNSON
> *The Idler*, November 11, 1758

JOYCE, JAMES

My God, what a clumsy olla putrida James Joyce is! Nothing but old fags and cabbage stumps of quotations from the Bible and the rest, stewed in the juice of deliberate, journalistic dirty-mindedness.

> D. H. LAWRENCE
> Letter, August 15, 1928

JUDGES

Judges are apt to be naïve, simple-minded men.

> OLIVER WENDELL HOLMES, JR.
> Speech in New York,
> February 15, 1913

JURY

Then went the jury out, whose names were Mr. Blind-man, Mr. No-good, Mr. Malice, Mr. Love-lust, Mr. Live-loose, Mr. Heady, Mr. High-mind, Mr. Enmity, Mr. Liar, Mr. Cruelty, Mr. Hate-light, and Mr. Implacable, who every one gave in his private verdict against him among themselves, and afterwards unanimously concluded to bring him in guilty before the judge.

JOHN BUNYAN
Pilgrim's Progress, 1678

We have a criminal jury system which is superior to any in the world; and its efficiency is only marred by the difficulty of finding twelve men every day who don't know anything and can't read.

MARK TWAIN
"After-Dinner Speech,"
Sketches New and Old, 1875

The jury system puts a ban upon intelligence and honesty, and a premium upon ignorance, stupidity and perjury.

MARK TWAIN
Roughing It, 1872

JUSTICE

It is beyond our power to explain either the prosperity of the wicked or the afflictions of the righteous.

TALMUD

Justice is the sanction of established injustice.

ANATOLE FRANCE
Crainquebille, 1901

I tell ye Hogan's r-right whin he says: "Justice is blind." Blind she is, an' deef an' dumb an' has a wooden leg!

FINLEY PETER DUNNE
Mr. Dooley's Opinions, 1901

NOW HATRED IS BY FAR THE
LONGEST PLEASURE;
MEN LOVE IN HASTE, BUT THEY
DETEST AT LEISURE.

LORD BYRON
DON JUAN, 1819–1824

KEATS, JOHN

That dirty little blackguard.

LORD BYRON, 1820

Such writing is mental masturbation—he is always fr-gg--g his Imagination. I don't mean he is indecent, but viciously soliciting his own ideas into a state, which is neither poetry nor anything else but a Bedlam vision produced by raw pork and opium.

LORD BYRON
Letter to John Murray,
October 12, 1820

KEROUAC, JACK

That's not writing, that's typing.

TRUMAN CAPOTE
Quoted in Myrick Land's *The Fine
Art of Literary Mayhem*, 1963

KINGS

Let us strangle the last king with the guts of the last priest.

DENIS DIDEROT
"Dithyrambe sur la fête des rois,"
c. 1750

Kings is mostly rapscallions.
MARK TWAIN
Huckleberry Finn, 1884

KISS

The kiss originated when the first male reptile licked the first female reptile, implying in a subtle, complimentary way that she was as succulent as the small reptile he had for dinner the night before.
F. SCOTT FITZGERALD
The Crack-Up, serialized in *Esquire*, 1936

Oh, what lies there are in kisses.
HEINRICH HEINE
"In den Küssen, welche Lüge," 1827

Kissing don't last; cookery do!
GEORGE MEREDITH
The Ordeal of Richard Feverel, 1859

Lord! I wonder what fool it was that first invented kissing.
Attributed to
JONATHAN SWIFT

KNOWLEDGE

A young man who desires to know all that in all ages and in all lands has been thought by the best minds, and wishes to make a synthesis of those thoughts for the future benefit of mankind, is laying up for himself a very miserable old age.
MAX BEERBOHM
Music Halls of My Youth, 1942

Knowledge is not happiness, and science
But an exchange of ignorance for that which is another kind of ignorance.
LORD BYRON
Manfred, 1817

Everything has been said.
JEAN DE LA BRUYÈRE
Les Caractères, 1688

KORAN

A wearisome confused jumble, crude, incondite; endless iterations, long-windedness, entanglement; most crude, incondite—insupportable stupidity, in short! Nothing but a sense of duty could carry any European through the Koran.

THOMAS CARLYLE
Heroes and Hero Worship, 1840

WHAT WE NEED IS HATRED—
FROM IT OUR IDEAS ARE BORN.

JEAN GENÊT
EPIGRAPH TO *THE BLACKS*, 1960

LABOR

Labor is the curse of the world, and nobody can meddle with it without becoming proportionately brutified.

NATHANIEL HAWTHORNE
American Notebooks, entry of August
12, 1841

LAMB, CHARLES

Insuperable proclivity to gin in poor old Lamb. His talk contemptibly small, indicating wondrous ignorance and shallowness, even when it was serious and good-mannered, which it seldom was, usually ill-mannered (to a degree), screwed into frosty artificialities, ghastly make-believe of wit, in fact more like "diluted insanity" (as I defined it) than anything of real jocosity, humor, or geniality.

THOMAS CARLYLE
Letter to Jane Welsh Carlyle, 1866

LANGUAGE

Language—human language—after all, is but little better than the croak and cackle of fowls, and other utterances of brute nature—sometimes not so adequate.

NATHANIEL HAWTHORNE
American Notebooks,
entry of July 14, 1850

LAS VEGAS

A monument to the Mafia's ability to cater to the lowest forms of lust in the souls of the American people; to give the suckers what they want. It's the biggest joke that's ever been played on the people of the United States.

THOMAS PERRY
The Butcher's Boy, 1982

LATINS

Latins Are Lousy Lovers
HELEN LAWRENSON
Title of magazine article,
Esquire, October 1936

LAUGHTER

Laughter, while it lasts, slackens and unbraces the mind, weakens the faculties, and causes a kind of remissness and dissolution in all the powers of the soul.

JOSEPH ADDISON
The Spectator, December 15, 1712

He who laughs has not yet heard the bad news.

BERTOLT BRECHT
The Caucasion Chalk Circle, 1943–45

In my mind, there is nothing so illiberal and so ill-bred, as audible laughter.

LORD CHESTERFIELD
Letter to his son, March 9, 1748

Laughter has its springs in some kind of meanness or deformity.

CICERO
De Oratore, 55 B.C.

LAW

Law is a bottomless pit.
JOHN ARBUTHNOT, M.D.
Title of pamphlet, 1712

Every law is an evil, for every law is an infraction of beauty.

JEREMY BENTHAM
Principals of Legislation, 1789

Most people have come to recognize the law as the deadly enemy of justice.

DAVID CORT
Revolution by Cliché, 1970

The law is a ass, a idiot.

CHARLES DICKENS
Oliver Twist, 1838

The law in its majestic equality, forbids the rich as well as the poor to sleep under bridges, to beg in the streets, and to steal bread.

ANATOLE FRANCE
Le Lys rouge, 1894

Laws are inherited like diseases.

JOHANN WOLFGANG VON GOETHE
Faust, 1808

The law is a sort of hocus-pocus science, that smiles in yer face while it picks yer pocket.

CHARLES MACKLIN
Love à la Mode, 1759

Laws were made to be broken.

CHRISTOPHER NORTH (JOHN WILSON)
Noctes Ambrosianae, No. 20,
May 1830

Law is born from despair of human nature.

Attributed to
JOSÉ ORTEGA Y GASSET

Laws, like cobwebs, entangle the weak, but are broken by the strong.

Attributed to
SOLON, c. 575 B.C.

LAWYER

You're an attorney. It's your duty to lie, conceal and distort everything, and slander everybody.

JEAN GIRAUDOUX
The Madwoman of Chaillot, 1945

There's no better way of exercising the imagination than the study of law. No poet ever interpreted nature as freely as a lawyer interprets truth.

JEAN GIRAUDOUX
Tiger at the Gates, 1935

Lawyers are always more ready to get a man into troubles than out of them.

OLIVER GOLDSMITH
The Good Natur'd Man, 1768

A lawyer's relationship to justice and wisdom ... is on a par with a piano tuner's relationship to a concert. He neither composes the music, nor interprets it—he merely keeps the machinery running.

LUCILLE KALLEN
Introducing C. B. Greenfield, 1979

I think we may class the lawyer in the natural history of monsters.

JOHN KEATS
Letter to George and Georgiana Keats,
March 13, 1819

Woe unto ye also, ye lawyers! for ye lade men with burdens grievous to be born, and ye yourselves touch not the burdens with one of your fingers.

Luke 11:46

The first thing we do, let's kill all the lawyers.

WILLIAM SHAKESPEARE
Henry VI, Part II, 1597–98

LEARNING

A learned man is an idler who kills time by study.

GEORGE BERNARD SHAW
Maxims for Revolutionists, 1903

Words are but wind; and learning is nothing but words; ergo, learning is nothing but wind.

JONATHAN SWIFT
A Tale of a Tub, 1704

Most learned men are like courtiers. Sometimes they are just as greedy, intriguing, treacherous, and cruel; and the only difference between the pests of the court and the pests of the school is that the latter are the more ridiculous.

VOLTAIRE
Letter to Frederick the Great,
August 26, 1736

LECTURERS

A lecturer is a literary strumpet, subject for a greater than whore's fee to prostitute himself.

OLIVER WENDELL HOLMES
Remark made to Herman Melville

LEISURE

The secret of being miserable is to have leisure to bother about whether you are happy or not.

GEORGE BERNARD SHAW
Misalliance, preface, 1914

LENTILS

I hate with a bitter hatred the names of lentils and haricots—those pretentious cheats of the appetite, those tabulated humbugs, those certificated aridities calling themselves human food!

GEORGE GISSING
The Private Papers of Henry Ryecroft,
1903

LEONARDO DA VINCI

He bores me. He ought to have stuck to his flying machines.

Attributed to
AUGUSTE RENOIR

LETTERS

I have received no more than one or two letters that were worth the postage.

HENRY DAVID THOREAU
Walden, 1854

LEVANT, OSCAR

Pearl is a disease of oysters. Levant is a disease of Hollywood.

Attributed to
KENNETH TYNAN

LEXICOGRAPHER

Lexicographer: a writer of dictionaries, a harmless drudge.

SAMUEL JOHNSON
In 1755, quoted in James Boswell's
Life of Samuel Johnson, 1791

LIBERACE

This deadly, winking, sniggering, snuggling, scent-impregnated, chromium-plated, luminous, quivering, giggling, fruit-flavored, mincing, ice-covered heap of mother-love . . . the summit of sex—the pinnacle of Masculine, Feminine and Neuter.

CASSANDRA (WILLIAM CONNOR)
Daily Mirror, London,
October 1956

Such dimpling and winking! Such tossing of blond curls, and fluttering of eyelashes and flashing of teeth! Such nausea.

FAYE EMERSON
Reviewing *The Liberace Show* in
the *New York World-Telegram*,
July 1952

LIBERTY

The great half truth, liberty.
WILLIAM BLAKE
The Marriage of Heaven and Hell, 1790

LIBERTY, STATUE OF

You have set up in New York harbor a monstrous idol which you call Liberty. The only thing that remains to complete that monument is to put on its pedestal the inscription written by Dante on the gate of Hell: "All hope abandon, ye who enter here."

GEORGE BERNARD SHAW
Address in New York,
April 11, 1933

LIBRARY

For myself, public libraries possess a special horror, as of lonely wastes and dragon-haunted fens. The stillness and the heavy air, the feeling of restriction and surveillance, the mute presence of these other readers, "all silent and all damned," combine to set up a nervous irritation fatal to quiet study.

KENNETH GRAHAME
Pagan Papers, 1893

LIFE

Life is divided into the horrible and the miserable.
WOODY ALLEN
Annie Hall, 1977

Not only is there no God, but try getting a plumber on weekends.
WOODY ALLEN
Getting Even, 1972

Life is a wonderful thing to talk about, or to read about in history books—but it is terrible when one has to live it.
JEAN ANOUILH
Time Remembered, 1939

Why do we live? But to make sport for our neighbours and laugh at them in return.
JANE AUSTEN
Pride and Prejudice, 1813

Nothing matters very much, and very few things matter at all.
Attributed to
ARTHUR JAMES BALFOUR

It is a misery to be born, a pain to live, a trouble to die.
SAINT BERNARD OF CLAIRVAUX
De consideratione, III, c. 1145

Life is an incurable disease.
ABRAHAM COWLEY
To Dr. Scarborough, 1656

Life is a zoo in a jungle.
PETER DE VRIES
The Vale of Laughter, 1967

Life is a God-damned, stinking, treacherous game and nine hundred and ninety-nine men out of a thousand are bastards.
THEODORE DREISER
A Book About Myself, 1922

We are born crying, live complaining, and die disappointed.
THOMAS FULLER
Gnomologia, 1732

There are three events in a man's life: birth, life and death; he is not conscious of being born, he dies in pain, and he forgets to live.
JEAN DE LA BRUYÈRE
Les Caractères, 1588

So little time and so little to do.
Attributed to
OSCAR LEVANT

Life is a long headache in a noisy street.
JOHN MASEFIELD
The Widow in the Bye Street, 1912

It is not true that life is one thing after another—it is one damn thing over and over.
Attributed to
EDNA ST. VINCENT MILLAY

Life is just one damned thing after another.
Attributed to
FRANK WARD O'MALLEY

Living is dangerous to your health. . . . For one thing, living brings on age, and we know how debilitating age can be. It's something everyone should avoid.

ANDREW A. ROONEY
And More by Andy Rooney, 1982

Nothing is so false as human life, nothing so treacherous. God knows no one would have accepted it as a gift, if it had not been given without our knowledge.

SENECA
Ad marciam de consolatione,
1st century A.D.

Life is as tedious as a twice-told tale,
Vexing the dull ear of a drowsy man.
WILLIAM SHAKESPEARE
King John, c. 1596

Out, out brief candle! Life's but a walking shadow, a poor player that struts and frets his hour upon the stage, and then is heard no more; it is a tale told by an idiot, full of sound and fury, signifying nothing.
WILLIAM SHAKESPEARE
Macbeth, c. 1605

Life is a disease; and the only difference between one man and another is the stage of the disease at which he lives.
GEORGE BERNARD SHAW
Back to Methuselah, 1921

People say that life is the thing, but I prefer reading.
LOGAN PEARSALL SMITH
Afterthoughts, 1931

Life is a gamble, at terrible odds—if it was a bet you wouldn't take it.
TOM STOPPARD
*Rosencrantz and Guildenstern Are
Dead*, 1967

LINCOLN, ABRAHAM

God damn your god damned old hellfired god damned soul to hell god damn you and goddam your god damned family's god damned hellfired god damned soul to hell and good damnation god damn them and god damn your god damn friends to hell.

> Letter to Abraham Lincoln
> dated Fillmore, Louisiana,
> November 25, 1860,
> signed PETE MUGGINS

LINGUIST

Men who can speak a number of different tongues are notorious for having little to say in any of them.

> H. R. HUSE
> *The Illiteracy of the Literate*, 1933

LISZT, FRANZ

Composition indeed! Decomposition is the proper word for such hateful fungi, which choke up and poison the fertile plains of harmony, threatening the world with drought.

> ANONYMOUS
> *Musical World*, London,
> June 30, 1855

LITERACY

If there's one major cause for the spread of mass illiteracy, it's the fact that everybody can read and write.

> PETER DE VRIES
> *The Tents of Wickedness*, 1959

A great many people now reading and writing would be better employed keeping rabbits.

> EDITH SITWELL
> *The Observer*, London,
> May 13, 1923

LITERARY PRIZES

Prizes are for the birds. They fill the head of one author with vanity and 30 others with misery.

> LOUIS AUCHINCLOSS
> Quoted in *Time*, September 21, 1981

LITERATURE

Literature is printed nonsense.
> AUGUST STRINDBERG
> *Zones of the Spirit,* 1913

Literature is the orchestration of platitudes.
> THORNTON WILDER
> *Time,* January 12, 1953

LIVINGSTON, EDWARD

He is a man of splendid abilities, but utterly corrupt. He shines and stinks like rotten mackerel by moonlight.
> JOHN RANDOLPH
> Speech, 1822 or 1823, in which
> Randolph described Livingston as
> the corrupting intellectual force
> behind Andrew Jackson

LOGIC

The application of whips, racks, gibbets, galleys, dungeons, fire and faggot in a dispute may be looked upon as popish refinements upon the old heathen logic.
> JOSEPH ADDISON
> *The Spectator,* December 4, 1711

"LOHENGRIN"

The banging and slamming and booming and crashing were something beyond belief. The racking and pitiless pain of it remains stored up in my memory alongside the memory of the time that I had my teeth fixed.
> MARK TWAIN
> *A Tramp Abroad,* 1880

LONDON

The monstrous tuberosity of civilized life, the capital of England.
> THOMAS CARLYLE
> *Sartor Resartus,* 1836

London, that great cesspool into which all the loungers of the Empire are irresistibly drained.
> SIR ARTHUR CONAN DOYLE
> *A Study in Scarlet,* 1887

Crowds without company, and dissipation without pleasure.

> EDWARD GIBBON
> *Memoirs of My Life and Writings,*
> 1796

That great foul city of London there—rattling, growling, smoking, stinking—a ghastly heap of fermenting brickwork, pouring out poison at every pore—you fancy it is a city of work? Not a street of it! It is a great city of play; very nasty play, and very hard play, but still play.

> JOHN RUSKIN
> *The Crown of Wild Olive,* 1866

London, that like a bowl of viscid human fluid, boils sullenly over the rim of its encircling hills and slops messily and uglily into the home counties.

> H. G. WELLS
> *The Future of America,* 1906

LONG, HUEY P.

The trouble with Senator Long is that he is suffering from halitosis of the intellect.

> HAROLD L. ICKES
> Press conference, April 18, 1935

LONGEVITY

Longevity, n. Uncommon extension of the fear of death.

> AMBROSE BIERCE
> *The Devil's Dictionary,* 1906, 1911

Do not try to live forever. You will not succeed.

> GEORGE BERNARD SHAW
> *The Doctor's Dilemma,* preface, 1911

Nothing that lasts too long is very agreeable, not even life.

> MARQUIS DE VAUVENARGUES
> *Réflexions et maximes,* 1747

LOS ANGELES

I mean, who would want to live in a place where the only cultural advantage is that you can turn right on a red light.

> WOODY ALLEN
> *Annie Hall,* 1977

The difference between Los Angeles and yoghurt is that yoghurt has an active, living culture.

ANONYMOUS

Seventeen suburbs in search of a city.
ANONYMOUS

Thought is barred in this city of Dreadful Joy, and conversation is unknown.

Attributed to
ALDOUS HUXLEY

It is hereby earnestly proposed that the U.S.A. would be much better off if that big, sprawling, incoherent, shapeless, slobbering civic idiot in the family of American communities, the City of Los Angeles, could be declared incompetent and placed in charge of a guardian like any individual mental defective.

WESTBROOK PEGLER
New York World-Telegram,
November 22, 1938

The city [from the air] seems dead as putrefying squid with plastic varicose veins stapled into a plastic belly . . .

HARRISON SALISBURY
Travels Around America, 1976

. . . Too many freeways, too much sun, too much abnormality taken normally, too many pink stucco houses and pink stucco consciences.

CLANCY SIGAL
Going Away, 1962

When it's five below in New York, it's 78 in Los Angeles, and when it's 110 in New York, it's 78 in Los Angeles. There are two million interesting people in New York—and only 78 in Los Angeles.

NEIL SIMON
Playboy, February 1979

Louis XIV

Strip your Louis Quatorze of his king-gear, and there is left nothing but a poor forked radish with a head fantastically carved.

THOMAS CARLYLE
On Heroes, Hero-Worship, and the
Heroic in History, 1841

LOVE

What is annoying about love is that it is a crime in which one cannot do without an accomplice.

CHARLES BAUDELAIRE
Intimate Journals, 1887

Love is mainly an affair of short spasms. If these spasms disappoint us, love dies. It is very seldom that it weathers the experience and becomes friendship.

JEAN COCTEAU
The Difficulty of Being, 1957

Heaven has no rage like love to hatred turned,
Nor Hell a fury like a woman scorned.

WILLIAM CONGREVE
The Mourning Bride, 1697

A woman who has never been hit by a man has never been loved.

ZSA ZSA GABOR
Quoted in *Vanity Fair,*
December 1983

Love is a universal migraine,
A bright stain on the vision,
Blotting out reason.

ROBERT GRAVES
"Symptoms of Love,"
Collected Poems, 1961

Love, love, love—all the wretched cant of it, masking egotism, lust, masochism, fantasy under a mythology of sentimental postures, a welter of self-induced miseries and joys, blinding and masking the essential personalities in the frozen gestures of courtship, in the kissing and the dating and the desire, the compliments and the quarrels which vivify its barrenness.

GERMAINE GREER
The Female Eunuch, 1970

Falling in love with love is falling for make-believe.

LORENZ HART
Song, 1938

We've practiced loving long enough,
Let's come at last to hate.

GEORGE HERWEGH
"Lied vom Hasse," 1841

Love between the sexes is a sin in theology, a forbidden intercourse in jurisprudence, a mechanical insult in medicine, and a subject philosophy has no time for.

KARL KRAUS
Quoted in
The Viking Book of Aphorisms,
edited by W. H. Auden and Louis
Kronenberger, 1962

. . . a state of mental misery which has a restricting, impoverishing and paralyzing effect upon the development of consciousness.

JOSÉ ORTEGA Y GASSET
On Love, 1957

Scratch a lover, and find a foe!
DOROTHY PARKER
Enough Rope, 1926

How miserable is the man who loves.
PLAUTUS
Asinaria, c. 200 B.C.

Love is an incurable malady like those pathetic states in which rheumatism affords the sufferer a brief respite only to be replaced by epileptiform headaches.

MARCEL PROUST
The Captive, 1923

O brawling love! O hating love!
WILLIAM SHAKESPEARE
Romeo and Juliet, c. 1596

Stay me with flagons, comfort me with apples: for I am sick of love.
The Song of Solomon 2:5, c. 200 B.C.

Love is a sour delight, a sugared grief,
A living death, an ever-dying life,
A breach of reason's law.
THOMAS WATSON
Hecatompathia, 1582

LUTHER, MARTIN

Luther was the foulest of monsters.
POPE GREGORY XV
Bull canonizing Ignatius Loyola,
1622

M.A.

A Master of Art
Is not worth a fart.

ANDREW BOORDE
The Jests of Scoggin, 1690

MACAULAY, THOMAS BABINGTON

An ugly, cross-made, splay-footed, shapeless little dumpling of a fellow, with a featureless face too—except indeed a good expansive forehead—sleek, puritanical, sandy hair—large glimmering eyes—and a mouth from ear to ear. He has a lisp and a burr.

ANONYMOUS
In *Blackwood's Magazine,* 1831

He has occasional flashes of silence that make his conversation perfectly delightful.

SYDNEY SMITH
In *A Memoir of the
Reverend Sydney Smith,*
by Lady Holland, 1855

McCORMICK, ROBERT R.

That great overgrown lummox of a Colonel McCormick, mediocre in ability, less than average in brains, and a damn physical coward in spite

159

of his size, sitting in the tower of the Tribune Building with his guards protecting him while he squirts sewage . . . at men whom he happens to dislike. He is the most foul, cowardly person that I think I have ever known. His public record would not bear light on a day of heaviest fog.

HAROLD L. ICKES
Secret Diary, 1954

MACDONALD, JAMES RAMSAY

We know that he has, more than any other man, the gift of compressing the largest number of words into the smallest amount of thought.

WINSTON S. CHURCHILL
Speech, March 23, 1933

MACHIAVELLI, NICCOLÒ

Out of his surname they have coined an epithet for a knave, and out of his Christian name a synonym for the Devil.

THOMAS BABINGTON MACAULAY
Machiavelli, 1827

MACHINERY

The world is dying of machinery; that is the great disease, that is the plague that will sweep away and destroy civilization; man will have to rise against it sooner or later.

GEORGE MOORE
Confessions of a Young Man, 1888

McKINLEY, WILLIAM

McKinley has no more backbone than a chocolate éclair.

THEODORE ROOSEVELT
On McKinley's reluctance to enter
upon war with Spain, 1898

McPHERSON, AIMEE SEMPLE

She is a frank and simple fraud, somewhat like Texas Guinan, but more comical and not quite so cheap.

MORROW MAYO
New Republic, December 25, 1929

MAILER, NORMAN

Mailer . . . decocts matters of the first philosophical magnitude from an examination of his own ordure, and I am not talking about his books.

WILLIAM F. BUCKLEY, JR.
National Review, July 2, 1968

MAJORITY

The majority, compose them how you will, are a herd, and not a very nice one.

WILLIAM HAZLITT
Butts of Different Sorts, 1829

The most dangerous foe to truth and freedom in our midst is the compact majority. Yes, the damned, compact, liberal majority.

HENRIK IBSEN
An Enemy of the People, 1882

MANKIND

More than any other time in history, mankind faces a crossroads. One path leads to despair and utter hopelessness. The other, to total extinction. Let us pray we have the wisdom to choose correctly.

WOODY ALLEN
Side Effects, 1981

Cursed is every one who placeth his hope in man.

SAINT AUGUSTINE
On the Christian Instruction, c. 397

Men have never been good, they are not good, they never will be good.

KARL BARTH
Time, April 12, 1954

Man is nothing else than . . . a sack of dung, the food of worms.

SAINT BERNARD OF CLAIRVAUX
Meditationes pussimae, c. 1140

Man is a puny, slow, awkward, unarmed animal.

JACOB BRONOWSKI
The Ascent of Man, 1974

O man! thou feeble tenant of an hour,
Debased by slavery, or corrupt by power,
Who knows thee well must quit thee with disgust,
Degraded mass of animated dust!
Thy love is lust, thy friendship all a cheat,
Thy smiles hypocrisy, thy word deceit!
By nature vile, ennobled out by name,
Each kindred brute might bid thee blush for shame.

LORD BYRON
*On the Monument of a
Newfoundland Dog,* 1808

The belief in a supernatural source of evil is not necessary; men alone are quite capable of every wickedness.

JOSEPH CONRAD
Under Western Eyes, 1911

What is man, when you come to think upon him, but a minutely set, ingenious machine for turning, with infinite artfulness, the red wine of Shiraz into urine?

ISAK DINESEN
Seven Gothic Tales, 1934

The majority of mankind is lazy-minded, incurious, absorbed in vanities, and tepid in emotion, and is therefore incapable of either much doubt or much faith.

T. S. ELIOT
Introduction, Pascal's *Pensées,* 1931

We are afraid of truth, afraid of fortune, afraid of death and afraid of each other.

RALPH WALDO EMERSON
Self-Reliance, 1841

Man is nature's sole mistake.

W. S. GILBERT
The Princess Ida, 1884

Lord, what are we, and what are our children, but a generation of vipers?

OLIVER WENDELL HOLMES
"The Medical Profession in
Massachusetts,"
1869 lecture in Boston

Of all the creatures that creep and breathe on earth there is none more wretched than man.

HOMER
Iliad, c. 8th century B.C.

Men, my dear, are very queer animals—a mixture of horse-nervousness, ass-stubbornness and camel-malice.

THOMAS HENRY HUXLEY
Letter to Mrs. W. K. Clifford,
February 10, 1895

Thus saith the Lord: Cursed be the man that trusteth in man . . .

Jeremiah 17:5, c. 625 B.C.

Speaking generally, men are ungrateful, fickle, hypocritical, fearful of danger and covetous of gain.

NICCOLÒ MACHIAVELLI
The Prince, 1513

... and only man is vile.
BISHOP REGINALD HEBER
Hymns, c. 1823

Men are the only animals that devote themselves, day in and day out, to making one another unhappy. It is an art like any other. Its virtuosi are called altruists.

H. L. MENCKEN
A Mencken Chrestomathy, 1949

The earth has skin, and that skin has diseases. One of those diseases is called man.

FRIEDRICH WILHELM NIETZSCHE
Thus Spake Zarathustra, 1883

Trust not a man; we are by nature false,
Dissembling, subtle, cruel and unconstant.

THOMAS OTWAY
The Orphan, 1680

Who are we? We find that we live on an insignificant planet of a humdrum star lost in a galaxy tucked away in some forgotten corner of a universe in which there are far more galaxies than people.

CARL SAGAN
Quoted in *Time*,
October 20, 1980

He'll swim a river of snot, wade nostril deep through a mile of vomit, if he thinks there'll be a friendly pussy awaiting him. He'll screw a woman he despises, any snaggle-toothed hag, and further, pay for the opportunity. And he'll also screw babies and corpses.

VALERIE SOLANAS
S.C.U.M. Manifesto, 1967–68

The world could get along very well without literature; it could get along even better without man.

JEAN-PAUL SARTRE
Situations, 1947–49

Man originates in muck, wades a while in muck, makes muck, and in the end returns to muck.

JOHANN CHRISTOPH FRIEDRICH VON
SCHILLER
The Robbers, 1781

Man is little inferior to the tiger and the hyena in cruelty and savagery.

ARTHUR SCHOPENHAUER
Parerga und Paralipomena, 1851

Lord, what fools these mortals be!

WILLIAM SHAKESPEARE
A Midsummer Night's Dream,
1595–96

There's no trust,
No faith, no honesty in men; all perjured,
All forsworn, all naught, all dissemblers.

WILLIAM SHAKESPEARE
Romeo and Juliet, c. 1596

The most pernicious race of little odious vermin that nature ever suffered to crawl upon the surface of the earth.

JONATHAN SWIFT
Gulliver's Travels, 1726

A creature squalid, vengeful, and impure;
Remorseless, and submissive to no law
But superstitious fear and abject sloth.

WILLIAM WORDSWORTH
The Excursion, 1814

MANNERS

Manners are the hypocrisy of a nation.

HONORÉ DE BALZAC
Quoted, 1911,
in André Gide's *Journals*,
published 1947–51

No one can be as calculatedly rude as the British, which amazes Americans, who do not understand studied insult and can only offer abuse as a substitute.

PAUL GALLICO
Quoted in *The New York Times*,
January 14, 1962

MANSFIELD, KATHERINE

I loathe you. You revolt me stewing in your consumption . . . the Italians were quite right to have nothing to do with you. You are a loathesome reptile—I hope you will die.

D. H. LAWRENCE
Letter to Katherine Mansfield,
received on or about February 7, 1919

MANUSCRIPT

Manuscript: something submitted in haste and returned at leisure.

Attributed to
OLIVER HERFORD

MARCHING

That a man can take pleasure in marching in fours to the strains of a band is enough to make me despise him.

ALBERT EINSTEIN
The World as I See It, 1934

MARRIAGE

Husband! thou dull unpitied miscreant,
Wedded to noise, to misery, and want;
Sold an eternal vassal for thy life,
Oblig'd to cherish and to heat a wife:
Repeat thy loath'd embraces every night
Prompted to act by duty not delight.

ANONYMOUS
Against Marriage, c. 1690

Marriage. The beginning and the end are wonderful. But the middle part is hell.

ENID BAGNOLD
The Chinese Prime Minister, 1964

Of all serious things, marriage is the most ludicrous.

BEAUMARCHAIS
The Marriage of Figaro, 1778

Marriage, n. A master, a mistress and two slaves, making in all, two.

AMBROSE BIERCE
The Devil's Dictionary, 1906, 1911

One was never married, and that's his hell; another is, and that's his plague.

> ROBERT BURTON
> *The Anatomy of Melancholy,* 1621

Oh! how many torments lie in the small circle of a wedding-ring!

> COLLEY CIBBER
> *The Double Gallant,* 1707

Every woman should marry—and no man.

> BENJAMIN DISRAELI
> *Lothair,* 1870

Nothing to me is more distasteful than that entire complacency and satisfaction which beam in the countenances of a newly married couple.

> CHARLES LAMB
> *Essays of Elia,* 1823

[Marriage is] a triumph of habit over hate.

> OSCAR LEVANT
> *Memoirs of an Amnesiac,* 1965

When two people are under the influence of the most violent, most insane, most delusive, and most transient of passions, they are required to swear that they will remain in that excited, abnormal, and exhausting condition continuously until death do them part.

> GEORGE BERNARD SHAW
> Preface to *Getting Married,* 1908

A system could not well have been devised more studiously hostile to human happiness than marriage.

> PERCY BYSSHE SHELLEY
> *Queen Mab,* notes, 1813

There is a poor sordid slavery in marriage that turns the flowing tide of honour, and sinks it to the lowest ebb of infamy. 'Tis a corrupted soil; ill-nature, avarice, sloth, cowardice and dirt are all its product.

> JOHN VANBRUGH
> *The Provok'd Wife,* 1697

Take my wife—please!

> HENNY YOUNGMAN

MARTYR

It is often pleasant to stone a martyr, nor matter how much we may admire him.

> JOHN BARTH
> *The Floating Opera,* 1956

There is a certain impertinence in allowing oneself to be burned for an opinion.

ANATOLE FRANCE
The Revolt of the Angels, 1914

Martyrdom, sir, is what these people like: it is the only way in which a man can become famous without ability.

GEORGE BERNARD SHAW
The Devil's Disciple, 1897

MASS

The mass is the greatest blaspheming of God, and the highest idolatry upon earth, an abomination the like to which has never been in Christendom since the time of the Apostles.

MARTIN LUTHER
Table Talk, 1569

MATHEMATICS

I have hardly ever known a mathematician who was able to reason.

PLATO
The Republic, c. 370 B.C.

Mathematics may be defined as the subject in which we never know what we are talking about, nor whether what we are saying is true.

BERTRAND RUSSELL
Mysticism and Logic, 1918

MATURITY

I think age is a very high price to pay for maturity.

TOM STOPPARD
Quoted in *Goodbye Baby & Amen*,
by David Bailey, 1969

MAUSOLEUM

Mausoleum, n. The final and funniest folly of the rich.

AMBROSE BIERCE
The Devil's Dictionary, 1906, 1911

MAXIM

It is unbecoming for young men to utter maxims.

ARISTOTLE
Rhetoric, c. 322 B.C.

I detest any attempt to bring the law into maxims. Maxims are invariably wrong, that is, they are so general and large that they always include something which is not intended to be included.

> LORD ESHER
> Judgment in *Yarmouth v. France*,
> 1887

Nothing is so useless as a general maxim.

> THOMAS BABINGTON MACAULAY
> *On Machiavelli,* 1827

MAYER, LOUIS B.

The reason so many people turned up at his funeral is that they wanted to make sure he was dead.

> Attributed to
> SAMUEL GOLDWYN

MEAT

I did *not* say this meat was tough. I just said I didn't see the horse that usually stands outside.

> W. C. FIELDS
> In *Never Give a Sucker an Even Break,* 1941

It is only by softening and disguising dead flesh by culinary preparation that it is rendered susceptible of mastication or digestion; and that the sight of its bloody juices and raw horror does not excite intolerable loathing and disgust.

> PERCY BYSSHE SHELLEY
> *Queen Mab,* notes, 1813

MEDIA

The media. It sounds like a convention of spiritualists.

> TOM STOPPARD
> *Jumpers,* 1972

At last Ike was giving it to those Commie-wierdo-Jew-fags [the media] who did not believe in the real America of humming electric chairs, well-packed prisons, and kitchens filled with every electric device that a small brown person of extranational provenance might successfully operate at a fraction of the legal minimum wage.

> GORE VIDAL
> In a review of *Make-Believe: The Story of Nancy and Ronald Reagan* in *The New York Review of Books,*
> September 29, 1983

MEDICINE

Just think of it. A hundred years ago there were no bacilli, no ptomaine poisoning, no diphtheria, and no appendicitis. Rabies was but little known, and only imperfectly developed. All of these we owe to medical science. Even such things as psoriasis and parotitus and trypanosomiasis, which are now household names, were known only to the few, and were quite beyond the reach of the great mass of people.

STEPHEN LEACOCK
"How to Be a Doctor,"
Literary Lapses, 1912

Nearly all men die of their medicines, not of their diseases.

MOLIÈRE
Le Malade imaginaire, 1673

Throw physic to the dogs; I'll none of it.
WILLIAM SHAKESPEARE
Macbeth, c. 1605

MEEKNESS

Meekness is the mask of malice.
ROBERT C. INGERSOLL
Prose-Poems and Selections, 1884

"MEISTERSINGER, DIE"

Of all the affected, sapless, soulless, beginningless, endless, topless, bottomless, topsiturviest, scrannel-pipiest, tongs and boniest doggrel of sounds I ever endured the deadliest of, that eternity of nothing was the deadliest.

JOHN RUSKIN
On *Die Meistersinger*, June 30, 1892

MENCKEN, H. L.

With a pig's eyes that never look up, with a pig's snout that loves muck, with a pig's brain that knows only the sty, and a pig's squeal that cries only when he is hurt, he sometimes opens his pig's mouth, tusked and ugly, and lets out the voice of God, railing at the whitewash that covers the manure about his habitat.

WILLIAM ALLEN WHITE
Quoted by H. L. Mencken,
A Schimpflexikon, 1928

MERCOURI, MELINA

As for Miss Mercouri, her blackly mascaraed eye-sockets gape like twin craters, unfortunately extinct.

JOHN SIMON
Private Screenings, 1967

MERCY

Kick him again; he's down.
AMERICAN PROVERB

Nothing emboldens sin so much as mercy.
WILLIAM SHAKESPEARE
Timon of Athens, 1607–8

MEREDITH, GEORGE

In George Meredith there is nothing but crackjaw sentences, empty and unpleasant in the mouth as sterile nuts. I do not know any book more tedious than *Tragic Comedians*, more pretentious, more blatant; it struts and screams, stupid in all its gaud and absurdity as a cockatoo.
GEORGE MOORE
Confessions of a Young Man, 1888

His style is chaos illuminated by flashes of lightning. As a writer he has mastered everything except language; as a novelist he can do everything except tell a story; as an artist he is everything, except articulate.
OSCAR WILDE
The Decay of Lying, 1889

METAPHYSICIAN

A metaphysician is a man who goes into a dark cellar at midnight without a light looking for a black cat that isn't there.

Attributed to
CHARLES BOWEN,
Baron of Colwood

METAPHYSICS

Metaphysics is almost always an attempt to prove the incredible by an appeal to the unintelligible.

H. L. MENCKEN
*Minority Report: H. L. Mencken's
Notebooks*, 1956

MIAMI BEACH

Miami Beach is where neon goes to die.
LENNY BRUCE
Quoted by Barbara Gordon in
Saturday Review, May 20, 1972

MICE

These mice are a brazen crew, entirely without fear. No room is inviolate, no conference so weighty as to be spared their squeaky presence. They have no morals. No decency. Their presence is an outrage to the dignity of Congress, an affront to basic human rights everywhere.
SENATOR WILLIAM PROXMIRE
Commenting on the presence of mice
in the Senate Office Building,
Washington, D.C., as reported by
United Press International,
September 15, 1978

MICHELANGELO'S "PIETÀ"

The figure of Christ is as much emaciated as if He had died of consumption: besides, there is something indelicate, not to say indecent in the attitude and design of a man's body, stark naked, lying upon the knees of a woman.
TOBIAS SMOLLETT
Travels in France and Italy, 1766

MIDDLE AGE

He was fifty. It's the age when clergymen first begin to be preoccupied with the underclothing of little schoolgirls in trains, the age when eminent archaeologists start taking a really passionate interest in the Scout movement.
ALDOUS HUXLEY
Brief Candles, 1930

MIDDLE AGES

We owe to the Middle Ages the two worst inventions of humanity—romantic love and gunpowder.
ANDRÉ MAUROIS
Quoted in *Reader's Digest*,
August 1961

MIDDLE CLASS

The Booboisie

Attributed to
H. L. MENCKEN

In the middle classes, where the segregation of the artificially limited family in its little brick box is horribly complete, bad manners, ugly dresses, awkwardness, cowardice, peevishness and all the petty vices of unsociability flourish like mushrooms in a cellar.

GEORGE BERNARD SHAW
Getting Married, 1908

MIDDLEMAN

It is well known what a middle man is: he is a man who bamboozles one party and plunders the other.

BENJAMIN DISRAELI
Speech, Maynooth, April 11, 1845

I remember a time when a cabbage could sell itself just by being a cabbage. Nowadays it's no good being a cabbage—unless you have an agent and pay him a commission. Nothing is free anymore to sell itself or give itself away. These days, . . . every cabbage has its pimp.

JEAN GIRAUDOUX
The Madwoman of Chaillot, 1945

MIDDLE OF THE ROAD

We know what happens to people who stay in the middle of the road. They get run over.

ANEURIN BEVAN
The Observer, London,
December 9, 1953

Damned Neuters, in their Middle way of Steering,
Are neither Fish, nor Flesh, nor good Red Herring.

JOHN DRYDEN
Absalom and Achitophel, 1680

The middle of the road is where the white line is—and that's the worst place to drive.

ROBERT FROST
Quoted in *Collier's,*
April 27, 1956

"MIDSUMMER NIGHT'S DREAM"

To the King's theatre, where we saw "Midsummer Night's Dream," which I had never seen before, nor shall ever again, for it is the most insipid, ridiculous play that ever I saw in my life.

SAMUEL PEPYS
Diary, entry for
September 29, 1662

MIDWEST

... those flat lands of compromise and mediocre self-expression, those endless half-pretty, repetitive small towns of the Middle and the West.

NORMAN MAILER
Superman Comes to the Supermarket,
1960

I doubt if there is anything in the world uglier than a Midwestern city.

FRANK LLOYD WRIGHT
Address in Evanston, Illinois,
August 8, 1954

MILITARISM

You cannot organize civilization around the core of militarism and at the same time expect reason to control human destinies.

FRANKLIN D. ROOSEVELT
Radio address, October 26, 1938

MILITARY

The existence of the soldier, next to capital punishment, is the most grievous vestige of barbarism which survives among men.

ALFRED DE VIGNY
Servitude et grandeur militaires, 1835

There is nothing on earth so stupid as a gallant officer.

Attributed to
ARTHUR WELLESLEY,
Duke of Wellington

The professional military mind is by necessity an inferior and unimaginative mind; no man of high intellectual quality would willingly imprison his gifts in such a calling.

H. G. WELLS
The Outline of History, 1920

We want to get rid of the militarist not simply because he hurts and kills, but because he is an intolerable thick-voiced blockhead who stands hectoring and blustering in our way to achievement.

H. G. WELLS
The Outline of History, 1920

MILITARY INTELLIGENCE

Military intelligence is a contradiction in terms.

Attributed to
GROUCHO MARX

MILITARY JUSTICE

Military justice is to justice what military music is to music.

Attributed to
GEORGES CLEMENCEAU

MILNE, A. A.

Tonstant Weader fwowed up.

DOROTHY PARKER
Review in *The New Yorker*,
October 20, 1928,
of Milne's *House at Pooh Corner*
(Parker signed her book reviews
"Constant Reader.")

MINNEAPOLIS

May your soul be forever tormented by fire and your bones dug up by dogs and dragged through the streets of Minneapolis.

GARRISON KEILLOR
Happy to Be Here, 1982

MIRACLE

A Miracle: An event described by those to whom it was told by men who did not see it.

ELBERT HUBBARD
A Thousand and One Epigrams, 1911

MISSIONARY

If I were a cassowary
  On the plains of Timbuctoo,
I would eat a missionary,
  Bible and hymn-book too.

Attributed to
SAMUEL WILBERFORCE

Mississippi River

But what words shall describe the Mississippi, great father of waters, who (praise to Heaven) has no children like him! An enormous ditch, sometimes two or three miles wide, running liquid mud, . . . its strong and frothy current choked and obstructed everywhere by huge logs and whole forest trees . . . now rolling past like monstrous bodies, their tangled roots showing like matted hair . . . or wounded snakes . . .

For two days we toiled up this foul stream.

Charles Dickens
American Notes, 1842

Moderation

Fear and dull disposition, lukewarmness and sloth, are not seldom wont to cloak themselves under the affected name of moderation.

John Milton
An Apology for Smectymnuus, 1642

Moderation is a fatal thing. Nothing succeeds like excess.

Oscar Wilde
A Woman of No Importance, 1894

Modern Art

So-called modern or contemporary art in our modern beloved country contains all the isms of depravity, decadence and destruction. Cubism aims to destroy by designed disorder. Futurism aims to destroy by a machine myth. Dadaism aims to destroy by ridicule. Expressionism aims to destroy by aping the primitive and insane. Klee, one of its three founders, went to the insane asylums for this inspiration. Abstractionism aims to destroy by the creation of brainstorms. Surrealism aims to destroy by the denial of reason. Salvador Dali, . . . Spanish surrealist, is now in the United States. He is reported to carry with him at all times a picture of Lenin. Abstractionism, or non-objectivity in so-called modern art, was spawned as a simon-pure, Russian Communist product. . . . Who has brought down this curse upon us; who has let into our homeland this horde of germ-carrying art vermin?

Representative George A.
Dondero
of Michigan
Speech to Congress, August 16, 1949

Anybody who sees and paints a sky green and pastures blue ought to be sterilized.

Adolf Hitler
Quoted in the *New York Post,*
January 3, 1944

Skill without imagination is craftsmanship and gives us many useful objects such as wickerwork picnic baskets. Imagination without skill gives us modern art.

TOM STOPPARD
Artist Descending a Staircase, 1972

I am of the opinion that so-called modern art is merely the vaporing of half-baked lazy people. There is no art at all in connection with the modernists.

HARRY S. TRUMAN
Quoted in *Trivializing America*,
by Norman Corwin, 1983

MODESTY

Modesty and diffidence make a man unfit for public affairs; they also make him unfit for brothels.

WALTER SAVAGE LANDOR
Imaginary Conversations, 1824–53

MOHAMMED

The kingdom of Mohammed is a kingdom of revenge, of wrath, and desolation.

MARTIN LUTHER
Table Talk, 1569

MONASTERY

Monastic incarceration is castration.
VICTOR HUGO
Les Misérables, 1862

MONEY

If you would know what the Lord God thinks of money, you have only to look at those to whom he gives it.

MAURICE BARING
Quoted by Dorothy Parker in
Writers at Work, First Series, 1958

You Can't Take It with You
MOSS HART AND GEORGE S.
KAUFMAN
Title of play, 1936

Money costs too much.
ROSS MacDONALD
The Goodbye Look, 1969
Money lays waste cities; it sets men to roaming from home; it seduces
and corrupts honest men and turns virtue to baseness; it teaches villainy
and impiety.

SOPHOCLES
Antigone, c. 440 B.C.

. . . filthy lucre.
1 TIMOTHY 3:8, c. A.D. 60
The love of money is the root of all evil.

1 TIMOTHY 6:10

MONOGAMY

Accursed from birth they be
Who seek to find monogamy,
Pursuing it from bed to bed—
I think they would be better dead.
DOROTHY PARKER
Sunset Gun, 1928

MONROE, MARILYN

Can't act . . . Voice like a tight squeak . . . Utterly unsure of herself . . .
unable even to take refuge in her own insignificance.
COLUMBIA PICTURES
Studio comment, c. 1948

She was a fruitcake.
TONY CURTIS
Of Marilyn Monroe to an interviewer
on BBC Television in the 1960s

As far as talent goes, Marilyn Monroe was so minimally gifted as to be
almost unemployable, and anyone who holds to the opinion that she
was a great natural comic identifies himself immediately as a dunce.
CLIVE JAMES
Commentary, October 1973
I don't think she could act her way out of a paper script. She has no
charm, delicacy or taste. She's just an arrogant little tail-twitcher who's
learned to throw sex in your face.
NUNNALLY JOHNSON
Quoted in *Popcorn in Paradise,*
edited by John Robert Colombo, 1979

Hollywood didn't kill Marilyn Monroe; it's the Marilyn Monroes who are killing Hollywood. Marilyn was mean. Terribly mean. The meanest woman I have ever met around this town. I have never met anybody as mean as Marilyn Monroe or as utterly fabulous on the screen.

Attributed to
BILLY WILDER

MORALITY

I never came across anyone in whom the moral sense was dominant who was not heartless, cruel, vindictive, log-stupid and entirely lacking in the smallest sense of humanity.

OSCAR WILDE
Letter to Leonard Smithers, 1897

MORALIZING

A man who moralizes is usually a hypocrite, and a woman who moralizes is invariably plain.

OSCAR WILDE
Lady Windermere's Fan, 1892

MOSES

Moses with his law is most terrible; there never was any equal to him in perplexing, affrighting, tyrannizing, threatening, preaching, and thundering.

MARTIN LUTHER
Table Talk, 1569

MOTHER

The Great American Mom—a juggernaut whose toll of crippled lives is greater than all our wounded in two world wars.

ANONYMOUS
Dust jacket copy for
Their Mothers' Sons,
by Dr. Edward A. Streiker, 1946

If a writer has to rob his mother he will not hesitate; the "Ode on a Grecian Urn" is worth any number of old ladies.

WILLIAM FAULKNER
Quoted by Malcolm Cowley in
And I Worked at the Writer's Trade,
1978

The mealy look of men today is the result of momism and so is the pinched and baffled fury in the eyes of womankind.

PHILIP WYLIE
Generation of Vipers, 1942

MOTHER-IN-LAW

I know a mother-in-law who sleeps in her spectacles, the better to see her son-in-law suffer in her dreams.

Attributed to
ERNEST COQUELIN

However much you dislike your mother-in-law you must not set fire to her.

ERNEST WILD, Recorder of London
To a culprit before him, c. 1925

Distrust all mothers-in-law. They are completely unscrupulous in what they say in court. The wife's mother is always more prejudiced against the husband than even the most ill-treated wife. If I had my way, I am afraid I would abolish mothers-in-law entirely.

SIR GEOFFREY WRANGHAM
Boston Herald, October 10, 1960

MOUNTAIN CLIMBING

Above all, young traveller, take my advice, and never, *never*, be such a fool as to go up a mountain, a tower, or a steeple. I have tried it. Men still ascend eminences, even to this day, and descending, say they have been delighted. But it is a lie. They have been miserable the whole day. Keep you down: and have breakfast while the asinine hunters after the picturesque go braying up the hill.

WILLIAM MAKEPIECE THACKERAY
Punch, August, 1844

MOUNTAINS

No, I can't do with mountains at close quarters—they are always in the way, and they are so stupid, never moving and never doing anything but obtrude themselves.

D. H. LAWRENCE
Letter to Lady Cynthia Asquith,
October 23, 1913

Ms.

A syllable which sounds like a bumble bee breaking wind.

HORTENSE CALISHER
Quoted in *The New York Times,*
September 22, 1974

I'm perplexed when people adopt the modish abbreviation "Ms.,"
which doesn't abbreviate anything except common sense.

DICK CAVETT
Eye on Cavett, 1983

MULTITUDE

If there be any among those common objects of hatred I do condemn
and laugh at, it is that great enemy of reason, virtue, and religion, the
multitude; that numerous piece of monstrosity, which, taken asunder,
seem men, and the reasonable creatures of God, but, confused together,
make but one great beast, and a monstrosity more prodigious than
Hydra.

THOMAS BROWNE
Religio Medici, 1642

The multitude is always in the wrong.

WENTWORTH DILLON,
Earl of Roscommon
Essay on Translated Verse, 1684

The blunt monster with uncounted heads,
The still-discordant wavering multitude.

WILLIAM SHAKESPEARE
Henry IV, Part V, c. 1598

MURALS IN RESTAURANTS

The murals in restaurants are on a par with the food in museums.

PETER DE VRIES
Madder Music, 1977

MUSEUM

The Museum is not meant either for the wanderer to see by accident or
for the pilgrim to see with awe. It is meant for the mere slave of a routine of self-education to stuff himself with every sort of incongruous intellectual food in one indigestible meal.

GILBERT KEITH CHESTERTON
All Is Grist, 1931

I am weary of museums, those graveyards of the arts.
> ALPHONSE DE LAMARTINE
> *Voyage en Orient,* 1835

An artist may visit a museum, but only a pedant can live there.
> GEORGE SANTAYANA
> *Reason in Art,* 1935

MUSIC

If any person or persons . . . commonly called Fiddlers or Minstrels shall be taken playing, fiddling, or making music, in any Inn, Alehouse, or Tavern, . . . or shall be taken intreating any person . . . to hear them play, . . . that every such person shall be adjudged rogues, vagabonds, and sturdy beggars . . . and be punished as such.
> ACT OF PARLIAMENT,
> England, 1642

A *great* fondness for music is a mark of great weakness, great vacuity of mind: not of hardness of heart; not of vice; not of downright folly; but of a want of capacity, or inclination, for sober thought.
> WILLIAM COBBETT
> *Advice to Young Men and*
> *(Incidentally)*
> *to Young Women, in the Middle and*
> *Higher Ranks of Life,* 1820

The ear disapproves but tolerates certain musical pieces; transfer them into the domain of our nose, and we will be forced to flee.
> Attributed to
> JEAN COCTEAU

Music is almost as dangerous as gunpowder; and it maybe requires looking after no less than the press, or the mint. 'Tis possible a public regulation might not be amiss.
> JEREMY COLLIER
> *A Short View of the Immorality and*
> *Profaneness of the English State,* 1698

Cocktail music he accepts as audible wallpaper.
> ALISTAIR COOKE
> "The Innocent American," *Holiday,*
> July 1962

Music, to a nice ear, is a hazardous amusement, as long attention to it is very fatiguing.
> WILLIAM CULLEN
> *First Lines of the Practice of Physic,*
> 1774

I hate music—especially when it's played.
Attributed to
JIMMY DURANTE

Music sweeps by me like a messenger carrying a message that is not for me.
GEORGE ELIOT
The Spanish Gypsy, 1868

Music was invented to deceive and delude mankind.
EPHORUS
Preface to the *History,*
4th century B.C.

The worst kind of music is that which is insipid to the ear. Even that which has an aggressively vulgar flavour is preferable to it. And when the former cloaks itself either in cheap morality or in cheap sentiment, it reaches the pinnacle of bad taste.
EDWIN EVANS
The Margin of Music, 1924

. . . Bestial cries are heard: neighing horses, the squeal of a brass pig, crying jackasses, amorous quacks of a monstrous toad . . . This excruciating medley of brutal sounds is subordinated to a barely perceptible rhythm. Listening to this screaming music for a minute or two, one conjures up an orchestra of madmen, sexual maniacs, led by a man-stallion beating time with an enormous phallos.
MAXIM GORKY
In America, 1906

The public doesn't want new music; the main thing it demands of a composer is that he be dead.
Attributed to
ARTHUR HONEGGER

In the judgment of Reason music has less worth than any other of the beautiful arts.
IMMANUEL KANT
Critique of Judgment, 1790

Music is a treason to the country, a treason to our youth, and we should cut out this music and replace it with something instructive.
AYATOLLAH RUHOLLAH KHOMEINI
Quoted in Norman Lebrect's
Discord, 1983

A carpenter's hammer, in a warm summer noon, will fret me into more than midsummer madness. But those unconnected, unset wounds are nothing to the measured malice of music.

CHARLES LAMB
"A Chapter of Ears,"
Essays of Elia, 1820–25

Modern music is as dangerous as cocaine.

PIETRO MASCAGNI
Interview in Berlin, December 1927

What strange impulse is it which induces otherwise trustful people to say they like music when they do not, and thus expose themselves to hours of boredom?

AGNES REPPLIER
Under Dispute, 1924

Music is essentially useless, as life is.

GEORGE SANTAYANA
The Life of Reason, 1905–6

Hell is full of musical amateurs: music is the brandy of the damned.

GEORGE BERNARD SHAW
Man and Superman, 1903

I shall hate sweet music my whole life long.

ALGERNON CHARLES SWINBURNE
The Triumph of Time, 1866

Music has two ills, the one mortal, the other wasting; the mortal is ever allied with the instant which follows that of the music's utterance, the wasting lies in its repetition, making it seem contemptible and mean.

LEONARDO DA VINCI
Notebooks, 1508–18

Musical people are so absurdly unreasonable. They always want one to be perfectly dumb at the very moment when one is longing to be absolutely deaf.

OSCAR WILDE
An Ideal Husband, 1895

If one hears bad music, it is one's duty to drown it by one's conversation.

OSCAR WILDE
The Picture of Dorian Gray, 1891

Most people wouldn't know music if it came up and bit them on the ass.

> Attributed to
> FRANK ZAPPA

MUSICIANS

A Musitian is his own Syren that turns himself into a beast with musick of his own making. His perpetual study to raise passion has utterly debased his reason; and musick is wont to set false values upon things, the constant use of it has render'd him a stranger to all true ones.

> SAMUEL BUTLER
> *Characters: A Musitian*, 1759

Music might tame and civilize wild beasts, but 'tis evident it never yet could tame and civilize musicians.

> JOHN GAY
> *Polly*, 1729

Show me an orchestra that likes its conductor and I'll show you a lousy conductor.

> GODDARD LIEBERSON
> Quoted by Herbert Kupferberg,
> *Those Fabulous Philadelphians*, 1969

Let a short Act of Parliament be passed, placing all street musicians outside the protection of the law, so that any citizen may assail them with stones, sticks, knives, pistols, or bombs without incurring any penalties—except, of course, in the case of the instrument itself being injured; for Heaven forbid that I should advocate any disregard of the sacredness of property . . .

> GEORGE BERNARD SHAW
> *Morning Leader*, November 27, 1893

Orchestras only need to be sworn at, and a German is consequently at an advantage with them, as English profanity, except in America, has not gone beyond a limited technology of perdition.

> GEORGE BERNARD SHAW
> Quoted by Harold C. Schonberg in
> *The Great Conductors*, 1967

After I die, I shall return to earth as the doorkeeper of a bordello and I won't let a one of you in.

> Attributed to
> ARTURO TOSCANINI
> To his orchestra during a difficult rehearsal

God tells me how the music should sound, but *you* stand in the way!
ARTURO TOSCANINI
To a trumpet player
Quoted in *The New York Times*,
April 11, 1954

Assassins!
Attributed to
ARTURO TOSCANINI
To his orchestra after
an unsatisfactory performance

MUSSOLINI, BENITO

Sawdust Caesar
GEORGE SELDES
Title of biography of
Benito Mussolini, 1932

MYTH

There is something feeble and a little contemptible about a man who cannot face the perils of life without the help of comfortable myths.
BERTRAND RUSSELL
*Human Society in Ethics
and Politics*, 1954

NAPOLEON

Bonaparte was a lion in the field only. In civil life, a cold-blooded, calculating, unprincipled usurper, without a virtue; no statesman, knowing nothing of commerce, political economy, or civil government, and supplying ignorance by bold presumption.

THOMAS JEFFERSON
Letter to John Adams, July 1814

NATION

A nation is a society united by a delusion about its ancestry and by a common hatred of its neighbors.

Attributed to
DEAN WILLIAM RALPH INGE

NATIONALISM

Nationalism is a silly cock crowing on its own dunghill.

RICHARD ALDINGTON
The Colonel's Daughter, 1931

Nationalism is our form of incest, is our idolatry, is our insanity. "Patriotism" is its cult.

ERICH FROMM
The Sane Society, 1955

Every nation thinks its own madness normal and requisite; more passion and more fancy it calls folly, less it calls imbecility.

GEORGE SANTAYANA
Dialogues in Limbo, 1925

NATURE

The true artist . . . is seldom an accurate observer of nature; he leaves that gross and often revolting exploration to geologists, engineers and anatomists. The last thing he wants to see is a beautiful woman in the bright, pitiless sunlight.

H. L. MENCKEN
Prejudices, Fourth Series, 1924

Nature is one with rapine, a harm no preacher can heal;
The Mayfly is torn by the swallow, the sparrow speared by the shrike,
And the whole little wood where I sit is a world of plunder and prey.

ALFRED, LORD TENNYSON
Maud: A Monodrama, 1856

A vacuum is a hell of a lot better than some of the stuff that nature replaces it with.

TENNESSEE WILLIAMS
Cat on a Hot Tin Roof, 1955

NECESSITY

Necessity is the plea for every infringement of human freedom. It is the argument of tyrants; it is the creed of slaves.

WILLIAM PITT
Speech, 1783

NECKTIES

Neckties strangle clear thinking.

LIN YUTANG
News summary, February 22, 1954

NEIGHBOR

Your next-door neighbour . . . is not a man; he is an environment. He is the barking of a dog; he is the noise of a pianola; he is a dispute about a party wall; he is drains that are worse than yours, or roses that are better than yours.

GILBERT KEITH CHESTERTON
The Uses of Diversity, 1920

NEW ENGLAND

I wonder if anybody ever reached the age of thirty-five in New England without wanting to kill himself.

BARRETT WENDELL
Barrett Wendell and His Letters, 1924

NEW JERSEY

The cities are indifferent and dingy; the people are seedy and dull, a kind of sloppiness and mediocrity seems to have fallen on the fields themselves, as if Nature herself had turned slattern and could no longer keep herself dressed.

EDMUND WILSON
These United States, 1924

NEWS

No news, good news.

LUDOVIC HALÉVY
La Belle Hélène, 1864

NEWSPAPERS

I am unable to understand how a man of honor could take a newspaper in his hands without a shudder of disgust.

Attributed to
CHARLES BAUDELAIRE

That ephemeral sheet of paper, the newspaper, is the natural enemy of the book, as the whore is of the decent woman.

EDMOND AND JULES DE GONCOURT
Journal, July 1858

The man who never looks into a newspaper is better informed than he who reads them, inasmuch as he who knows nothing is nearer to truth than he whose mind is filled with falsehoods and errors.

THOMAS JEFFERSON
Letter to John Norvell, 1807

Every newspaper editor pays tribute to the Devil.

JEAN DE LA FONTAINE
Letter to Simon de Troyes, 1686

All successful newspapers are ceaselessly querulous and bellicose. They never defend anyone or anything if they can help it; if the job is forced upon them, they tackle it by denouncing someone or something else.

H. L. MENCKEN
Prejudices, First Series, 1919

To the best of my knowledge and belief, the average American newspaper, even of the so-called better sort, is not only quite as bad as Upton Sinclair says it is, but ten times worse—ten times as ignorant, ten times as unfair and tyrannical, ten times as complaisant and pusillanimous, and ten times as devious, hypocritical, disingenuous, deceitful, pharisaical, pecksniffian, fraudulent, slippery, unscrupulous, perfidious, lewd and dishonest.

> H. L. MENCKEN
> Review of Upton Sinclair's
> *The Brass Check,* 1919

The newspapers! Sir, they are the most villainous—licentious—abominable—infernal—not that I ever read them—no—I make it a rule never to look into a newspaper.

> RICHARD BRINSLEY SHERIDAN
> *The Critic,* 1779

I have been reading the morning paper. I do it every morning—well knowing that I shall find in it the usual depravities and baseness and hypocrisies and cruelties that make up civilization, and cause me to put in the rest of the day pleading for the damnation of the human race.

> MARK TWAIN
> Letter to novelist William Dean
> Howells, 1899

NEW YEAR'S EVE

New Year's Eve rings a false bell in my brain because it seems contrived. . . . And that's the trouble with the New Year's Eve kind of fun. It's phony. There's nothing spontaneous about it. The noisemakers were bought at the five-and-ten. The confetti was cut by machine and sold in boxes. The fun is compulsory.

> ANDREW A. ROONEY
> *And More by Andy Rooney,* 1982

NEW YORK

The only real advantage of New York is that all its inhabitants ascend to heaven right after their deaths, having served their full term in hell right on Manhattan Island.

> *Barnard Bulletin* (Barnard College
> newspaper), September 22, 1967

This muck heaves and palpitates. It is multidirectional and has a mayor.

> DONALD BARTHELME
> Quoted in *Loose Talk,* compiled by
> Linda Botts, 1981

New York is appalling, fantastically charmless and elaborately dire.

HENRY JAMES
Letter to W. E. Norris,
December 15, 1904

New York, like London, seems to be cloacina of all the depravities of human nature.

THOMAS JEFFERSON, 1823

I don't like the life here. There is no greenery. It would make a stone sick.

NIKITA S. KHRUSHCHEV
On a visit to New York, *Time,*
October 10, 1960

NEW YORK YANKEES

Hating the Yankees is as American as pizza pie, unwed mothers and cheating on your income tax.

MIKE ROYKO
Chicago Sun-Times, 1981

NIAGARA FALLS

When I first saw the falls I was disappointed in the outline. Every American bride is taken there, and the sight must be one of the earliest, if not the keenest, disappointments in American married life.

OSCAR WILDE
Press interview in New York, 1882

NICE GUYS

Nice guys finish last.

LEO DUROCHER
In an interview with Frank Graham,
1945

NICKNAMES

A nickname is the heaviest stone that the devil can throw at a man . . . of all eloquence the most concise of all arguments . . . the most unanswerable.

WILLIAM HAZLITT
Sketches and Essays, 1839

NIETZSCHE, FRIEDRICH WILHELM

An agile but unintelligent and abnormal German, possessed of the mania of grandeur.

LEO TOLSTOY
What Is Religion?, 1902

NIGHTINGALE

Nightingales sing badly.
Attributed to JEAN COCTEAU

NINETEENTH CENTURY

We are all fakes and charlatans. Pretense, affectation, humbug everywhere—the crinoline has falsified the buttocks. Our century is a century of whores, and so far what is least prostituted is the prostitute.

GUSTAVE FLAUBERT
Letter to Louise Colet, 1854

NIXON, RICHARD M.

For years I've regarded [Nixon's] very existence as a monument to all the rancid genes and broken chromosomes that corrupt the possibilities of the American Dream; he was a foul caricature of himself, a man with no soul, no inner convictions, with the integrity of a hyena, and the style of a poison food.

HUNTER S. THOMPSON
The Great Shark Hunt, 1979

That Richard Nixon, boys, is a no-good lying son-of-a-bitch.

HARRY S. TRUMAN
At a Presidential press conference
Quoted in *Newsweek*, May 12, 1975

NONSMOKER

Nobody can be so revoltingly smug as the man who has just given up smoking.

SYDNEY J. HARRIS
Strictly Personal, 1953

NORMALCY

Society values its normal man. It educates children to lose themselves and to become absurd and thus be normal. Normal men have killed perhaps 100,000,000 of their fellow normal men in the last fifty years.

R. D. LAING
The Politics of Experience, 1967

NOSE

[The nose is] generally the organ in which stupidity is most readily displayed.

> MARCEL PROUST
> *Remembrance of Things Past,*
> 1913–27

NOSTALGIA

That's what hell must be like, small chat to the babbling of Lethe about the good old days when we wished we were dead.

> SAMUEL BECKETT
> *Embers,* 1959

Those were the good old days—I was so unhappy then.

> Attributed to
> CLAUDE-CARLOMAN DE RULHIÈRE

NOVEL

The love of novels is the preference of sentiment to the senses.

> RALPH WALDO EMERSON
> Journal, 1831

Novels are receipts to make a whore.

> MATTHEW GREEN
> *The Spleen,* 1737

The novel is a prose narrative of some length that has something wrong with it.

> Attributed to
> RANDALL JARRELL

NOVEMBER

The gloomy month of November, when the people of England hang and drown themselves.

> JOSEPH ADDISON
> *The Spectator,* May 23, 1712

November, n. The eleventh twelfth of a weariness.

> AMBROSE BIERCE
> *The Devil's Dictionary,* 1906, 1911

Now

Ours is the age of substitutes: instead of language, we have jargon; instead of principles, slogans; and, instead of genuine ideas, bright ideas.

ERIC BENTLEY
The Dramatic Event, 1954

These are the times that try men's souls.

THOMAS PAINE
The American Crisis, 1776

Nudity

Bare breasts, get dressed! Bottomless go-goers, begone! Four-letter words, shut up! The same goes for all you sensuous women and glib obscenity lawyers and leering TV hosts and naked cellists . . . I'm sick of it.

SHANA ALEXANDER
Newsweek, February 5, 1973

A mass of naked figures does not move us to empathy, but to disillusion and dismay.

SIR KENNETH CLARK
The Nude, 1972

Nun

A nun, at best, is only half a woman, just as a priest is only half a man.

H. L. MENCKEN
*Minority Report: H. L. Mencken's
Notebooks,* 1956

OATH

Nothing like a solemn oath. People always think you mean it.

NORMAN DOUGLAS
An Almanac, 1945

OBEDIENCE

. . . obedience,
Bane of all genius, virtue, freedom, truth
Makes slaves of men, and of the human frame
A mechanized automaton.

PERCY BYSSHE SHELLEY
Queen Mab, 1813

OBOE

The oboe is an ill wind that nobody blows good.

ANONYMOUS

OCCIDENT

Occident, n. The part of the world lying west (or east) of the Orient. It is largely inhabited by Christians, a powerful sub-tribe of the Hypocrites, whose principal industries are murder and cheating, which they are pleased to call "war" and "commerce." These, also, are the principal industries of the Orient.

AMBROSE BIERCE
The Devil's Dictionary, 1906, 1911

O'HARA, MAUREEN

She looked as though butter wouldn't melt in her mouth—or anywhere else.

Attributed to
ELSA LANCHESTER

OLD AGE

Believe me, all evil comes from the old. They grow fat on ideas and young men die of them.

JEAN ANOUILH
Catch as Catch Can, 1960

It is the ugliness of old age I hate. Being old is not bad if you keep away from mirrors; but broken-down feet, bent knees, peering eyes, rheumatic knuckles, withered skin, these are *ugly*, hard to tolerate with patience.

EMILY CARR
Revelations: Diaries of Women,
Edited by Mary Jane Moffat and
Charlotte Painter, 1974

Nature abhors the old.
RALPH WALDO EMERSON
Essays, 1841

O harsh old age! How hateful is your reign!
EURIPIDES
The Suppliants, c. 424 B.C.

My diseases are an asthma and a dropsy, and what is less curable, seventy-five.

SAMUEL JOHNSON
Letter to W. S. Hamilton,
October 20, 1784

Life protracted is protracted woe.
SAMUEL JOHNSON
The Vanity of Human Wishes, 1749

Have you not a moist eye, a dry hand, a yellow cheek, a white beard, a decreasing leg, an increasing belly? Is not your voice broken, your wind short, your chin double, your wit single, and every part about you blasted with antiquity?

> WILLIAM SHAKESPEARE
> *Henry IV*, Part II, c. 1598

OLD MASTERS

I am glad the old masters are all dead, and I only wish they had died sooner.

> MARK TWAIN
> Letter to the *Alta Californian*,
> May 28, 1867

OPERA

I do not mind what language an opera is sung in so long as it is a language I don't understand.

> SIR EDWARD APPLETON
> *The Observer*, London,
> "Sayings of the Week,"
> August 28, 1955

Opera, n. A play representing life in another world, whose inhabitants have no speech but song, no motions but gestures and no postures but attitudes. All acting is simulation, and the word simulation is from simia, an ape; but in opera the actor takes for his model Simia audibilis (or Pithecanthropus stentor)—the ape that howls.

> AMBROSE BIERCE
> *The Devil's Dictionary*, 1906, 1911

People are wrong when they say that the opera isn't what it used to be. It *is* what it used to be. That's what's wrong with it.

> NOËL COWARD
> *Design for Living*, 1933

The opera . . . is to music what a bawdy house is to a cathedral.

> H. L. MENCKEN
> Letter to Isaac Goldberg,
> May 6, 1925

OPINION

Opinion has caused more trouble on this little earth than plagues or earthquakes.

> VOLTAIRE
> Letter to an unknown correspondent,
> January 5, 1759

OPTIMISM

Cheer up, the worst is yet to come.
>PHILANDER CHASE JOHNSON
>"Shooting Stars," *Poems,* 1942

The basis of optimism is sheer terror.
>Attributed to
>OSCAR WILDE

ORATORIO

Nothing can be more disgusting than an oratorio. How absurd to see five hundred people fiddling like madmen about the Israelites in the Red Sea!
>SYDNEY SMITH
>Letter to Lady Holland, 1823

ORATORY

He can best be described as one of those orators who, before they get up, do not know what they are going to say; when they are speaking, do not know what they are saying; and when they have sat down, do not know what they have said.
>WINSTON S. CHURCHILL
>Of Charles Beresford in a speech,
>December 20, 1911

Oratory is the huffing and blustering spoiled child of a semi-barbarous age.
>CHARLES CALEB COLTON
>*Lacon,* 1820

What orators lack in depth they make up to you in length.
>CHARLES DE SECONDAT
>DE MONTESQUIEU
>*Letters,* 1767

Oratory is just like prostitution: you must have little tricks.
>VITTORIO EMANUELE ORLANDO
>*Time,* December 8, 1952

ORCHIDS

Nasty things! Their flesh is too much like the flesh of men. Their perfume has the rotten sweetness of corruption.
>WILLIAM FAULKNER,
>LEIGH BRACKETT AND
>JULES FURTHMAN
>Screenplay, *The Big Sleep,* 1946

ORIGINALITY

Originality is too often only undetected and frequently unconscious plagiarism.

Attributed to
DEAN WILLIAM INGE

ORPHAN

Orphan, n. A living person whom death has deprived of the power of filial ingratitude—a privation appealing with a particular eloquence to all that is sympathetic in human nature. When young the orphan is commonly sent to an asylum, where by careful cultivation of its rudimentary sense of locality it is taught to know its place. It is then instructed in the arts of dependence and servitude and eventually turned loose to prey upon the world as a bootblack or scullery maid.

AMBROSE BIERCE
The Devil's Dictionary, 1906, 1911

OXFORD UNIVERSITY

A sanctuary in which exploded systems and obsolete prejudices find shelter and protection after they have been hunted out of every corner of the world.

ADAM SMITH
The Wealth of Nations, 1794

OYSTERS

I will not eat oysters. They're alive when you eat them. I want my food dead—not sick, not wounded—dead.

WOODY ALLEN
Don't Drink the Water, 1966

Oysters, n. A slimy, gobby shellfish which civilization gives men the hardihood to eat without removing its entrails! The shells are sometimes given to the poor.

AMBROSE BIERCE
The Devil's Dictionary, 1906, 1911

PACIFISM

The peace of the man who has forsworn the use of the bullet seems to me not quite peace, but a canting impotence.

RALPH WALDO EMERSON
Journal, 1839

Pacifism is simply undisguised cowardice.

ADOLF HITLER
Speech at Nürnberg,
August 21, 1926

The parlor pacifist, the white-handed or sissy type of pacifist, represents decadence, represents the rotting out of the virile virtues among people who typify the unlovely, senile side of civilization. The rough-neck pacifist, on the contrary, is a mere belated savage who has not been educated to the virtues of national patriotism.

THEODORE ROOSEVELT
Speech in Minneapolis,
September 28, 1917

PAINE, THOMAS

For such a mongrel between pig and puppy, begotten by a wild boar on a bitch wolf, never before in any age of the world was suffered by the poltroonery of mankind, to run through such a career of mischief. Call it then the Age of Paine.

JOHN ADAMS
Letter, October 29, 1805,
objecting to calling the period
the Age of Reason.

That dirty little atheist.

Attributed to
THEODORE ROOSEVELT

PAINTING

Painting, v. The art of protecting flat surfaces from the weather and exposing them to the critic.

AMBROSE BIERCE
The Devil's Dictionary, 1906, 1911

. . . I know nothing of painting—& that I detest it . . . I spit upon & abhor all the saints and subjects of one half the impostures I see in the churches and palaces . . . Depend upon it, of all the arts it is the most artificial and unnatural—& that by which the nonsense of mankind is the most imposed upon.

LORD BYRON
Letter to John Murray,
April 14, 1817

PARADES

Parades should be classed as a nuisance and participants should be subject to a term in prison. They stop more work, inconvenience more people, stop more traffic, cause more accidents, entail more expense, and commit and cause I don't remember the other hundred misdemeanors.

WILL ROGERS
The Illiterate Digest, 1924

PARENTS

Lizzie Borden took an axe
And gave her mother forty whacks.
Then when she saw what she had done
She gave her father forty-one.

ANONYMOUS

There are orphanages for children who have lost their parents—oh! why, why, why, are there no harbors of refuge for grown men who have not yet lost them?

SAMUEL BUTLER
The Way of All Flesh, 1903

There are times when parenthood seems nothing but feeding the mouth that bites you.

PETER DE VRIES
Tunnel of Love, 1954

PARIS

Paris is what it has always been: a pedant-ridden failure in everything that it pretends to lead.

GEORGE BERNARD SHAW
London Music, 1888–90

PARSLEY

. . . any dish that has either a taste or an appearance that can be improved by parsley is ipso facto a dish unfit for human consumption.

OGDEN NASH
I'm a Stranger Here Myself, 1938

PARTY

You call this a party? The beer is warm, the women are cold and I'm hot under the collar. In fact, a more poisonous little barbecue I've never attended.

S. J. PERELMAN AND
WILL B. JOHNSTONE
Monkey Business, screenplay, 1931

PASSION

Eternal passion!
Eternal pain!

MATTHEW ARNOLD
Philomela, 1853

You must make a serious effort to change, my dear Clara. . . . Passions are not a natural adjunct to human nature, they are always exceptional or aberrant . . . Look on yourself as ill, dear Clara, seriously ill . . .

JOHANNES BRAHMS
Letter to Clara Schumann,
October 11, 1857

PAST

Look Back in Anger
JOHN OSBORNE
Title of play, 1956

And all our yesterdays have lighted fools
The way to dusty death.

WILLIAM SHAKESPEARE
Macbeth, c. 1605

You Can't Go Home Again
THOMAS WOLFE
Title of novel, 1941

PATERNITY

There is no good father, that's the rule. Don't lay the blame on men but on the bond of paternity, which is rotten. To beget children, nothing better; to *have* them, what iniquity!

JEAN-PAUL SARTRE
The Words, 1964

PATIENCE

Patience, n. A minor form of despair, disguised as a virtue.

AMBROSE BIERCE
The Devil's Dictionary, 1906, 1911

PATRIOTISM

... the religion of hell.
JAMES BRANCH CABELL
Jurgen, 1919

Treason is in the air around us everywhere. It goes by the name of patriotism.

THOMAS CORWIN
Letter from Washington, D.C.,
January 16, 1861

If I had to choose between betraying my country and betraying my friend, I hope I should have the guts to betray my country.

E. M. FORSTER
Two Cheers for Democracy, 1951

Patriotism is the last refuge of a scoundrel.

> SAMUEL JOHNSON
> April 7, 1775, quoted in Boswell's
> *Life of Samuel Johnson,* 1791

Love makes fools, marriage cuckolds and patriotism malevolent imbeciles.

> PAUL LÉAUTAUD
> *Journal,* 1954

Patriotism is often an arbitrary veneration of real estate above principles.

> GEORGE JEAN NATHAN
> *Testament of a Critic,* 1931

Patriotism is a pernicious, psychopathic form of idiocy.

> Attributed to
> GEORGE BERNARD SHAW

Talking of patriotism, what humbug it is; it is a word which always commemorates a robbery. There isn't a foot of land in the world which doesn't represent the ousting and re-ousting of a long line of successive owners.

> MARK TWAIN
> *Mark Twain's Notebooks,* 1935

Patriotism is the virtue of the vicious.

> Attributed to
> OSCAR WILDE

PATRON

Commonly, a wretch who supports with insolence and is paid with flattery.

> SAMUEL JOHNSON
> *Dictionary of the English Language,*
> 1775

PAX ROMANA

Pax Romana. Where they made a desolation they called it a peace. What absolute nonsense! It was a nasty, vulgar sort of civilization, only dignified by being hidden under a lot of declensions.

> ANTHONY BURGESS
> *Inside Mr. Enderby,* 1963

PEACE

Peace, n. In international affairs, a period of cheating between two periods of fighting.

AMBROSE BIERCE
The Devil's Dictionary, 1906, 1911

Mankind has grown strong in eternal struggles and it will only perish through eternal peace.

ADOLF HITLER
Mein Kampf, 1924

PEALE, NORMAN VINCENT

I find Paul appealing but Peale appalling.
Attributed to
ADLAI E. STEVENSON

PENOLOGY

Penology . . . has become torture and foolishness, a waste of money and a cause of crime . . . a blotting out of sight and heightening of social anxiety.

Attributed to
PAUL GOODMAN

PEOPLE

He who speaks of the people, speaks of a madman; for the people is a monster full of confusion and mistakes; and the opinions of the people are as far removed from the truth as, according to Ptolemy, the Indies are from Spain.

FRANCESCO GUICCIARDINI
Storia d'Italia, 1564

The people are a many-headed beast.
ALEXANDER POPE
*The First Epistle of the First
Book of Horace*, 1735

I love mankind—it's people I can't stand.
CHARLES M. SCHULZ
Go Fly a Kite, Charlie Brown, 1963

Other people are quite dreadful. The only possible society is one's self.
OSCAR WILDE
An Ideal Husband, 1895

PERELMAN, S. J.

Under a forehead roughly comparable to that of Javanese and Piltdown man are visible a pair of tiny pig eyes, lit up alternately by greed and concupiscence.

S. J. PERELMAN
On himself in *Quest*,
November 1978

PERFECTION

Perfection has one grave defect: it is apt to be dull.

W. SOMERSET MAUGHAM
The Summing Up, 1938

PERSEVERANCE

Of all the thirty-six alternatives, running away is best.

CHINESE PROVERB

PHILANTHROPY

Proffered service stinketh.

GEOFFREY CHAUCER
The Canterbury Tales, c. 1386

I owe much; I have nothing; I give the rest to the poor.

FRANÇOIS RABELAIS
Last Will, 1553

Philanthropy [has become] simply the refuge of people who wish to annoy their fellow-creatures.

OSCAR WILDE
An Ideal Husband, 1895

PHILOSOPHY

Philosophy, n. A route of many roads leading from nowhere to nothing.

AMBROSE BIERCE
The Devil's Dictionary, 1906, 1911

All philosophies, if you ride them home, are nonsense; but some are greater nonsense than others.

SAMUEL BUTLER
Note-Books, 1912

There is no statement so absurd that no philosopher will make it.

CICERO
De Divinatione, 45–44 B.C.

The various opinions of philosophers have scattered through the world as many plagues of the mind as Pandora's box did those of the body; only with this difference, that they have not left hope at the bottom.

JONATHAN SWIFT
A Critical Essay upon the
Faculties of the Mind, 1707

PHONOGRAPH

Phonograph, n. An irritating toy that restores life to dead noises.

AMBROSE BIERCE
The Devil's Dictionary, 1906, 1911

Dear Mr. Edison,
For myself, I can only say that I am astonished and somewhat terrified at the result of this evening's experiment. Astonished at the wonderful form you have developed and terrified at the thought that so much hideous and bad music will be put on records forever.

SIR ARTHUR SULLIVAN
On a "phonogram" to
Thomas Alva Edison, 1888

PHOTOGRAPHY

For half a century photography has been the "art form" of the untalented.

GORE VIDAL
"On Prettiness," *New Statesman,*
March 17, 1978

PIANO

Piano, n. A parlor utensil for subduing the impenitent visitor. It is operated by depressing the keys of the machine and the spirits of the audience.

AMBROSE BIERCE
The Devil's Dictionary, 1906, 1911

PIANO, UPRIGHT

A musical growth found adhering to the walls of most semi-detached houses in the provinces.

SIR THOMAS BEECHAM
Beecham Stories, edited by
Harold Atkins and Archie Newman,
1978

PIE

Pie, n. An advance agent of the reaper whose name is Indigestion.
AMBROSE BIERCE
The Devil's Dictionary, 1906, 1911

PIERCE, FRANKLIN

. . . a man who cannot be befriended; whose miserable administration admits but of one excuse, imbecility. Pierce was either the worst, or he was the weakest of all our Presidents.
RALPH WALDO EMERSON
Quoted by Mark Van Doren in
Nathaniel Hawthorne, 1949

PIGEONS

. . . flying rodents.
ANONYMOUS

PILL, THE

When you take your pill it's like a mine disaster. I think of all the people lost inside you.
RICHARD BRAUTIGAN
*The Pill versus the Springhill
Mine Disaster*, 1968

PITTSBURGH, PENNSYLVANIA

Abandon it.
FRANK LLOYD WRIGHT
The New York Times,
November 27, 1955

PITY

The response man has the greatest difficulty in tolerating is pity, especially when he warrants it. Hatred is a tonic, it makes one live, it inspires vengeance, but pity kills, it makes our weakness weaker.
HONORÉ DE BALZAC
"La Peau de chagrin," 1831

Pity costs nothin' and ain't worth nothin'.
JOSH BILLINGS
Complete Comical Writings, 1876–77

Pity! the scavenger of misery.

> GEORGE BERNARD SHAW
> *Major Barbara*, 1905

PLATO

Fashion and authority apart, and bringing Plato to the test of reason, take from him his sophisms, futilities and incomprehensibilities and what remains? His foggy mind is forever presenting the semblances of objects which, half seen through a mist, can be defined neither in form nor dimensions.

> THOMAS JEFFERSON
> Letter to John Adams,
> July 5, 1814

Plato is a bore.

> FRIEDRICH WILHELM NIETZSCHE
> *The Twilight of the Idols*, 1889

PLEASURE

Pleasure, n. The least hateful form of dejection.

> AMBROSE BIERCE
> *The Devil's Dictionary*, 1906, 1911

Love of pleasure is the disease which makes men most despicable.

> LONGINUS
> *On the Sublime*, c. 250

Who loves pleasure shall be a poor man.

> Proverbs 21:17

POETS AND POETRY

Poetry is the Devil's wine.

> SAINT AUGUSTINE
> *Contra Academicos*, c. 387

All poets are mad.

> ROBERT BURTON
> *The Anatomy of Melancholy*, 1621

I do not find that God has made you a poet; and I am very glad that he has not.

> LORD CHESTERFIELD
> Letter to his son,
> November 24, 1749

I know that poetry is indispensable, but to what I could not say.
JEAN COCTEAU
The Observer, London,
October 23, 1955

Turn pimp, flatterer, quack, lawyer, parson, be chaplain to an atheist, or stallion to an old woman, anything but poet; for a poet is worse, more servile, timorous and fawning than any I have named.
WILLIAM CONGREVE
Love for Love, 1695

Poets arguing about modern poetry: jackals snarling over a dried-up well.
CYRIL CONNOLLY
The Unquiet Grave, 1945

Poetry's unnat'ral; no man ever talked poetry 'cept a beadle on boxin' day.
CHARLES DICKENS
Pickwick Papers, 1836–37

Immature poets imitate; mature poets steal.
THOMAS STEARNS ELIOT
Philip Massinger, 1920

As things are, and as fundamentally they must always be, poetry is not a career, but a mug's game. No honest poet can ever feel quite sure of the permanent value of what he has written: he may have wasted his time and messed up his life for nothing.
THOMAS STEARNS ELIOT
*The Uses of Poetry and the
Use of Criticism*, 1933

I hate all boets and bainters.
Attributed to
KING GEORGE I OF ENGLAND

I was moved to go and speak to one of the wickedest men in the country, one who was a common drunkard, a noted whoremaster, and a rhyme-maker; and I reproved him in the dread of the mighty God for his evil courses.
GEORGE FOX
Journal, 1694

The man is either crazy or he is a poet.
HORACE
Satires, c. 25 B.C.

Whenever a poet praises the verses of another poet you may be sure that they are stupid and of no real value.

JEAN DE LA BRUYÈRE
Caractères, 1688

Perhaps no person can be a poet, or even can enjoy poetry, without a certain unsoundness of mind.

THOMAS BABINGTON MACAULAY
On Milton, 1825

Publishing a volume of poetry today is like dropping a rose-petal down the Grand Canyon and waiting for the echo.

DON MARQUIS
New York *Sun*
in the 1920s

Poetry is a comforting piece of fiction set to more or less lascivious music.

H. L. MENCKEN
Prejudices, Third Series, 1922

Poetry and consumption are the most flattering of diseases.

WILLIAM SHENSTONE
On Writing and Books, 1764

What poet would not grieve to see
His brother write as well as he?
But rather than they should excel,
Would wish his rivals all in Hell?

JONATHAN SWIFT
On the Death of Dr. Swift, 1731

Ye gods, what crime had my poor father
   done
That you should make a poet of his son?

JOHN VANBRUGH
The Confederacy, 1705

Poets, like whores, are only hated by each other.

WILLIAM WYCHERLEY
The Country Wife, c. 1673

POLITENESS

Politeness, n. The most acceptable hypocrisy.

AMBROSE BIERCE
The Devil's Dictionary, 1906, 1911

Politeness is fictitious benevolence.
SAMUEL JOHNSON
August 21, 1773, quoted in
James Boswell's *Tour to the Hebrides,*
1786

Politeness is organized indifference.
PAUL VALÉRY
Tel Quel, 1943

POLITICS AND POLITICIANS

Politics, as a practice, whatever its professions, has always been the systematic organization of hatreds.
HENRY ADAMS
The Education of Henry Adams, 1907

All political parties die at last of swallowing their own lies.
JOHN ARBUTHNOT
Quoted in Richard Garnett's
Life of Emerson, 1887

My deepest feeling about politicians is that they are dangerous lunatics to be avoided when possible and carefully humored: people, above all, to whom one must never tell the truth.
W. H. AUDEN
In *The English Auden,* edited by
Edward Mendelson, 1978

In politics, as in high finance, duplicity is regarded as a virtue.
Attributed to
MIKHAIL A. BAKUNIN

The standard of intellect in politics is so low that men of moderate mental capacity have to stoop in order to reach it.
Attributed to
HILAIRE BELLOC
After a term in the
House of Commons

Politics ruins the character.
Attributed to
OTTO VON BISMARCK

An honest politician is one who, when he is bought, will stay bought.
Attributed to
SIMON CAMERON

It was as dark as the inside of a Cabinet Minister.

> JOYCE CARY
> *The Horse's Mouth,* 1944

Contact with the affairs of state is one of the most corrupting of the influences to which men are exposed.

> JAMES FENIMORE COOPER
> *The American Democrat,* 1838

A politician is an arse upon which every one has sat except a man.

> Attributed to
> E. E. CUMMINGS

I have come to the conclusion that politics is too serious a matter to be left to the politicians.

> Attributed to
> CHARLES DE GAULLE

There is no act of treachery or meanness of which a political party is not capable; for in politics there is no honor.

> BENJAMIN DISRAELI
> *Vivian Grey,* 1824

Spare me the sight of this thankless breed, these politicians who cringe for favors from a screaming mob and do not care what harm they do their friends, providing they can please a crowd!

> EURIPIDES
> *Hecuba,* c. 425 B.C.

Politics is such a torment that I would advise every one I love not to mix with it.

> THOMAS JEFFERSON
> Letter to Martha Jefferson Randolph,
> 1800

Successful democratic politicians are insecure and intimidated men. They advance politically only as they placate, appease, bribe, seduce, bamboozle, or otherwise manage to manipulate the demanding and threatening elements in their constituencies.

> WALTER LIPPMANN
> *The Public Philosophy,* 1955

If experience teaches us anything at all, it teaches us this: that a good politician, under democracy, is quite as unthinkable as an honest burglar.

> H. L. MENCKEN
> *Prejudices,* Fourth Series, 1924

One has to be a lowbrow, a bit of a murderer, to be a politician, ready and willing to see people sacrificed, slaughtered, for the sake of an idea, whether a good one or a bad one.

HENRY MILLER
Interview, *Writers at Work,*
Second Series, 1963

Politics is the diversion of trivial men who, when they succeed at it, become important in the eyes of more trivial men.

GEORGE JEAN NATHAN
News summaries, July 9, 1954

Politicians . . . are the semi-failures in business and the professions, men of mediocre mentality, dubious morality and magnificent commonplaceness.

WALTER B. PITKIN
The Twilight of the American Mind,
1928

Get thee glass eyes;
And, like a scurvy politician, seem
To see the thing thou dost not.
WILLIAM SHAKESPEARE
King Lear, 1606

Politics, as the word is commonly understood, are nothing but corruptions.

JONATHAN SWIFT
Thoughts on Various Subjects, 1706

You can fool too many of the people too much of the time.

JAMES THURBER
The Thurber Carnival, 1945

A politician imitates the Devil, as the Devil imitates a cannon: whereso-ever he comes to do mischief, he comes with his backside towards you.

JOHN WEBSTER
The White Devil, c. 1608

The members who composed it [a typical Democratic national convention of the pre–Civil War era] were, seven-eighths of them, the meanest kind of bawling and blowing office-holders, office-seekers, pimps, malignants, conspirators, murderers, fancy-men, custom-house clerks, contractors, kept-editors, spaniels well-train'd to carry and fetch, jobbers, infidels, disunionists, terrorists, mail-riflers, slave-catchers, pushers of slavery, creatures of the President, creatures of would-be Presidents, spies, bribers, compromisers, lobbyers, sponges, ruin'd sports, expell'd gamblers, policy-backers, monte-dealers, duellists, carriers of conceal'd weapons, deaf men, pimpled men, scarr'd inside with vile disease, gaudy outside with gold chains made from the people's money and harlots' money twisted together; crawling, serpentine men, the lousy combinings and born freedom-sellers of the earth.

WALT WHITMAN
Origins of Attempted Secession,
c. 1880

POLYGAMY

Polygamy may well be held in dread,
Not only as a sin, but as a bore.
LORD BYRON
Don Juan, 1823

POPE, ALEXANDER

There are two ways of disliking poetry, one way is to dislike it, the other is to read Pope.

Attributed to
OSCAR WILDE

POPPINS, MARY

Mary Poppins is a junkie.
GRAFFITO

POPULARITY

When the multitude detests a man, inquiry is necessary; when the multitude likes a man, inquiry is equally necessary.

CONFUCIUS
Analects, 6th century B.C.

Popularity is a crime from the moment it is sought; it is only a virtue where men have it whether they will or no.

MARQUESS OF HALIFAX
Moral Thoughts and Reflections,
17th century

Popularity? Three-penny fame.
VICTOR HUGO
Ruy Blas, 1838

POPULAR PSYCHOLOGY

Popular psychology is a mass of cant, of slush, and of superstition worthy of the most flourishing days of the medicine man.

Attributed to
JOHN DEWEY

PORNOGRAPHIC FILMS

My reaction to porno films is as follows: After the first ten minutes, I want to go home and screw. After the first twenty minutes, I never want to screw again as long as I live.

ERICA JONG
Quoted in *Trivializing America,* by
Norman Corwin, 1983

POSITIVE

Positive, n. Mistaken at the top of one's voice.

AMBROSE BIERCE
The Devil's Dictionary, 1906, 1911

POSTERITY

We are always doing something for posterity, but I would fain see posterity doing something for us.

JOSEPH ADDISON
The Spectator, August 20, 1714

To invoke one's posterity is to make a speech to maggots.

LOUIS-FERDINAND CÉLINE
Voyage to the End of Night, 1932

POVERTY

Those who have not, and live in want, are a menace,
Ridden with envy and fooled by demagogues.

EURIPIDES
The Suppliant Women, c. 421 B.C.

POWER

Power tends to corrupt and absolute power corrupts absolutely.

LORD ACTON
Letter to Mandell Creighton,
April 5, 1887

How are the mighty fallen.
                    II Samuel 1:25

Power, like a desolating pestilence,
Pollutes whate'er it touches.
                    PERCY BYSSHE SHELLEY
                    Queen Mab, 1813

No one is fit to be trusted with power. . . . No one. . . . Any man who
has lived at all knows the follies and wickedness he's capable of. If he
does not know it, he is not fit to govern others. And if he does know it,
he knows also that neither he nor any man ought to be allowed to decide a single human fate.
                    SIR CHARLES PERCY SNOW
                    The Light and the Dark, 1961

PRAISE

Woe unto you, when all men shall speak well of you!
                    Luke 6:26, 50

Do you want to injure someone's reputation? Don't speak ill of him,
speak too well.
                    ANDRÉ SIEGFRIED
                    Quelques Maximes, 1943

PRAYER

Pray, v. To ask that the laws of the universe be annulled in behalf of a
single petitioner confusedly unworthy.
                    AMBROSE BIERCE
                    The Devil's Dictionary, 1906, 1911

Prayers are to men as dolls are to children. They are not without use
and comfort, but it is not easy to take them very seriously.
                    SAMUEL BUTLER
                    Note-Books, 1912

. . . when the gods wish to punish us they answer our prayers.
                    OSCAR WILDE
                    An Ideal Husband, 1895

PREDECESSORS

We have to hate our immediate predecessors to get free of their authority.

                    D. H. LAWRENCE
                    Quoted in Henry Miller's
                    The Wisdom of the Heart, 1941

PREDICTION

Prediction is very difficult, especially about the future.

NIELS BOHR
Quoted in *Time*, April 26, 1982

PRESBYTERIANISM

Not a religion for a gentleman.

Attributed to
KING CHARLES II of England

PRESENT

Present, n. That part of eternity dividing the domain of disappointment from the realm of hope.

AMBROSE BIERCE
The Devil's Dictionary, 1906, 1911

PRESLEY, ELVIS

Elvis Presley—bloated, over the hill, adolescent entertainer—had nothing to do with excellence, just myth.

MARLON BRANDO
Playboy, January 1979

PRESS

The press is the hired agent of the monied system, and set up for no other purpose than to tell lies where their interests are involved. One can trust nobody and nothing.

HENRY ADAMS
The Letters of Henry Adams, 1918

The press is like the air, a chartered libertine.

WILLIAM PITT THE ELDER
Letter to Lord Grenville, 1757

PRETTY

It is not easy to be a pretty woman without causing mischief.

Attributed to
ANATOLE FRANCE

PRIDE

God hates those who praise themselves.

SAINT CLEMENT
First Epistle to the Corinthians, c. 125

PRIESTS

Hell is paved with priests' skulls.
                    SAINT JOHN CHRYSOSTOM
                    De sacerdotio, c. 390

Priests are no more necessary to religion than politicians to patriotism.
                    JOHN HAYNES HOLMES
                    The Sensible Man's View of Religion,
                    1933

You robbers of the poor, you assassins, you brigands, you sacrilegious scoundrels!

                    JAN HUS
                    Simony, 1442

In all ages, hypocrites, called priests, have put crowns upon the heads of thieves, called kings.

                    Attributed to
                    ROBERT G. INGERSOLL

In every country and in every age the priest has been hostile to liberty. He is always in alliance with the despot, abetting his abuses in return for protection to his own.

                    THOMAS JEFFERSON
                    Letter to Horatio Gates Spafford, 1814

How ludicrous the priest's dogmatic roar!
The weight of his exterminating curse,
How light! and his affected charity,
To suit the pressure of the changing times,
What a palpable deceit!
                    PERCY BYSSHE SHELLEY
                    Queen Mab, 1813

PRIMA DONNA

My own objection to the prima donna is that, as a rule, she represents merely tone and technique without intelligence.
                    SIR ERNEST NEWMAN
                    A Musical Motley, 1919

PRIORITIES

From the cradle to the coffin, underwear comes first.
                    BERTOLT BRECHT
                    The Threepenny Opera, 1928

PRIVILEGE

One of the privileges of the great is to witness catastrophes from a terrace.

JEAN GIRAUDOUX
Tiger at the Gates, 1935

PRIZEFIGHTING

Hurting people is my business.

SUGAR RAY ROBINSON
To the New York State Boxing
Commission, May 23, 1962

PRIZES

Prizes bring bad luck. Academic prizes, prizes for virtue, decorations, all these inventions of the devil encourage hypocrisy, and freeze the spontaneous upsurge of a free heart.

CHARLES BAUDELAIRE
Curiosités esthétiques, 1868

PROFESSIONS

All professions are conspiracies against the laity.

GEORGE BERNARD SHAW
The Doctor's Dilemma, 1913

PROFESSOR

Whenever the cause of the people is entrusted to professors it is lost.

NIKOLAI LENIN
Political Parties and the Proletariat,
1917

Our American professors like their literature clear and cold and pure and very dead.

SINCLAIR LEWIS
Nobel Prize address, 1930

PROGRESS

What we call progress is the exchange of one nuisance for another nuisance.

Attributed to
HAVELOCK ELLIS

Industrialism is the systematic exploitation of wasting assets ... progress is merely an acceleration in the rate of that exploitation. Such prosperity as we have known up to the present is the consequence of rapidly spending the planet's irreplaceable capital.

ALDOUS HUXLEY
Themes and Variations, 1950

Is it progress if a cannibal uses knife and fork?

STANISLAW LEM
Unkempt Thoughts, 1962

Progress might have been all right once, but it's gone on too long.

OGDEN NASH
Quoted in *Reader's Digest,*
February 1975

PROLETARIAT

What the proletariat needs is a bath of blood.

BENITO MUSSOLINI
Speech in Milan, July 22, 1919

PROMISE

To make a vow for life is to make oneself a slave.

VOLTAIRE
Philosophical Dictionary, 1764

PROMISING

Whom the gods wish to destroy they first call promising.

CYRIL CONNOLLY
Enemies of Promise, 1938

PROOFREADER

Proofreader, n. A malefactor who atones for making your writing non-sense by permitting the compositor to make it unintelligible.

AMBROSE BIERCE
The Devil's Dictionary, 1906, 1911

PROPERTY

Property is theft.

PIERRE-JOSEPH PROUDHON
Qu'est-ce que la propriété?, 1940

PROPHECY

. . . a denial of possibility, of adventure, of the dream of becoming.

ANATOLE BROYARD
The New York Times,
October 16, 1977

Prophecy is the most gratuitous form of error.

GEORGE ELIOT
Middlemarch, 1871–72

PROPHET

If you keep saying things are going to be bad, you have a chance of being a prophet.

ISAAC BASHEVIS SINGER
Interview, *The Dick Cavett Show,*
July 17, 1978

PROSE

There are too many words in prose, and they take up altogether too much room.

EDWARD ARLINGTON ROBINSON
In conversation, 1912

PROTESTANT

The chief contribution of Protestantism to human thought is its massive proof that God is a bore.

H. L. MENCKEN
*Minority Report: H. L. Menken's
Notebooks,* 1956

Definition of Protestantism: hemiplegic paralysis of Christianity—and of reason.

FRIEDRICH WILHELM NIETZSCHE
The Antichrist, 1888

PROUST, MARCEL

I was reading Proust for the first time. Very poor stuff. I think he was mentally defective.

EVELYN WAUGH
Letter to John Betjeman,
February 1948

Reading Proust is like bathing in someone else's dirty water.
Attributed to
ALEXANDER WOOLLCOTT

PROVERB

I do not say a proverb is amiss when aptly and reasonably applied, but to be forever discharging them, right or wrong, hit or miss, renders conversation insipid and vulgar.
MIGUEL DE CERVANTES
Don Quixote, 1605

Proverbs may be called the literature of the illiterate.
FREDERICK S. COZZENS
Sayings, Wise and Otherwise, 1880

The use of proverbs is characteristic of an unlettered people. They are invaluable treasures to dunces with good memories.
JOHN HAY
Castilian Days, 1872

PRUDENCE

Prudence is a rich, ugly old maid courted by Incapacity.
WILLIAM BLAKE
The Marriage of Heaven and Hell,
1790

PSYCHOANALYSIS

Why should I tolerate a perfect stranger at the bedside of my mind?
VLADIMIR NABOKOV
Strong Opinions, 1973

Let the credulous and the vulgar continue to believe that all mental woes can be cured by a daily application of old Greek myths to their private parts.
VLADIMIR NABOKOV
Wisconsin Studies in Contemporary
Literature, Spring 1967

PUBLIC

There is not a more mean, stupid, dastardly, pitiful, selfish, spiteful, envious, ungrateful animal than the public. It is the greatest of cowards, for it is afraid of itself.
WILLIAM HAZLITT
Table-Talk, 1821–22

The public is pusillanimous and cowardly because it is weak. It knows itself to be a great dunce, and that it has no opinions but upon suggestion.

WILLIAM HAZLITT
Table-Talk, 1821–22

The public is a fool.

ALEXANDER POPE
*The First Epistle of the Second
Book of Horace*, 1737

The public be damned.

W. H. VANDERBILT
To two newspaper reporters aboard his
special train, approaching Chicago,
October 8, 1882

The public is a ferocious beast: one must either chain it up or flee from it.

VOLTAIRE
Letter to Mademoiselle Quinault,
August 16, 1738

PUBLICITY

The art of publicity is a black art.

Attributed to
JUDGE LEARNED HAND

PUBLIC LIBRARY

No place affords a more striking conviction of the vanity of human hopes than a public library.

SAMUEL JOHNSON
The Rambler, March 23, 1751

PUBLIC OPINION

There is nothing that makes more cowards and feeble men than public opinion.

HENRY WARD BEECHER
Proverbs from Plymouth Pulpit, 1887

Public opinion, a vulgar, impertinent, anonymous tyrant who deliberately makes life unpleasant for anyone who is not content to be the average man.

WILLIAM RALPH INGE
Outspoken Essays, First Series, 1919

Public opinion, in its raw state, gushes out in the immemorial form of the mob's fears. It is piped into central factories, and there it is flavored and colored, and put into cans.

H. L. MENCKEN
Notes on Democracy, 1926

That great compound of folly, weakness, prejudice, wrong feeling, right feeling, obstinacy, and newspaper paragraphs, which is called public opinion.

SIR ROBERT PEEL in 1820

One should respect public opinion insofar as is necessary to avoid starvation and keep out of prison, but anything that goes beyond this is voluntary submission to an unnecessary tyranny.

BERTRAND RUSSELL
The Conquest of Happiness, 1930

PUBLIC PLEASURES

The public pleasures of far the greater part of mankind are counterfeit.

SAMUEL JOHNSON
The Idler, August 12, 1758

PUBLIC RELATIONS

Don't tell the bastards anything.

WILLIAM FAULKNER
Letter to an agent, 1930, quoted in
Faulkner, by Joseph Blotner, 1974

PUBLIC SCHOOLS

Public schools are the nurseries of all vice and immorality.

HENRY FIELDING
Joseph Andrews, 1742

PUBLISHERS

As repressed sadists are supposed to become policemen or butchers so those with irrational fear of life become publishers.

CYRIL CONNOLLY
Enemies of Promise, 1938

If a man makes money by publishing a newspaper, by poisoning the wells of information, by feeding the people a daily spiritual death, he is the greatest criminal I can conceive.

FERDINAND LASSALLE, 1863

One of the signs of Napoleon's greatness is the fact that he once had a publisher shot.

SIEGFRIED UNSELD
The Author and His Publisher, 1980

I could show you all society poisoned by this class of person—a class unknown to the ancients—who, not being able to find any honest occupation, be it manual labor or service, and unluckily knowing how to read and write, become the brokers of literature, live on our works, steal our manuscripts, falsify them, and sell them.

VOLTAIRE
The Portable Voltaire, 1977

PURITANISM

Puritanism—the haunting fear that someone, somewhere, may be happy.

H. L. MENCKEN
A Book of Burlesques, 1920

PURPLE

Purple belongs to shady years, jewels to ugly women; a pretty girl is prettier undressed than dressed in purple.

PLAUTUS
Mostellaria, c. 251–184 B.C.

PYRAMIDS

As for the pyramids, there is nothing to wonder at in them so much as the fact that so many men could be found degraded enough to spend their lives constructing a tomb for some ambitious booby, whom it would have been wiser and manlier to have drowned in the Nile, and then given his body to the dogs.

HENRY DAVID THOREAU
Walden, 1854

I'M MAD AS HELL, AND I'M NOT
GOING TO TAKE IT ANY MORE.

PADDY CHAYEVSKY
SCREENPLAY, *NETWORK*, 1976

QUAKER

Quakers are under the strong delusion of Satan.

INCREASE MATHER
Remarkable Providences, 1684

QUEUE

"O, for an axe!" my soul cries out in railway stations, "to hew limb
from limb all the friends and Jezabels between me and the ticket office."

LOGAN PEARSALL SMITH
All Trivia, 1933

QUOTATIONS

I hate quotations. Tell me what you know.

RALPH WALDO EMERSON
Journal, May 1849

. . . a collection of a hundred good intellects produces collectively one
idiot.

CARL JUNG
In a book review, 1934

NEXT TO GENIUS, NOTHING IS MORE CLEAR-SIGHTED THAN HATRED.

CLAUDE BERNARD
PENSÉES, 1937

RADICALISM

Radicalism, n. The conservatism of tomorrow injected into the affairs of today.

AMBROSE BIERCE
The Devil's Dictionary, 1906, 1911

RADIO

Radio is a bag of mediocrity where little men with carbon minds wallow in sluice of their own making.

FRED ALLEN
Letters to Abe Burrows, 1945

Dictators have only become possible through the invention of the microphone.

SIR THOMAS INSKIP
The Observer, London, 1936

The gift of broadcasting is, without question, the lowest human capacity to which any man could attain.

HAROLD NICOLSON
The Observer, London, 1947

227

RATIONALISM

You can't be a rationalist in an irrational world. It isn't rational.

JOE ORTON
What the Butler Saw, 1969

RAVEL'S "BOLERO"

Ravel's *Bolero* I submit as the most insolent monstrosity ever perpetrated in the history of music. From the beginning to the end of its 339 measures it is simply the incredible repetition of the same rhythm . . . and above it the blatant recurrence of an overwhelmingly vulgar cabaret tune that is little removed . . . from the wail of an obstreperous back-alley cat.

EDWARD ROBINSON
The American Mercury, May 1932

READING

A well-read fool is the most pestilent of blockheads: his learning is a flail which he knows not how to handle, and with which he breaks his neighbor's shins as well as his own.

STANISLAS LESZCZYŃSKI,
King of Poland
Oeuvres du philosophe bienfaisant,
1763

I see no point in reading.

Attributed to
LOUIS XIV

There are some people who read too much: the bibliobibuli. I know some who are constantly drunk on books, as other men are drunk on whiskey or religion. They wander through this most diverting and stimulating of worlds in a haze, seeing nothing and hearing nothing.

H. L. MENCKEN
*Minority Report: H. L. Mencken's
Notebooks*, 1956

Much reading is an oppression of the mind, and extinguishes the natural candle, which is the reason of so many senseless scholars in the world.

WILLIAM PENN
Advice to His Children, 1699

REAGAN, RONALD

> . . . a triumph of the embalmer's art.
>> Attributed to
>> GORE VIDAL

REAL ESTATE

> What we call real estate—the solid ground to build a house on—is the broad foundation on which nearly all the guilt of the world rests.
>> NATHANIEL HAWTHORNE
>> *The House of the Seven Gables*, 1851

REALITY

> Everything is a dangerous drug except reality, which is unendurable.
>> CYRIL CONNOLLY
>> *The Unquiet Grave*, 1945

REASON

> I'll not listen to reason . . . Reason always means what someone else has got to say.
>> ELIZABETH CLEGHORN GASKELL
>> *Cranford*, 1853

> Reason? That dreary shed, that hutch for grubby schoolboys.
>> THEODORE ROETHKE
>> *The Collected Verse of Theodore Roethke*, 1961

> But is this struggle for a healthy mind in a maggoty world really after all worth it! Are there not soporific dreams and sweet deliriums more soothing than Reason?
>> LOGAN PEARSALL SMITH
>> *Trivia*, 1921

REFORM

> Every reform is only a mask under cover of which a more terrible reform, which dares not yet name itself, advances.
>> RALPH WALDO EMERSON
>> *Journals*, 1909–14

REFORMER

> A creature effeminate without being either masculine or feminine; unable to beget or bear; possessing neither fecundity nor virility; endowed

with the contempt of men and the derision of women; and doomed to sterility, isolation and extinction.

J. J. INGALLS
Speech in the Senate, c. 1885

RELATIVES

A poor relation is an odious approximation,—a preposterous shadow, lengthening in the noontide of your prosperity,—an unwelcome remembrancer,—a rebuke to your rising,—a stain in your blood, a blot on your scutcheon,—a rent in your garment,—a death's head at your banquet,—a lion in your path,—a frog in your chamber,—a fly in your ointment,—a mote in your eye,—a triumph to your enemy,—an apology to your friends,—the one thing not needful,—the hail in harvest,—the ounce of sour in a pound of sweet.

CHARLES LAMB
Poor Relations, 1823

The worst hatred is that of relatives.

TACITUS
Annales, c. 110

Relations are simply a tedious pack of people who haven't got the remotest knowledge of how to live, nor the smallest instinct about when to die.

OSCAR WILDE
The Importance of Being Earnest,
1895

RELIGION

And of all plagues with which mankind are cursed,
Ecclesiastic tyranny's the worst.

DANIEL DEFOE
The True-Born Englishman, 1701

All religions are ancient monuments to superstition, ignorance, ferocity; and modern religions are only ancient follies rejuvenated.

BARON D'HOLBACH
*Le Bon Sens, ou Idées naturelles
opposées aux idées surnaturelles*, 1772

You never see animals going through the absurd and often horrible fooleries of magic and religion. . . . Only man behaves with such gratuitous folly. It is the price he has to pay for being intelligent but not, as yet, quite intelligent enough.

ALDOUS HUXLEY
Texts and Pretexts, 1932

No man with any sense of humor ever founded a religion.
ROBERT G. INGERSOLL
Prose-Poems and Selections, 1884

Religion is a monumental chapter in the history of human egotism.
WILLIAM JAMES
The Varieties of Religious Experience,
1902

What excellent fools
Religion makes of men!
BEN JONSON
Sejanus, 1603

How many evils have flowed from religion!
LUCRETIUS
De rerum natura, c. 60 B.C.

Religion is the sign of the oppressed creature, the sentiment of a heart-less world, and the soul of soulless conditions. It is the opium of the people.
KARL MARX
Introduction to *Contribution to
the Critique of Hegel's Philosophy
of Right,* 1884

We have just enough religion to make us hate, but not enough to make us love one another.
Attributed to
JONATHAN SWIFT

Most religious teachers spend their time trying to prove the unproven by the unprovable.
OSCAR WILDE
In conversation

REPENTANCE

Repentance is the virtue of weak minds.
JOHN DRYDEN
The Indian Emperor, 1665

REPOSE

There is nothing so insupportable to man as complete repose, without passion, occupation, amusement, care. Then it is that he feels his nothingness, his isolation, his insufficiency, his dependence, his impotence, his emptiness.

BLAISE PASCAL
Pensées, 1670

RESEARCH

If you copy from one author, it's plagiarism. If you copy from two, it's research.

WILSON MIZNER
Quoted in *The Legendary Mizners,* by
Alva Johnson, 1953

RESIGNATION

What's all this resignation business? Doesn't anyone get fired anymore? You read the business pages of the paper, and presidents of corporations are always resigning. . . . Come on, fellas, we're not business tycoons, but we're not that dumb. You got canned.

ANDREW A. ROONEY
And More by Andy Rooney, 1982

RESPONSIBILITY

Responsibility, n. A detachable burden easily shifted to shoulders of God, Fate, Fortune, Luck or one's neighbor. In the days of astrology it was customary to unload it upon a star.

AMBROSE BIERCE
The Devil's Dictionary, 1906, 1911

REST

Rest is for the dead.

THOMAS CARLYLE
Journal, June 22, 1830

Too much rest becomes a pain.

HOMER
Odyssey, c. 8th century B.C.

Men tire themselves in the pursuit of rest.

Attributed to
LAURENCE STERNE

RETIREMENT

. . . statutory senility.

GENERAL EMMETT O'DONNELL
Newsweek, January 10, 1972

REVOLUTION

Every revolution evaporates and leaves behind only the slime of a new bureaucracy.

Attributed to
FRANZ KAFKA

"RHAPSODY IN BLUE"

How trite and feeble and conventional the tunes are; how sentimental and vapid the harmonic treatment, under its disguise of fussy and futile counterpoint! . . . Weep over the lifelessness of the melody and harmony, so derivative, so stale, so inexpressive.

LAWRENCE GILMAN
New York Tribune, February 13, 1924

RHETORIC

That pestilent cosmetic, rhetoric.
THOMAS HENRY HUXLEY
Science and Morals, 1886

RHUBARB

Rhubarb, n. Vegetable essence of stomach ache.
AMBROSE BIERCE
The Devil's Dictionary, 1906, 1911

RHYME

. . . no necessary adjunct or true ornament of poem or good verse, in longer works especially, but the invention of a barbarous age, to set off wretched matter and lame meter.

JOHN MILTON
Preface to *Paradise Lost*, 1667

RICH

The rich are the scum of the earth in every country.
GILBERT KEITH CHESTERTON
The Flying Inn, 1914

The rich aren't like us, they pay less taxes.

PETER DE VRIES
I Hear America Swinging, 1976

Go to now, ye rich men, weep and howl for your miseries that shall come upon you.

James 5:1, c. 60

It is easier for a camel to go through the eye of a needle, than for a rich man to enter into the kingdom of God.

>   Mark 10:25, c. 70

It is the wretchedness of being rich that you have to live with rich people.

>   LOGAN PEARSALL SMITH
>   *All Trivia*, 1949

RIGG, DIANA

Diana Rigg is built like a brick mausoleum with insufficient flying buttresses.

>   JOHN SIMON
>   Referring to Miss Rigg in a nude
>   scene in *Abelard and Heloise*,
>   by Ronald Millar; in *New York*
>   magazine, May 1970

ROAD

Road, n. A strip of land along which one may pass from where it is futile to go.

>   AMBROSE BIERCE
>   *The Devil's Dictionary*, 1906, 1911

ROCK AND ROLL

Commercial rock and roll music is a brutalization of one stream of contemporary Negro church music . . . an obscene looting of a cultural expression.

>   RALPH ELLISON
>   *Shadow and Act*, 1964

You have to blame Thomas Alva Edison for today's rock and roll. He invented electricity.

>   Attributed to
>   STAN GETZ

Rock is a corruption of Rhythm and Blues which was a dilution of the blues, so that today's mass-marketed noise is a vulgarization of a vulgarization.

>   BENNY GREEN
>   Notes for a Joe Turner album, 1976

Youth has many glories, but judgement is not one of them, and no amount of electronic amplification can turn a belch into an aria.

>   ALAN JAY LERNER
>   *The Street Where I Live*, 1978

Rock lyrics are doggerel, maybe.
> DAVE MARSH AND KEVIN STEIN
> *The Book of Rock Lists,* 1981

Rock and roll might best be summed up as monotony tinged with hysteria.
> VANCE PACKARD
> Testimony, Interstate Commerce
> Committee, U.S. Senate, 1958

It fosters almost totally negative and destructive reactions in young people. It smells phony and false. It is sung, played and written for the most part by cretinous goons and by means of its almost imbecilic reiterations and sly—lewd—in plain fact, dirty lyrics, and . . . it manages to be the martial music of every sideburned delinquent on the face of the earth. This rancid aphrodisiac I deplore.
> FRANK SINATRA
> Quoted in a lecture by Russell
> Sanjek, "The War on Rock," 1971

ROCK DRUMMERS

They should put them cats in a capsule and lose their asses in outer space.
> Attributed to
> ELVIN JONES

ROCK JOURNALISM

Rock journalism is people who can't write interviewing people who can't talk for people who can't read.
> FRANK ZAPPA
> *Rolling Stone,* December 28, 1978

ROCK MUSIC FESTIVALS

Those kids don't know anything. They're lying around in mud listening to a shitty sound system and eating day-old garbage, and they think they're having a good time. They're just being had, mister, had.
> BILL GRAHAM, rock "impresario"
> Quoted in *Loose Talk,* compiled by
> Linda Botts, 1981

ROGERS, WILL

This bosom friend of senators and congressmen was about as daring as an early Shirley Temple movie.
> Attributed to
> JAMES THURBER

ROMAN EMPIRE

The barbarians who broke up the Roman Empire did not arrive a day too soon.

RALPH WALDO EMERSON
"Considerations by the Way,"
The Conduct of Life, 1860

ROMANCE

When one is in love one begins by deceiving oneself, one ends by deceiving others. That is what the world calls romance.

OSCAR WILDE
The Picture of Dorian Gray, 1891

The worst of having a romance is that it leaves one so unromantic.

OSCAR WILDE
The Picture of Dorian Gray, 1891

ROUSSEAU, JEAN-JACQUES

He is surely the blackest and most atrocious villain, beyond comparison, that now exists in the world; and I am heartily ashamed of anything I ever wrote in his favor.

DAVID HUME
Letter to Hugh Blair, July 1, 1766

RUSSIA

The essential clue to Russian literature, as indeed to the mysterious Russian character, is that all Russians are shits. . . . They know they are shits, that their whole repulsive society is based on a succession of lies which nobody really believes. . . . The only proof that they are not, as Hitler believed, morally sub-human, is to be found in their occasional propensity to despair and suicide.

AUBERON WAUGH
Quoted in *Harper's*, December 1980

SABBATH

The "Sabbath" was born of asceticism, hatred of human joy, fanaticism, ignorance, egotism of priests and the cowardice of people.

ROBERT G. INGERSOLL
Some Mistakes of Moses, 1879

SAINT

Saint, n. A dead sinner revised and edited.

AMBROSE BIERCE
The Devil's Dictionary, 1906, 1911

The invocation of saints is a most abominable blindness and heresy; yet the papists will not give it up. The pope's greatest profit arises from the dead; for the calling on dead saints brings him infinite sums of money and riches, far more than he gets from the living.

MARTIN LUTHER
Table Talk, 1569

The history of the saints is mainly the history of insane people.

BENITO MUSSOLINI
Speech in Lausanne, July 1904

Saints should always be judged guilty until they are proved innocent.

GEORGE ORWELL
Shooting an Elephant, 1950

ST. PETER'S BASILICA, ROME

As a whole St. Peter's is fit for nothing but a ballroom, and it is a little too gaudy even for that.

JOHN RUSKIN
Letter to the Reverend Thomas Dale,
December 31, 1840

SAINT-SAËNS, CAMILLE

I'm told that Saint-Saëns has informed a delighted public that since the war began he has composed music for the stage, melodies, an elegy and a piece for the trombone. If he'd been making shell-cases instead it might have been all the better for music.

MAURICE RAVEL
Letter to Jean Marnold,
October 7, 1916

SARCASM

Sarcasm [is] the language of the Devil.
THOMAS CARLYLE
Sartor Resartus, 1836

"SARTOR RESARTUS"

Sartor Resartus is simply unreadable, and for me that always sort of spoils a book.

Attributed to
WILL CUPPY

SATIRE

Satire is what closes on Saturday night.
Attributed to
GEORGE S. KAUFMAN

Satire [is] always as sterile as it is shameful and is impotent as it is insolent.

OSCAR WILDE
The English Renaissance of Art, 1882

SATISFACTION

As long as I have a want, I have a reason for living. Satisfaction is death.
GEORGE BERNARD SHAW
Overruled, 1912

SAXOPHONE

The saxophone is a long metal instrument bent at both ends. It is alleged to be musical. The creature has a series of tiny taps stuck upon it, apparently at random. These taps are very sensitive; when touched they cause the instrument to utter miserable sounds, suggesting untold agony. At either end there is a hole. People, sometimes for no reason at all, blow down the small end of the saxophone, which then shrieks and moans as if attacked by a million imps of torture.

ANONYMOUS
London *Daily News*, 1927

The saxophone is the embodied spirit of beer.

Attributed to
ARNOLD BENNETT

SCAB

A scab is a two-legged animal with corkscrew soul, a waterlogged brain, a combination backbone of jelly and glue. Where others have hearts, he carries a tumor of rotten principles.

Attributed to
JACK LONDON

SCHILLER, FRIEDRICH VON

Schiller's blank verse is bad. He moves in it as a fly in a glue bottle. His thoughts have their connection and variety, it is true, but there is no sufficiently corresponding movement in the verse.

SAMUEL TAYLOR COLERIDGE
Table-Talk, June 2, 1834

SCHOLAR

Scholars are wont to sell their birthright for a mess of learning.

HENRY DAVID THOREAU
*A Week on the Concord and
Merrimack Rivers*, 1849

SCHOOL

School days, I believe, are the unhappiest in the whole span of human existence. They are full of dull, unintelligible tasks, new and unpleasant ordinances, brutal violations of common sense and common decency.

H. L. MENCKEN
"Travail," *The Baltimore Evening Sun*,
October 8, 1928

Show me the man who has enjoyed his schooldays and I will show you a bully and a bore.

> ROBERT MORLEY
> *Robert Morley: Responsible*
> *Gentleman,* 1966

Thou hast most traitorously corrupted the youth of the realm in erecting a grammar school: and whereas, before, our forefathers had no other books but the score and the tally, thou hast caused printing to be used.

> WILLIAM SHAKESPEARE
> *Henry VI,* Part II, c. 1591

At boarding schools . . . the relaxation of the junior boys is mischief; and of the senior, vice.

> MARY WOLLSTONECRAFT
> *A Vindication of the Rights of*
> *Woman,* 1792

SCHUMANN, ROBERT

A pathological case, a literary man turned composer.

> JAMES HUNEKER
> *Old Fogy,* 1913

SCIENCE

I hate and fear science because of my conviction that, for long to come if not for ever, it will be the remorseless enemy of mankind. I see it destroying all simplicity and gentleness of life, all the beauty of the world; I see it restoring barbarism under a mask of civilization: I see it darkening men's minds and hardening their hearts.

> GEORGE GISSING
> *The Private Papers of Henry Ryecroft,*
> 1903

If science produces no better fruits than tyranny, murder, rapine and destitution of national morality, I would rather wish our country to be ignorant, honest and estimable, as our neighboring savages are.

> THOMAS JEFFERSON
> Letter to John Adams, 1812

I am sorry to say that there is too much point to the wisecrack that life is extinct on other planets because their scientists were more advanced than ours.

> JOHN F. KENNEDY
> Address, Washington, D.C.,
> December 11, 1959

Science? Pooh! Whatever good has science done the world? Damned bosh!

GEORGE MOORE
To Philip Gosse, 1932

I almost think it is the ultimate destiny of science to exterminate the human race.

THOMAS LOVE PEACOCK
Gryll Grange, 1860

What is called science today consists of a haphazard heap of information, united by nothing, often utterly unnecessary, and not only failing to present one unquestionable truth, but as often as not containing the grossest errors, today put forward as truths, and tomorrow overthrown.

LEO TOLSTOY
What Is Religion?, 1902

Science robs men of wisdom and usually converts them into phantom beings loaded up with facts.

MIGUEL DE UNAMUNO
Essays and Soliloquies, 1925

SCOLD

A frank scold is a devil of the feminine gender; a serpent perpetually hissing, and spitting of venom; a composition of ill-nature and clamor. You may call her animated gunpowder, a walking Mount Etna that is always belching forth flames of sulphur, or a real Purgatory, more to be dreaded in this world than the pope's imaginary hothouse in the next.

ANONYMOUS
*Poor Robin's True Character of a
Scold,* 1678

SCOTLAND

A land of meanness, sophistry and mist.

LORD BYRON
The Curse of Minerva, 1815

I have been trying all my life to like Scotchmen, and am obliged to desist from the experiment in despair.

CHARLES LAMB
"Imperfect Sympathies," *Essays of
Elia,* 1820–23

The whole nation hitherto has been void of wit and humor, and even incapable of relishing it.

HORACE WALPOLE
Letter to Sir Horace Mann, 1778

SCREENWRITER

[Screen] writers are a little like gypsies swimming in an aquarium filled with sharks, killer whales, squid, octopuses and other creatures of the deep. And plenty of squid shit.

JOSEPH WAMBAUGH
Playboy, July 1979

SCULPTURE

Sculpture: mudpies which endure.

CYRIL CONNOLLY
Enemies of Promise, 1938

A fellow will hack half a year at a block of marble to make something in stone that hardly resembles a man. The value of statuary is owing to its difficulty. You would not value the finest head cut upon a carrot.

SAMUEL JOHNSON
March 19, 1776, quoted in James
Boswell's *Life of Samuel Johnson*,
1791

SEA

There are certain things—as, a spider, a ghost,
The income-tax, gout, an umbrella for three—
That I hate, but the thing that I hate the most
Is a thing they call the sea.

LEWIS CARROLL
"A Sea Dirge," 1869

The snotgreen sea. The scroutumtightening sea.

JAMES JOYCE
Ulysses, 1922

There is nothing so desperately monotonous as the sea, and I no longer wonder at the cruelty of pirates.

JAMES RUSSELL LOWELL
Fireside Travels, 1864

The thing itself is dirty, wobbly and wet.

WALLACE STEVENS
Quoted in *Along Came the Witch*,
by Helen Bevington, 1976

SEASHORE

It is the drawback of all sea-side places that half the landscape is unavailable for purposes of human locomotion, being covered by useless water.

NORMAN DOUGLAS
An Almanac, 1945

SECURITY

. . . an invitation to indolence.

ROD MCKUEN
Speech, 1968

SELF

Every man is crucified upon the cross of himself.

WHITTAKER CHAMBERS
Witness, 1952

What is hell? Hell is oneself,
Hell is alone, the other figures in it
Merely projections.

T. S. ELIOT
The Cocktail Party, 1949

I abhor myself, and repent in dust and ashes.

Job 42:6, c. 325 B.C.

He who despises himself esteems himself as a self-despiser.

SUSAN SONTAG
Death Kit, 1967

SELF-KNOWLEDGE

Know thyself! A maxim as pernicious as it is ugly. Whoever observes himself arrests his own development. A caterpillar who wanted to know itself well would never become a butterfly.

ANDRÉ GIDE
Les Nouvelles Nourritures, 1935

Self-knowledge is a dangerous thing, tending to make man shallow or insane.

KARL SHAPIRO
The Bourgeois Poet, 1964

SENTIMENTALITY

. . . the ostentatious parading of excessive and spurious emotion . . . the mark of dishonesty, the inability to feel.

JAMES BALDWIN
Notes of a Native Son, 1955

. . . the emotional promiscuity of those who have no sentiment.

NORMAN MAILER
Cannibals and Christians, 1966

SEX

The difference between sex and death is, with death you can do it alone and nobody's going to make fun of you.

WOODY ALLEN
Quoted in *Loser Take All: The Comic
Art of Woody Allen,*
by Maurice Yacowar, 1979

I know of nothing which brings the manly mind down from the heights more than a woman's caresses and that joining of bodies without which one cannot have a wife.

SAINT AUGUSTINE
Soliloquies, c. 387

I've tried several varieties of sex. The conventional position makes me claustrophobic. And the others give me either a stiff neck or lockjaw.

TALLULAH BANKHEAD
Quoted in *Playboy,*
December 1977

And how many lovers, even the most infatuated and tender ones, leave a stiffened arm under the other's neck. One wakes up worrying about having snored. This *forgetfulness of the other* in sleep—whether by night or day—seems to me to be the greatest of discourtesies and dangers.

NATALIE BARNEY
Quoted in *The Intimate Sex Lives of
Famous People,* edited by Irving,
Amy and Sylvia Wallace and
David Wallechinsky, 1981

I could be content that we might procreate like trees, without conjunction, or that there were any way to perpetuate the world without this trivial and vulgar way of coition: it is the foolishest act a wise man commits in all his life.

THOMAS BROWNE
Religio Medici, 1642

The pleasure is momentary, the position ridiculous, and the expense damnable.

Attributed to
LORD CHESTERFIELD

Of all the animals on earth, none is so brutish as man when he seeks the delirium of coition.

EDWARD DAHLBERG
The Edward Dahlberg Reader, 1967

We have too much sex on the brain, and too little of it elsewhere.

NORMAN DOUGLAS
An Almanac, 1945

The man takes a body that is not his, claims it, sows his so-called seed, reaps a harvest—he colonizes a female body, robs it of its natural resources, controls it . . .

ANDREA DWORKIN
In *Ms.* magazine, December 1976

Men and women, women and men. It will never work.

ERICA JONG
Fear of Flying, 1973

But in the Morning, No!
COLE PORTER
Song title, 1939

Coition sometimes called "the little death" is more like a slight attack of apoplexy.

PAULINE SHAPLER
The Feminist Guide, 1974

The act of procreation and the members employed therein are so repulsive, that if it were not for the beauty of the faces and the adornments of the actors and the pent-up impulse, nature would lose the human species.

LEONARDO DA VINCI
Notebooks, 1508–18

All this fuss about sleeping together. For physical pleasure I'd sooner go to my dentist any day.

EVELYN WAUGH
Vile Bodies, 1930

SHAKESPEARE, WILLIAM

Shakespeare never had six lines together without a fault. Perhaps you may find seven, but this does not refute my general assertion.

SAMUEL JOHNSON
October 19, 1769, quoted in James
Boswell's *Life of Samuel Johnson,*
1791

I think Shakespeare is shit. Absolute shit! He may have been a genius for his time, but I just can't relate to that stuff. "Thee" and "thou"—the guy sounds like a faggot.

GENE SIMMONS, member of the rock
group Kiss, in an interview

It was most injudicious in Johnson to select Shakespeare as one of his principal authorities [for his *Dictionary*]. Play-writers, in describing low scenes and vulgar characters use low language, language unfit for decent company; and their ribaldry has corrupted our speech, as well as the public morals.

NOAH WEBSTER
Letter to Thomas Dawes,
August 5, 1809

SHAW, GEORGE BERNARD

George Bernard Shaw, most poisonous of all the poisonous haters of England; despiser, distorter, and denier of the plain truths whereby men live; topsy-turvy perverter of all human relationships; a menace to ordered social thought and ordered social life; irresponsible braggart, blaring self-trumpeter; idol of opaque intellectuals and thwarted females; calculus of contrariwise; flipperty gibbet Pope of chaos; portent and epitome of this generation's moral and spiritual disorder.

HENRY ARTHUR JONES
My Dear Wells,
Letter XIX, 1921

I think Shaw, on the whole, is more bounder than genius; and though of course I admit him to be "forcible," I don't admit him to be "moral" . . . I couldn't get on with "Man and Superman": it disgusted me.

BERTRAND RUSSELL
Letter to G. L. Dickinson,
July 20, 1904

Bernard Shaw has no enemies but is intensely disliked by his friends.
OSCAR WILDE
Quoted in W. B. Yeats,
Autobiographies, 1926

SHELLEY, PERCY BYSSHE

Shelley I saw once. His voice was the most obnoxious squeak I ever was tormented with.

CHARLES LAMB
Letter to Bernard Barton,
October 9, 1822

He was a liar and a cheat; he paid no regard to truth, nor to any kind of moral obligation. It was mortifying to discover this, for I never saw a youth of whom I could have hoped better things.

ROBERT SOUTHEY
Letter to Henry Taylor,
February 29, 1830

SHIP

What is a ship but a prison?
ROBERT BURTON
The Anatomy of Melancholy, 1621

A ship is worse than a jail. There is, in jail, better air, better company, better conveniency of every kind; and a ship has the additional disadvantage of being in danger.

SAMUEL JOHNSON
March 18, 1776, quoted in James
Boswell's *Life of Samuel Johnson*,
1791

SILENCE

Silence is the wit of fools.
JEAN DE LA BRUYÈRE
Les Caractères, 1688

Sticks and stones are hard on bones.
Aimed with angry art,
Words can sting like anything.
But silence breaks the heart.
PHYLLIS MCGINLEY
The Love Letters of Phyllis McGinley, 1954

Silence is the most perfect expression of scorn.
GEORGE BERNARD SHAW
Back to Methuselah, 1921

SILK

If I kept a seraglio the ladies would all wear linen gowns, or cotton—I mean stuffs made of vegetable substances. I would have no silk: you cannot tell when it's clean.
SAMUEL JOHNSON
September 17, 1773, quoted in James
Boswell's *Tour to the Hebrides,* 1786

SIMPLICITY

Simplicity is the most deceitful mistress that ever betrayed man.
HENRY ADAMS
The Education of Henry Adams, 1907

SINCERITY

A little sincerity is a dangerous thing, and a great deal of it is absolutely fatal.
OSCAR WILDE
The Critic as Artist, 1891

SINGER

The tenor's voice is spoilt by affectation
and for the bass, the beast can only bellow;
In fact, he had no singing education, an ignorant,
noteless, timeless, tuneless fellow.
LORD BYRON
Don Juan, 1819–24

The lewd trebles squeak nothing but bawdy, and the basses roar blasphemy.
WILLIAM CONGREVE
The Way of the World, 1700

Her voice was precisely like a stringed instrument that one imagined to have fallen into disuse when the viola came along to replace it.
NOËL COWARD
Quoted by William Marchant in
The Privilege of His Company, 1975

He who sings worse let him begin first.
DESIDERIUS ERASMUS
Colloquia, 1516

All singers have this fault: if asked to sing among their friends they are never so inclined, if unasked they never leave off.

HORACE
Satires, 35 B.C.

Musicians have the reputation of being not overly bright. This happens to be only too fatally true in the case of singers.

ALEXANDER KING
Rich Man, Poor Man, 1965

Man was never meant to sing:
And all his mimic organs e'er expressed
Was but an imitative howl at best.
JOHN LANGHORNE
The Country Justice, c. 1766

A vile beastly rottenheaded foolbegotten, brazenthroated pernicious piggish screaming, tearing, roaring, perplexing, split-mecrackle crash-mecriggle insane ass of a woman is practicing howling below-stairs with a brute of a singing master so horribly that my head is nearly off.

EDWARD LEAR
Letter to Lady Strachey,
January 24, 1859

I am convinced that people applaud a prima donna as they do the feats of the strong man at a fair. The sensations are painfully disagreeable, hard to endure, but one is so glad when it is all over that one cannot help rejoicing.

JEAN-JACQUES ROUSSEAU
Discours sur les arts et sciences, 1750

I *hate* performers who debase great works of art: I long for their annihilation: if my criticisms were flaming thunderbolts, no prudent Life or Fire Insurance Company would entertain a proposal from any singer within my range, or from the lessee of any opera-house or concert-room within my circuit.

GEORGE BERNARD SHAW
May 30, 1894, in *Music in London,*
1890–94, 1931

SISTER

Big sisters are the crab grass in the lawn of life.

CHARLES M. SCHULZ
Peanuts, 1952

SITWELL, EDITH

I am fairly unrepentant about her poetry. I really think that three quarters of it is gibberish. However, I must crush down these thoughts otherwise the dove of peace will shit on me.

NOËL COWARD
Diary, November 21, 1962

So you've been reviewing Edith Sitwell's latest piece of virgin dung, have you? Isn't she a poisonous thing of a woman, lying, concealing, flipping, plagiarising, misquoting and being as clever a crooked literary publicist as ever?

DYLAN THOMAS
Letter to Glyn Jones, 1934

SIXTIES NOSTALGIA

I don't have one nostalgic bone in my body for the 1960s. I have no desire to go back to Woodstock and spend three days in the mud on "downers."

TIMOTHY LEARY
The New York Times,
October 19, 1976

SLANG

Slang, though humanly irreverent, tends to be inhumanly loveless. It lacks tenderness and compassion; its poetry has the effulgence of a soldier's brass buttons.

ANTHONY BURGESS
Quoted in *The New York Times*,
July 12, 1970

SLEEP

. . . an eight-hour peep show of infantile erotica.

J. G. BALLARD
*The Best Short Stories of J. G.
Ballard*, 1978

Sleep is gross, a form of abandonment, and it is impossible for anyone to awake and observe its sordid consequences save with a faint sense of recent dissipation, of minute personal disquiet and remorse.

PATRICK HAMILTON
Slaves of Solitude, 1947

Sleep is such a dull, stupid state of existence that even amongst mere animals we despise them most which are most drowsy.

WILLIAM LAW
*A Serious Call to a Devout and
Holy Life*, 1728

Sleep is the most moronic fraternity in the world, with the heaviest dues and the crudest rituals.

VLADIMIR NABOKOV
Quoted in *The New York Times*,
December 15, 1974

SMALL TALK

Where in this small-talking world can I find
A longitude with no platitude?

CHRISTOPHER FRY
The Lady's Not for Burning, 1948

SMITH, SYDNEY

A more profligate parson I never met.
Attributed to KING GEORGE IV

SMOKING

What smells so? Has somebody been burning a rag, or is there a dead mule in the backyard? No, the man is smoking a five-cent cigar.

EUGENE FIELD
The Tribune Primer, 1882

If you will study the history of almost any criminal, you will find he is an inveterate cigarette smoker.

HENRY FORD
Quoted by John Gunther in
Inside U.S.A., 1947

A custom loathsome to the eye, hateful to the nose, harmful to the brain, dangerous to the lungs, and in the black, stinking fume thereof nearest resembling the horrible Stygian smoke of the pit that is bottom-less.

> KING JAMES I OF ENGLAND
> *A Counterblast to Tobacco,* 1604

I want all hellions to quit puffing that hell fume in God's clean air.

> CARRY NATION
> Quoted in *Charmers and Cranks,*
> by Ishbel Ross, 1965

SOCIABILITY

Go very light on vices such as carrying on in society. The social ramble ain't restful.

> Attributed to SATCHEL PAIGE

The sole cause of man's unhappiness is that he does not know how to stay quietly in his room.

> BLAISE PASCAL
> *Pensées,* 1670

SOCIAL CONTRACT

. . . a vast conspiracy of human beings to lie to and humbug themselves and one another for the social good.

> H. G. WELLS
> *Love and Mrs. Lewisham,* 1900

SOCIALISM

The inherent vice of capitalism is the unequal sharing of blessings; the inherent virtue of socialism is the equal sharing of miseries.

> Attributed to WINSTON S. CHURCHILL

The function of socialism is to raise suffering to a higher level.

> Attributed to NORMAN MAILER

We should have had socialism already, but for the socialists.

> Attributed to GEORGE BERNARD
> SHAW

SOCIAL WORKERS

All those social workers are nigger lovers. You find me a social worker who ain't a nigger lover and I'll massage your ass, and I ain't queer.

> NORMAN WEXLER
> Screenplay, *Joe,* 1970

SOCIETY

Society is one vast conspiracy for carving one into the kind of a statue it likes, and then placing it in the most convenient niche it has.

RANDOLPH BOURNE
Youth and Life, 1913

Society is now one polish'd horde
Form'd of two mighty tribes, the bores and the bored.

LORD BYRON
Don Juan, 1823

Though the world contains many things which are thoroughly bad, the worst thing in it is society.

ARTHUR SCHOPENHAUER
Our Relation to Ourselves, 1851

Society is a madhouse whose wardens are the officials and the police.

AUGUST STRINDBERG
Zones of the Spirit, 1913

Society is always diseased, and the best is most so.

HENRY DAVID THOREAU
Excursions, 1863

SOCIOLOGY

Sociology is the science with the greatest number of methods and the least results.

JULES-HENRI POINCARÉ
La Science et l'hypothèse, 1903

These terrible sociologists, who are the astrologers and alchemists of our twentieth century.

MIGUEL DE UNAMUNO
Essays and Soliloquies, 1925

SOCRATES

The character of Socrates does not rise upon me. The more I read about him, the less I wonder that they poisoned him.

THOMAS BABINGTON· MACAULAY
Letter to T. F. Ellis,
May 29, 1835

Socrates belonged to the lowest of the low: he was the mob. You can
still see for yourself how ugly he was.

> FRIEDRICH WILHELM NIETZSCHE
> *The Twilight of the Idols,* 1889

SOLDIERS

A good soldier has his heart and soul in it. When he receives an order,
he gets a hardon, and when he drives his lance into the enemy's guts, he
comes.

> BERTOLT BRECHT
> *The Caucasian Chalk Circle,*
> translated by Eric Bentley, 1947

Soldiering, my dear madam, is the coward's art of attacking mercilessly
when you are strong, and keeping out of harm's way when you are weak.
This is the whole secret of successful fighting. Get your enemy at a disadvantage; and never, on any account, fight him on equal terms.

> GEORGE BERNARD SHAW
> *Arms and the Man,* 1894

SOLEMNITY

Solemnity is the shield of idiots.

> CHARLES DE SECONDAT DE
> MONTESQUIEU
> *Pensées et jugements,* 1899

SOLITUDE

Solitude is the playfield of Satan.

> VLADIMIR NABOKOV
> *Pale Fire,* 1962

SOLZHENITSYN, ALEXANDER I.

He is a bad novelist and a fool. The combination usually makes for
great popularity in the U.S.

> GORE VIDAL
> *Conversations with Gore Vidal,* 1980

SONG

Song: the licensed medium for bawling in public things too silly or sacred to be uttered in ordinary speech.

> Attributed to OLIVER HERFORD

SOPRANO

She was a town-and-country soprano of the kind often used for augmenting grief at a funeral.

Attributed to GEORGE ADE

Most of them sound like they live on seaweed.

SIR THOMAS BEECHAM
Newsweek, April 30, 1956

If she can strike a low G or F like a death rattle and a high F like the shriek of a little dog when you step on its tail, the house will resound with acclamations.

HECTOR BERLIOZ
À Travers Chants, 1862

The moment the human voice intrudes in an orchestral work, my dream-world of music vanishes. Mother Church is right in banishing from within the walls of her temples the female voice. The world, the flesh, and the devil lurk in the larynx of the soprano or alto, and her place is before the footlights, not as a vocal staircase to paradise.

JAMES GIBBONS HUNEKER
Ivory Apes and Peacocks, 1915

SOUL

The soul! That unhappy word has been the refuge of empty minds ever since the world began.

NORMAN DOUGLAS
An Almanac, 1945

SOUTH AFRICANS

Fancy, a whole nation of lower-middle-class Philistines!

OLIVE SCHREINER
Quoted by William Plomer in
Cecil Rhodes, 1933

SOUTH AND SOUTHERNERS

The palavery kind of Southerners; all that slushy gush on the surface, and no sensibilities whatever—a race without consonants and without delicacy.

WILLA CATHER
My Mortal Enemy, 1926

The South is one great brothel, where half a million of women are flogged to prostitution, or, worse still, are degraded to believe it honorable.

WENDELL PHILLIPS
Speech before the Massachusetts
Anti-Slavery Society, Boston,
January 27, 1853

SOUTHEY, ROBERT

Richard Porson: Yes Mr. Southey is a wonderful poet. He will be read when Homer and Virgil are forgotten.
Lord Byron: Yes, but not until then.

JOHN BERRYMAN
Love and Fame, 1970

SOUTH POLE

Great God! this is an awful place.
ROBERT FALCON SCOTT
Journal, January 17, 1912

SPACE

Outer space is no place for a person of breeding.
LADY VIOLET BONHAM CARTER
Consenting Adults, 1981

SPAIN

Spain imports tourists and exports chambermaids.
CARLOS FUENTES
The New York Times,
May 5, 1974

SPANISH

A feeble, imbecile, and superstitious race.

NAPOLEON I
To Barry E. O'Meara at St. Helena,
November 9, 1816

SPECIALIST

Specialized meaninglessness has come to be regarded in certain circles as a kind of hallmark of true science.
ALDOUS HUXLEY
Ends and Means, 1937

SPINACH

"It's broccoli, dear."
"I say it's spinach, and I say the hell with it."

E. B. WHITE
Caption of cartoon by Carl Rose,
The New Yorker, December 8, 1928

SPINOZA, BENEDICT

Let him be accursed by day, and accursed by night; let him be accursed in his lying down, and accursed in his rising up; accursed in going out and accursed in coming in. May the Lord never more pardon or acknowledge him; may the wrath and displeasure of the Lord burn henceforth against this man, load him with all the curses written in the Book of the Law, and blot out his name from under the sky. No one may speak to him, nor write to him. No one shall render him any service or stay under the same roof with him or within a distance of four yards, and none shall read anything written by him.

EDICT OF EXCOMMUNICATION
Amsterdam Synagogue, July 1656

SPORT

Sport begets tumultuous strife and wrath, and wrath begets fierce quarrels and war to the death.

Attributed to HORACE

I hate all sports as rabidly as a person who likes sports hates common sense.

H. L. MENCKEN
Heathen Days, 1943

Serious sport has nothing to do with fair play. It is bound up with hatred, jealousy, boastfulness, disregard of all rules and sadistic pleasure in witnessing violence: in other words it is war minus the shooting.

GEORGE ORWELL
Shooting an Elephant, 1950

SPORTSMAN

. . . a man who, every now and then, simply has to get out and kill something.

STEPHEN LEACOCK
Laugh with Leacock, 1943

SPRING

Spring Can Really Hang You Up the Most

> FRAN LANDESMAN
> Popular song, 1955

STATISTICS

Statistics are the triumph of the quantitative method, and the quantitative method is the victory of sterility and death.

> HILAIRE BELLOC
> *The Silence of the Sea*, 1941

The most exact of false sciences.

> JEAN CAU
> Quoted by Israel Shenker in
> *Words and Their Masters*, 1974

There are lies, damned lies, and statistics.

> Attributed to BENJAMIN DISRAELI

Statistics is the art of lying by means of figures.

> DR. WILHELM STEKEL
> *Essays*, 1922

STEELE, RICHARD

Steele might become a reasonably good writer if he would pay a little more attention to grammar, learn something about the propriety and disposition of words and, incidentally, get some information on the subject he intends to handle.

> Attributed to JONATHAN SWIFT

STEIN

I don't like the family Stein!
There is Gert, there is Ep, there is Ein.
Gert's writings are punk,
Ep's statues are junk,
Nor can anyone understand Ein.
Attributed to ARTHUR H. R. BULLER

STEIN, GERTRUDE

Miss Stein was a past master in making nothing happen very slowly.

> CLIFTON FADIMAN
> "Puzzlements," *Party of One*, 1955

Gertrude Stein's prose is a cold, black suet-pudding. We can represent it as a cold suet-roll of fabulously reptilian length. Cut it at any point, it is . . . the same heavy, sticky, opaque mass all through, and all along.

PERCY WYNDHAM LEWIS
Quoted in *The Third Rose: Gertrude
Stein and Her World,* by
John Malcolm Brinnin, 1959

STRANGER

Call no man foe, but never love a stranger.

STELLA BENSON
Poems, 1935

A wise man distrusts everyone he does not know.

JEAN DE LA FONTAINE
"The Fox, the Wolf and the Horse,"
1668

STRAUSS, RICHARD

Such an astounding lack of talent was never before united to such pretentiousness.

PETER ILYICH TCHAIKOVSKY
Letter to Modeste Tchaikovsky,
January 1888

STRAVINSKY, IGOR

His music used to be original. Now it is aboriginal.

SIR ERNEST NEWMAN
Musical Times, London, July 1921

STREISAND, BARBRA

. . . I realize with a gasp . . . that this progressively more belligerent caterwauling can sell anything—concerts, records, movies. And I feel as if our entire society were ready to flush itself down in something even worse than a collective death wish—a collective will to live in ugliness and self-debasement.

JOHN SIMON
Review of *A Star Is Born,* in *New
York* magazine, January 10, 1977

STUDENTS

Hard students are commonly troubled by gowts, catarrhes, rheums, cachexia, bradypepsia, bad eyes, stone, and collick, crudities, oppilations, vertigo, winds, consumptions, and all such diseases as come by over much sitting; they are most part lean, dry, ill-coloured; spend their fortunes, lose their wits, and many times their lives; and all through immoderate pains and extraordinary studies.

ROBERT BURTON
The Anatomy of Melancholy, 1621

STYLE

I am well aware that an addiction to silk underwear does not necessarily imply that one's feet are dirty. None the less, style, like sheer silk, too often hides eczema.

ALBERT CAMUS
The Fall, 1956

SUBJUNCTIVE

Damn the subjunctive. It brings all our writers to shame.

MARK TWAIN
Notebooks, 1924

SUBURBS

Slums may well be breeding-grounds of crime, but middle-class suburbs are incubators of apathy and delirium.

CYRIL CONNOLLY
The Unquiet Grave, 1945

SUCCESS

. . . the bitch goddess
WILLIAM JAMES
Letter to H. G. Wells,
September 11, 1906

Now that I'm here, where am I?
JANIS JOPLIN
Quoted in *Newsweek*,
March 28, 1977

Is it possible to succeed without any act of betrayal?

JEAN RENOIR
My Life and My Films, 1974

I think what's most disturbing about success is that it's very hazardous to your health, as well as to your daily routine. Not only are there intrusions on your time, but there is a kind of corrosion of your own humility and sense of necessary workmanship. You get the idea that anything you do is in some way marvelous.

JOHN UPDIKE
Time, October 18, 1982

It is not enough to succeed. Others must fail.

Attributed to GORE VIDAL

SUMMER

Do what we can, summer will have its flies. If we walk in the woods, we must feed mosquitoes.

RALPH WALDO EMERSON
"Prudence," *Essays*, First Series, 1841

SUN

Thank heavens, the sun has gone in, and I don't have to go out and enjoy it.

LOGAN PEARSALL SMITH
Afterthoughts, 1931

SUNDAY

The boredom of Sunday afternoons, which drove De Quincey to opium, also gave birth to surrealism: hours propitious for making bombs.

CYRIL CONNOLLY
The Unquiet Grave, 1945

SWIMMING POOL

I dislike immersing myself in a swimming pool. It is after all only a big tub where other people join you—makes one think of those horrible Japanese communal baths, full of a floating family, or a shoal of businessmen.

VLADIMIR NABOKOV
In a television interview, 1965

SWINBURNE, ALGERNON C.

Having read Mr. Swinburne's defense of his prurient poetics, Punch hereby gives him his royal license to change his name to what is evidently its true form—Swine-born.

ANONYMOUS REVIEW OF
SWINBURNE'S
Poems and Ballads in *Punch*, 1866

SWITZERLAND

Switzerland is a curst, selfish, swinish country of brutes, placed in the most romantic region of the world.

LORD BYRON
Letter to Thomas Moore,
September 19, 1821

In Italy, for thirty years under the Borgias, they had warfare, terror, murder and bloodshed, but they produced Michelangelo, Leonardo da Vinci and the Renaissance. In Switzerland, they had brotherly love; they had five hundred years of democracy and peace—and what did they produce? The cuckoo clock.

GRAHAM GREENE
Screenplay, *The Third Man*, 1949

The only interesting thing that can happen in a Swiss bedroom is suffocation by feather mattress.

DALTON TRUMBO
Additional Dialogue, 1970

SYMMETRY

Symmetry is ennui, and ennui is the very essence of grief and melancholy. Despair yawns.

VICTOR HUGO
Les Misérables, 1862

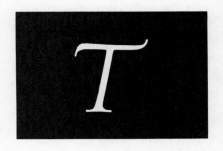

WE HAVE MET THE ENEMY AND
THEY ARE US.

WALT KELLY
POGO, 1949–60

TAFT-HARTLEY ACT

Every day I have matutinal indisposition that emanates from the nauseous effluvia of that oppressive slave statute.

JOHN L. LEWIS
Comment, news reports
of May 10, 1954

TALLEYRAND-PÉRIGORD, CHARLES-MAURICE DE

He is a silk stocking filled with dung.

NAPOLEON I
Comment, c. 1816

TAORMINA

It is a world of canaille: Absolutely. Canaille, Canaglia, Schweinhunderei, Stink-pots. Pfui!—pish, pshaw, Prrr! They all stink. . . . A curse, a murrain, a pox on this crawling, sniffling, spunkless brood of humanity.

D. H. LAWRENCE
Quoted by John Leonard in *The New
York Times*, September 4, 1980

TAPE RECORDERS

A monster with the appetite of a tapeworm ... through its creature, oral history, [it engenders] an artificial survival of trivia of appalling proportions.

> BARBARA TUCHMAN
> Quoted in *Newsweek*, August 5, 1974

TAYLOR, ELIZABETH

... she has a double chin and an overdeveloped chest and she's rather short in the leg. So I can hardly describe her as the most beautiful creature I've ever seen.

> RICHARD BURTON
> "Dubious Achievement Awards,"
> *Esquire*, December 1963

TEA

I view the tea-drinking as a destroyer of health, an enfeebler of the frame, an engenderer of effeminacy and laziness, a debaucher of youth and a maker of misery for old age.

> WILLIAM COBBETT
> "The Vice of Tea-Drinking," in
> *Cobbett's Weekly Political Register*,
> 1802–35

Teas, where small talk dies in agonies.

> PERCY BYSSHE SHELLEY
> *Peter Bell the Third*, 1819

Tea possesses an acrid astringent quality, peculiar to most leaves and exterior bark of trees, and corrodes and paralyzes the nerves.

> JESSE TORREY
> *The Moral Instructor*, 1819

TEACHER

I was, but am no more, thank God—a school teacher—I dreamed last night I was teaching again—that's the only bad dream that ever afflicts my sturdy conscience.

> D. H. LAWRENCE
> *Selected Letters of D. H. Lawrence*,
> 1932

The evil of men is that they like to be the teachers of others.

> MENG-TZU (MENCIUS)
> *Discourses*, c. 300 B.C.

The average schoolmaster is and always must be essentially an ass, for how can one imagine an intelligent man engaging in so puerile an avocation?

H. L. MENCKEN
Prejudices, Third Series, 1922

A fool is only troublesome, a pedant insupportable.

Attributed to NAPOLEON I

It is when the gods hate a man with uncommon abhorrence that they drive him into the profession of a schoolmaster.

SENECA
Epistolae ad Lucilium, A.D. 64

He who can does. He who cannot, teaches.

GEORGE BERNARD SHAW
Maxims for Revolutionists, 1903

Teaching has ruined more American novelists than drink.

GORE VIDAL
Oui magazine, April 1975

TELEPHONE

O misery, misery, mumble and moan!
Someone invented the telephone,
And interrupted a nation's slumbers,
Ringing wrong but similar numbers.

OGDEN NASH
"Look What You Did,
Christopher!" in
Many Long Years Ago, 1945

TELETHON

... the telethon evokes in me more terror than mirth. The spectacle of all that self-congratulatory yap masquerading as conscience, of all those chairmen of the board passing off public relations as altruism is truly sickening.

HARRY STEIN
Esquire, January 1982

TELEVISION

Television is a device that permits people who haven't anything to do to watch people who can't do anything. . . . [It is] radio fluoroscoped; the triumph of machinery over people; a "medium" because anything good on it is "rare."

Attributed to FRED ALLEN

Some television programs are so much chewing gum for the eyes.

JOHN MASON BROWN
Interview, July 28, 1955

Good heavens, television is something you appear on; you don't watch.

Attributed to NOËL COWARD

You have debased [my] child. . . . You have made him a laughingstock of intelligence . . . a stench in the nostrils of the gods of the ionosphere.

DR. LEE DE FOREST, inventor of the
audion tube, to the National
Association of Broadcasters.
Quoted in his obituary in *Time*,
July 7, 1961

It [television] is a medium of entertainment which permits millions of people to listen to the same joke at the same time, and yet remain lonesome.

T. S. ELIOT
New York Post, September 22, 1963

Television is an invention that permits you to be entertained in your living room by people you wouldn't have in your home.

DAVID FROST
Speaking on CBS-TV,
September 19, 1971

In an automobile civilization, which was one of constant motion and activity, there was almost no time to think; in a television one, there is small desire.

LOUIS KRONENBERGER
Company Manners, 1954.

I think anyone responsible for depicting violence on television should be kicked in the head, have his eyes gouged, his nose chopped off, be run through with a sword, and shot in the left hip.

GREGORY MCDONALD
Love Among the Mashed Potatoes,
1978

I invite you to sit down in front of your television set when your station goes on the air . . . and keep your eyes glued to that set until the station signs off. I can assure you that you will observe a vast wasteland.

NEWTON MINOW
In an address to the
National Association
of Broadcasters, May 10, 1961

Now that practically everybody is rioting around the world, what is to prevent the fifteen million American men and women now sixty-five years old or older from rising up in angry unison and beating the holy bejudas out of television? It is, as comforting thoughts go nowadays, a comforting thought.

JAMES THURBER
Credos and Curios, 1962

There are days when any electrical appliance in the house, including the vacuum cleaner, seems to offer more entertainment possibilities than the TV set.

HARRIET VAN HORNE
New York World-Telegram and Sun,
June 7, 1957

I hate television. I hate it as much as peanuts. But I can't stop eating peanuts.

ORSON WELLES
New York Herald Tribune,
October 12, 1956

TEMPERANCE

Damn temperance and he that first invented it.

CHARLES LAMB
Letter to Dorothy Wordsworth,
August 1810

TENNYSON, ALFRED, LORD

Tennyson is a beautiful half of a poet.

RALPH WALDO EMERSON
Journal, September 21, 1838

TENORS

Tenors are usually short, stout men (except when they are Wagnerian tenors, in which case they are large, stout men) made up predominantly of lungs, rope-sized vocal chords, large frontal sinuses, thick necks, thick heads, tantrums and *armour propre*. . . . It is certain that they are a race apart, a race that tends to operate reflexively rather than with due process of thought.

HAROLD C. SCHONBERG
Show, December 1961

A tenor is not a man but a disease.
HANS VON BÜLOW
Quoted by Harold C. Schonberg,
The Great Conductors, 1967

TEXAS

Texas is now the third most urbanized state (behind New York and California) with all the tangles, stench, random violence, architectural rape, historical pillage, neon blight, pollution and ecological imbalance the term implies.

LARRY KING
Atlantic, March 1975

If I owned Hell and Texas I'd rent out Texas and live in Hell.
GENERAL PHILIP H. SHERIDAN
Speech at Fort Clark, Texas, 1855

THEATER

There are no dull subjects, only dull playwrights.
ROBERT ANDERSON
Theater Arts, August 1955

I suppose I am not very serious; after all, I work in the theater.
JEAN ANOUILH
Preface to *Becket*, 1959

Stage plays are the most petulant, the most impure, imprudent, wicked, unclean, the most shameful and detestable atonements of filthy Devil-gods.

SAINT AUGUSTINE
Quoted by Diana Rigg,
No Turn Unstoned, 1983

The modern theater is a skin disease, a sinful disease of the cities. It must be swept away with a broom; it is unwholesome to love it.

ANTON CHEKHOV
Letter to I. L. Scheglov,
November 7, 1888

Spending time in the theaters produces fornication, intemperance, and every kind of impurity.

> SAINT JOHN CHRYSOSTOM
> *Homilies,* c. 388

You know, I go to the theatre to be entertained . . . I don't want to see plays about rape, sodomy and drug addiction . . . I can get all that at home.

> PETER COOK
> Caption to cartoon by Roger Law in
> *The Observer,* London, July 8, 1962

One should never take one's daughter to a theater. Not only are plays immoral; the house itself is immoral.

> Attributed to ALEXANDRE
> DUMAS FILS

With these summer shows, it isn't the heat, it's the bromidity.

> HERMAN MANKIEWICZ
> From a *New York Times* play review
> in the 1920s

To my mind there is no sadder spectacle of artistic debauchery than a London theatre; the overfed inhabitants of the villa in the stalls hoping for gross excitement to assist them through their hesitating digestions; an ignorant mob in the pit and gallery forgetting the miseries of life in imbecile stories reeking of the sentimentality of the backstairs.

> GEORGE MOORE
> *Confessions of a Young Man,* 1888

THEOLOGY

It [theology] is taught by demons, it teaches about demons, and it leads to demons.

> SAINT ALBERTUS MAGNUS
> *Summa theologiae,* 1280

Theologians are all alike, of whatever religion or country they may be; their aim is always to wield despotic authority over men's consciences; they therefore persecute all of us who have the temerity to unveil the truth.

> FREDERICK THE GREAT
> Letter to Voltaire,
> November 4, 1736

Whoever has theological blood in his veins is shifty and dishonorable in all things.

FRIEDRICH WILHELM NIETZSCHE
The Antichrist, 1888

The study of theology, as it stands in Christian churches, is the study of nothing; it is founded on nothing; it rests on no principles; it proceeds by no authorities; it has no data; it can demonstrate nothing; and it admits of no conclusion.

THOMAS PAINE
The Age of Reason, 1794

THINKING

Most people would die sooner than think; in fact, they do so.

BERTRAND RUSSELL
The Observer, London, 1925

Yond Cassius has a lean and hungry look;
He thinks too much: such men are dangerous.

WILLIAM SHAKESPEARE
Julius Caesar, 1599–1600

Thinking is the most unhealthy thing in the world, and people die of it just as they die of any other disease.

OSCAR WILDE
The Decay of Lying, 1889

THIRTY

Better than old beef is the tender veal;
I want no woman thirty years of age.

GEOFFREY CHAUCER
The Canterbury Tales, c. 1386

THOREAU

He [Thoreau] was unperfect, unfinished, inartistic; he was worse than provincial—he was parochial.

HENRY JAMES
Hawthorne, 1879

TIME

Tobacco, coffee, alcohol, hashish, prussic acid, strychnine, are weak dilutions; the surest poison is time.

RALPH WALDO EMERSON
"Old Age," *Society and Solitude*, 1870

TURKEY

What a shocking fraud the turkey is. In life preposterous, insulting—what foolish noise they make to scare you away! In death—unpalatable. The turkey has practically no taste except a dry fibrous flavor reminiscent of a mixture of warmed-up plaster of paris and horse hair. The texture is like wet sawdust and the whole vast feathered swindle has the piquancy of a boiled mattress.

CASSANDRA (WILLIAM CONNOR)
Daily Mirror, London,
December 24, 1953

TYPEWRITER

Typewriter quotha! . . . I could never say what I would if I had to pick out my letters like a learned pig.

JAMES RUSSELL LOWELL
Letter to Mrs. W. K. Clifford,
June 11, 1889

Someone gave me an electric typewriter but I can't write on it. There's no sense pretending you can use machinery that thinks faster than you do. An electric typewriter is ready to go before I have anything to say.

ANDREW A. ROONEY
Letter, August 23, 1983

I believe that composing on the typewriter has probably done more than anything else to deteriorate English prose.

EDMUND WILSON
Quoted in *The New York Times*,
November 10, 1976

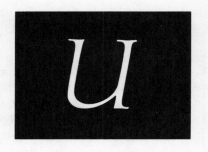

I HATE THEM WITH PERFECT
HATRED . . .

PSALMS 139:22

"ULYSSES" (JAMES JOYCE)

Ulysses is a dogged attempt to cover the universe with mud.

E. M. FORSTER
Aspects of the Novel, 1927

UMPIRE

Kill the umpire!

TRADITIONAL AMERICAN BASEBALL
DICTUM

UNDERTAKER

I have nothing against undertakers personally. It's just that I wouldn't want one to bury my sister.

JESSICA MITFORD
Saturday Review, February 1, 1964

UNITARIANISM

Unitarianism is, in effect, the worst of one kind of atheism joined to the worst of one kind of Calvinism, like two asses tied tail to tail.

SAMUEL TAYLOR COLERIDGE
Table Talk, April 4, 1832

276

UNITED NATIONS

. . . a forum in which nations meet in order handily to exchange insults, bribes, intimidations, and cynicisms.

WILLIAM F. BUCKLEY, JR.
National Review, November 16, 1957

UNSELFISHNESS

If people knew how much ill-feeling unselfishness occasions, it would not be so often recommended from the pulpit.

CLIVE STAPLES LEWIS
The Screwtape Letters, 1942

UPCOMING

If I read "upcoming" in the *Wall Street Journal* again, I will be down-coming and somebody will be outgoing.

BERNARD KILGORE,
former president of Dow Jones
(publisher of the *Wall Street Journal*)
Quoted by William Safire in
The New York Times Magazine,
April 29, 1979

VACUUM

A vacuum is repugnant to reason.

RENÉ DESCARTES
Principles of Philosophy, 1644

VAUDEVILLE

Vaudeville is a species of entertainment derived from the dregs of drama and musical comedy assembled in such wise that they shall appeal to the dregs of drama and musical comedy audiences.

GEORGE JEAN NATHAN
The American Mercury,
September 1929

VEBLEN, THORSTEIN

Tunnel under his great moraines and stalagmites of words, dig down into his vast kitchen midden of discordant and raucous polysyllables, blow up the hard, thick shell of his almost theological manner and what you will find in his discourse is chiefly a mass of platitudes—the self-evident made horrifying, the obvious in terms of the staggering.

H. L. MENCKEN
"Professor Veblen," *Prejudices,*
First Series, 1919

VEGETABLES

I have no truck with lettuce, cabbage and similar chlorophyll. Any dietitian will tell you that a running foot of apple strudel contains four times the vitamins of a bushel of beans . . . Every time I crush a stalk of celery, there is a whirring crash, a shriek of tortured capillaries, and my metabolism goes to the boneyard.

S. J. PERELMAN
Acres and Pains, 1947

VEGETARIANISM

Vegetarians have wicked, shifty eyes, and laugh in a cold and calculating manner. They pinch little children, steal stamps, drink water, favor beards . . . wheeze, squeak, drawl and maunder.

J. B. MORTON ("BEACHCOMBER")
By the Way, 1932

Vegetarianism isn't simply a distaste for animal products. It's a way of life: faddish, cranky and holier-than-thou.

HARRIET VAN HORNE
New York Post, June 23, 1978

VENICE

Venice would be a fine city if it were only drained.

Attributed to ULYSSES S. GRANT
During his visit to Venice, 1879

VICE-PRESIDENCY

It's about as much use as a pitcher of spit.

Attributed to JOHN NANCE GARNER

VICTIMS

I hate victims who respect their executioners.

JEAN-PAUL SARTRE
Les Séquestrés d'Altona, 1959

VICTORY

. . . a word to describe who is left alive in the ruins.

LYNDON B. JOHNSON
Speech, February 6, 1964

The technique of winning is so shoddy, the terms of winning are so ig-noble, the tenure of winning is so brief; and the specter of the has-been—a shameful rather than a pitiable sight today—brings a sudden chill even to our sunlit moments.

LOUIS KRONENBERGER
Company Manners, 1954

Nothing except a battle lost can be half so melancholy as a battle won.
ARTHUR WELLESLEY,
DUKE OF WELLINGTON
Dispatch, 1815

VIENNESE

The Viennese, speaking generally, dislike and misunderstand anything serious and sensible; they care only for trash—burlesques, harlequin-ades, magical tricks, farces and antics.

LEOPOLD MOZART
Letter to Lorenz Hagenauer,
February 3, 1768

VIGILANTE

No tin hat brigade of goose-stepping vigilantes or Bible-babbling mob of blackguarding and corporation-paid scoundrels will prevent the on-ward march of labor.

JOHN L. LEWIS
Time, September 9, 1937

VIOLIN

. . . when a man is not disposed to hear musick, there is not a more dis-agreeable Sound in Harmony than that of a violin.

RICHARD STEELE
The Tatler, April 1, 1710

He was a fiddler, and consequently a rogue.

JONATHAN SWIFT
Letter to Stella, July 25, 1711

VIRGIL

A crawling and disgusting parasite, a base scoundrel, and a pander to unnatural passion.

Attributed to WILLIAM COBBETT

VIRGINITY

Nature abhors a virgin—a frozen asset.

Attributed to CLARE BOOTH LUCE

Virginity is peevish, proud, idle, made of self-love, which is the most inhibited sin in the canon.

WILLIAM SHAKESPEARE
All's Well That Ends Well, c. 1600

VIRTUE

The extremes of vice and virtue are alike detestable; absolute virtue is as sure to kill a man as absolute vice is.

SAMUEL BUTLER
Note-Books, 1912

Punctuality, regularity, discipline, industry, thoroughness, are a set of "slave" virtues.

G. D. H. COLE
The Observer, London, 1922

Virtuous people are simply those who have either not been tempted sufficiently, because they live in a vegetative state, or, because their purposes are so concentrated in one direction, . . . not had leisure to glance around them.

ISADORA DUNCAN
My Life, 1927

I cannot praise a fugitive and cloistered virtue, unexercised and unbreathed, that never sallies out and sees her adversary, but slinks out of the race where that immortal garland is to be run for, not without dust and heat.

JOHN MILTON
Areopagitica, 1644

And be on thy guard against the good and the just! They would fain crucify those who devise their own virtues—they hate the lonesome ones.

FRIEDRICH WILHELM NIETZSCHE
Thus Spake Zarathustra, 1883

Women's virtue is man's greatest invention.

CORNELIA OTIS SKINNER
Paris '90, 1952

Virtue's an ass.
> JOHN VANBRUGH
> *The Provok'd Wife*, 1697

VIVALDI, ANTONIO

Vivaldi is greatly overrated—a dull fellow who would compose the same form so many times over.
> Attributed to IGOR STRAVINSKY

VOLTAIRE

The godless arch-scoundrel! Voltaire is dead—dead like a dog, like a beast.
> WOLFGANG AMADEUS MOZART
> Letter to his father, July 3, 1778

VOTING

I never vote *for* anyone. I always vote against.
> Attributed to W. C. FIELDS

VOX POPULI

Vox populi; vox humbug.
> GENERAL WILLIAM TECUMSEH
> SHERMAN
> Letter to his wife, June 2, 1863

WAGNER, RICHARD

I love Wagner, but the music I prefer is that of a cat hung up by its tail outside a window and trying to stick to the panes of glass with its claws.

Attributed to CHARLES BAUDELAIRE

The Prelude to [Wagner's] *Tristan und Isolde* reminds me of the old Italian painting of a martyr whose intestines are slowly unwound from his body on a reel.

EDUARD HANSLICK
Quoted in *Discord*,
by Norman Lebrect, 1983

This is not music—believe me! I have always flattered myself I know something about music—but this is chaos. This is demagogy, blasphemy, insanity, madness! It is a perfumed fog, shot through with lightning! It is the end of all honesty in art.

THOMAS MANN
A character in *Buddenbrooks*, 1901,
discussing *Tristan und Isolde*

Is Wagner actually a man? Is he not rather a disease? Everything he touches falls ill: he has made music sick.

FRIEDRICH WILHELM NIETZSCHE
The Twilight of the Idols, 1889

283

I like Wagner's music better than anybody's. It's so loud that one can talk the whole time without other people hearing what one says.

> OSCAR WILDE
> *The Picture of Dorian Gray,* 1891

WAITING FOR GODOT

. . . it is pretentious gibberish, without any claim to importance whatsoever. . . . It is nothing but phoney surrealism with occasional references to Christ and mankind. It has no form, no basic philosophy and absolutely no lucidity. It's too conscious to be written off as mad. It's just a waste of everybody's time and it made me ashamed to think that such balls could be taken seriously for a moment.

> NOËL COWARD
> Diary, August 6, 1960

WALES AND THE WELSH

The earth contains no race of human beings so totally vile and worthless as the Welsh.

> WALTER SAVAGE LANDOR
> Letter to Robert Southey

There are still parts of Wales where the only concession to gaiety is a striped shroud.

> GWYN THOMAS
> *Punch,* June 18, 1958

"The Welsh," said the Doctor, "are the only nation in the world that has produced no graphic or plastic art, no architecture, no drama. They just sing," he said with disgust, "sing and blow down wind instruments of plated silver."

> EVELYN WAUGH
> *Decline and Fall,* 1928

WALKING

I nauseate walking; 'tis a country diversion; I loathe the country.

> WILLIAM CONGREVE
> *The Way of the World,* 1700

WALTON, ISAAK

The quaint old cruel coxcomb, in his gullet
Should have a hook and a small trout to pull it.

LORD BYRON
Don Juan, 1823

WASHINGTON, GEORGE

As to you, sir, treacherous to private friendship (for so you have been to
me, and that in the day of danger) and a hypocrite in public life, the
world will be puzzled to decide whether you are an apostate or an im-
postor, whether you have abandoned good principles or whether you
ever had any.

THOMAS PAINE
Letter to George Washington,
July 30, 1796

WASHINGTON, D.C.

Washington is not a place to live in. The rents are high, the food is bad,
the dust is disgusting and the morals are deplorable.

HORACE GREELEY
New York Tribune,
July 13, 1865

Washington is an endless series of mock palaces clearly built for clerks.

ADA LOUISE HUXTABLE
The New York Times,
September 22, 1968

A city of southern efficiency and northern charm.

JOHN FITZGERALD KENNEDY
Quoted by William Manchester in
Portrait of a President, 1962

The loss of the physical city of Washington would be a benefit not only
to government, but to aesthetics.

PHILIP WYLIE
Generation of Vipers, 1942

WASHINGTON MONUMENT

Saw Washington monument. Phallic. Appalling. A national catas-
trophe ...

ARNOLD BENNETT
Journal, October 17, 1911

WATER

Fish fuck in it.
> Attributed to W. C. FIELDS
> When asked why he never drank water

And if from man's vile arts I flee
And drink pure water from the pump,
I gulp down infusoria
And quarts of raw bacteria,
And hideous rotatorae,
And wriggling polygastricae,
And slimy diatomacae,
And various animalculae
Of middle, high and low degree.
> WILLIAM JUNIPER
> *The True Drunkard's Delight*, 1933

Water taken in moderation cannot hurt anybody.
> MARK TWAIN
> *Mark Twain's Notebook*, 1935

Water ... doth very greatly deject the appetite, destroy the natural heat, and overthrow the strength of the stomach, and consequently, confounding the concoction, it is the cause of crudities, fluctuations, and windiness in the body.
> TOBIAS VENNER
> *Via recta*, 1620

WAUGH, EVELYN

You have no idea how much nastier I would be if I was not a Catholic. Without supernatural aid I would hardly be a human being.
> EVELYN WAUGH
> *Newsweek*, November 24, 1975

A disgusting common little man ... he had never been taught how to avoid being offensive.
> REBECCA WEST
> Quoted in *New York* magazine,
> November 11, 1980

WEALTH

In every dictatorship wealth is a sacred thing; in democracies it is the only sacred thing.
> ANATOLE FRANCE
> *Penguin Island*, 1908

What is true is that honesty is incompatible with the amassing of a large fortune.

MOHANDAS K. GANDHI
Non-Violence in Peace and War, 1948

Nothing is more intolerable than a wealthy woman.

JUVENAL
Satires, c. 110

Inherited wealth is a big handicap to happiness. It is as certain death to ambition as cocaine is to morality.

WILLIAM K. VANDERBILT
Press interview, 1905

WEATHER

Change of weather is the discourse of fools.

THOMAS FULLER
Gnomologia, 1732

WEBSTER'S DICTIONARY

Webster III, behind its front of passionless objectivity, is in truth a fighting document. And the enemy it is out to destroy is every obstinate vestige of linguistic punctilio, every surviving influence that makes for the upholding of standards, every criterion for distinguishing between better usages and worse. In other words, it has gone bodily to the school that construes traditions as enslaving, the rudimentary principles of syntax as crippling and taste as irrelevant.

WILSON FOLLETT
Atlantic Monthly, January 1962

WELL-BEING

There are moments when everything goes well; don't be frightened, it won't last.

JULES RENARD
Journal, c. 1900

WEST

What do we want with this worthless area, this region of savages and wild beasts, of shifting sands and whirlwinds of dust, of cactus and prairie dogs? To what use could we ever hope to put these great deserts and these endless mountain ranges?

DANIEL WEBSTER
As Secretary of State, 1852

WHISTLER, JAMES A. NCNEILL

For Mr. Whistler's own sake, no less than for the protection of the purchaser, Sir Coutts Lindsay ought not to have admitted works into the gallery in which the ill-educated conceit of the artist so nearly approached the aspect of willful imposture. I have seen, and heard, much of cockney impudence before now, but never expected to hear a coxcomb ask two hundred guineas for flinging a pot of paint in the public's face.

JOHN RUSKIN
Fors Clavigera, July 2, 1877

WHITMAN, WALT

Mr. Whitman's muse is at once indecent and ugly, lascivious and gawky, lubricious and coarse.

LAFCADIO HEARN
New Orleans Times-Democrat,
July 30, 1882

WIFE

If long, she is lazy;
   If little, she is loud;
If fair, she is sluttish;
   If foul, she is proud.

JOHN FLORIO
Second Frutes, 1591

Good wives and private soldiers should be ignorant.

WILLIAM WYCHERLEY
The Country Wife, 1673

WILDE, OSCAR

What a tiresome, affected sod.
NOËL COWARD
Diary, July 14, 1946

WINE

The point about white Burgundies is that I hate them myself . . . so closely resembling a blend of cold chalk soup and alum cordial with an additive or two to bring it to the color of children's pee.

KINGSLEY AMIS
The Green Man, 1970

The Spanish wine, my God, it is foul, catpiss is champagne compared, this is the sulphurous urination of some aged horse.

D. H. LAWRENCE
Letter to Rhys Davis, April 25, 1929

Look not thou upon the wine when it is red, when it giveth his color in the cup, when it moveth itself aright. At the last it biteth like a serpent, and stingeth like an adder.

Proverbs 23:31–32

The Germans are exceedingly fond of Rhine wines. . . . One tells them from vinegar by the label.

MARK TWAIN
A Tramp Abroad, 1880

WINTER

Winter changes into stone the water of heaven and the heart of man.
VICTOR HUGO
Les Misérables, 1862

WISDOM

What is all wisdom save a collection of platitudes.
NORMAN DOUGLAS
South Wind, 1917

WIT

Wit is educated insolence.
ARISTOTLE
Rhetoric, c. 322 B.C.

Fools are only laughed at; wits are hated.
ALEXANDER POPE
Prologue for Three Hours After
Marriage, 1717

WOLFE, THOMAS

If it must be Thomas, let it be Mann, and if it must be Wolfe let it be Nero, but let it never be Thomas Wolfe.

PETER DE VRIES
Comfort Me with Apples, 1956

WOMEN

As regards the individual nature, woman is defective and misbegotten.
SAINT THOMAS AQUINAS
Summa Theologica, c. 1265–74

There's nothing in the world worse than woman—save some other woman.
ARISTOPHANES
Thesmophoriazusae, 411 B.C.

Woman may be said to be an inferior man.
ARISTOTLE
Poetics, c. 322 B.C.

There is no other purgatory but a woman.
BEAUMONT AND FLETCHER
The Scornful Lady, c. 1614

The only position for women in SNCC is prone.
Attributed to
STOKELEY CARMICHAEL in 1966

A woman should be covered with shame by the thought that she is a woman.
CLEMENT OF ALEXANDRIA
Paedagogus, c. 190

Deceit is the game of small minds, and is thus the proper pursuit of women.
PIERRE CORNEILLE
Nicomède, 1651

Women, at best, are bad.
THOMAS DEKKER
The Honest Whore, 1604

The one thing civilization couldn't do anything about—women.
SHELAGH DELANEY
A Taste of Honey, 1958

The most winning woman I ever knew was hanged for poisoning three little children for their insurance money.
SIR ARTHUR CONAN DOYLE
The Sign of Four, 1890

All wickedness is but little to the wickedness of a woman.
Ecclesiasticus 25:19, c. 180 B.C.

Strange that God hath given to men salves for the venom of all creeping
   pests,
But none hath ever yet devised a balm
For venomous woman, worse than fire or viper.

EURIPIDES
Andromache, c. 426 B.C.

Neither earth nor ocean produces a creature as savage and monstrous as
woman.

EURIPIDES
Hecuba, c. 425 B.C.

Women are like elephants to me: I like to look at them, but I wouldn't
want to own one.

Attributed to W. C. FIELDS

A Woman Is a Sometime Thing
   DU BOSE HEYWARD
Song from *Porgy and Bess,* 1935

How can he be clean that is born of a woman?

Job c. 325 B.C.

The female of the species is more deadly than the male.

RUDYARD KIPLING
The Female of the Species, 1911

... a rag, a bone and a hank of hair.
   RUDYARD KIPLING
   The Vampire, 1897

The First Blast of the Trumpet Against the Monstrous Regiment of
Women.

JOHN KNOX
Title of pamphlet, 1558

A woman occasionally is quite a serviceable substitute for masturbation.
It takes an abundance of imagination, to be sure.

Attributed to KARL KRAUS

You needn't groan when a girl is born—she may in time be the mother
of a man!

D. H. LAWRENCE
Letter to Blanche Jennings,
May 13, 1908

There are many wild beasts on land and in the sea, but the beastliest of all is woman.

MENANDER
The Changeling, 4th–3rd century B.C.

Woman was God's second mistake.
FRIEDRICH WILHELM NIETZSCHE
The Antichrist, 1888

Thou goest to women? Forget not thy whip!

Attributed to
FRIEDRICH WILHELM NIETZSCHE

The female sex is in some respects inferior to the male sex, both as regards body and soul.

PLATO
The Republic, c. 370 B.C.

Two women are worse than one.
PLAUTUS
Curculio, c. 200 B.C.

There is a good principle which created order, light and man, and an evil principle which created chaos, darkness and women.

Attributed to PYTHAGORAS,
6th century B.C.

When a woman thinks, she thinks evil.
Attributed to SENECA, 1st century

Frailty, thy name is woman!
WILLIAM SHAKESPEARE
Hamlet, c. 1601

These anthropomorphs, these half apes, this horde of half-developed animals, these women whose intellects are of the Age of Bronze.
AUGUST STRINDBERG
Comrades, 1890

Woman is the lesser man.
ALFRED, LORD TENNYSON
Locksley Hall, 1886

I hate women because they always know where things are.
Attributed to JAMES THURBER

Woman is the very root of wickedness, the cause of the bitterest pain, a mine of suffering.

> TULSĪ DĀS
> *Rāmāyan*, 1574

Wicked women bother one. Good women bore one. That is the only difference between them.

> OSCAR WILDE
> *Lady Windermere's Fan*, 1892

WORDS

Religion—freedom—vengeance—what you will,
A word's enough to raise mankind to kill.

> LORD BYRON
> *Lara*, 1814

Articulate words are a harsh clamor and dissonance. When man arrives at his highest perfection, he will again be dumb!

> NATHANIEL HAWTHORNE
> *American Notebooks*,
> April 1841

She speaks poniards, and every word stabs: if her breath were as terrible as her terminations, there were no living near her; she would infect to the north star.

> WILLIAM SHAKESPEARE
> *Much Ado About Nothing*, c. 1599

WORK

I never forget that work is a curse—which is why I've never made it a habit.

> BLAISE CENDRARS
> *Writers at Work*, Third Series, 1967

I do not like work even when another person does it.

> Attributed to MARK TWAIN

Work is the curse of the drinking classes.

> Attributed to OSCAR WILDE
> In conversation

WORLD

That cold accretion called the world, so terrible in the mass, is so unformidable, even pitiable, in its units.

> THOMAS HARDY
> *Tess of the D'Urbervilles*, 1891

The world just doesn't work. It's an idea whose time is gone.
> JOSEPH HELLER
> *Something Happened,* 1974

The world is a comedy to those that think, a tragedy to those that feel.
> HORACE WALPOLE
> Letter to Sir Horace Mann,
> December 31, 1769

The world is a stage, but the play is badly cast.
> OSCAR WILDE
> *Lord Arthur Saville's Crime,* 1887

The world is too much with us . . .
> WILLIAM WORDSWORTH
> *Sonnets,* 1838

WRITERS AND WRITING

Against the disease of writing one must take special precautions, since it is a dangerous and contagious disease.
> PIERRE ABÉLARD
> Letter 8 to Héloïse, 12th century

All writing is pigshit.
Attributed to ANTONIN ARTAUD

Of all fatiguing, futile, empty trades, the worst, I suppose, is writing about writing.
> HILAIRE BELLOC
> *The Silence of the Sea,* 1941

No wonder the really powerful men in our society, whether politicians or scientists, hold writers and poets in contempt. They do it because they get no evidence from modern literature that anybody is thinking about any significant question.
> SAUL BELLOW
> *Writers at Work,* Third Series, 1967

Every writer without exception is a masochist, a sadist, a peeping Tom, an exhibitionist, a narcissist, an "injustice collector" and a depressed person constantly haunted by fears of unproductivity.
> EDMUND BERGLER, M.D.
> Quoted by Kenneth Tynan in *Tynan*
> *Right and Left,* 1967

Writers are always selling somebody out.
JOAN DIDION
Slouching Towards Bethlehem, 1968

There is no denying the fact that writers should be read but not seen.
Rarely are they a winsome sight.
EDNA FERBER
A Kind of Magic, 1963

Who knows whether in retirement I shall be tempted to the last infirmity of mundane minds, which is to write a book.
GEOFFREY FISHER
Final address as Archbishop of
Canterbury, May 12, 1961

To practice art in order to earn money, flatter the public, spin facetious or dismal yarns for reputation or cash—that is the most ignoble of professions.
GUSTAVE FLAUBERT
Letter to his mother, April 8, 1851

What! Another of those damned, fat, square, thick books! Always scribble, scribble, scribble, eh, Mr. Gibbon?
THE DUKE OF GLOUCESTER
To Edward Gibbon on
being presented a copy of Volume
III of *The Decline and Fall of
the Roman Empire*, 1781

Authors are easy enough to get on with—if you are fond of children.
MICHAEL JOSEPH
The Observer, London, 1949

Beware of the scribes, which love to go in long clothing, and love salutations in the marketplaces, and the chief seats in the synagogues, and the uppermost rooms at feasts: which devour widows' houses, and for a pretense make long prayers: these shall receive greater damnation.
Mark 12:38–40, c. A.D. 80

If you want to get rich from writing, write the sort of thing that's read by persons who move their lips when they're reading to themselves.
Attributed to DON MARQUIS

All writers are vain, selfish, and lazy, and at the very bottom of their motives there lies a mystery. Writing a book is a horrible, exhausting struggle, like a long bout of some painful illness. One would never undertake such a thing if one were not driven on by some demon whom one can neither resist nor understand. For all one knows that demon is simply the same instinct that makes a baby squall for attention.

GEORGE ORWELL
Why I Write, 1947

One reason the human race has such a low opinion of itself is that it gets so much of its wisdom from writers.

WILFRID SHEED
The Good Word, 1978

Writing is not a profession but a vocation of unhappiness.

GEORGES SIMENON
Writers at Work, First Series, 1958

Every author, however modest, keeps a most outrageous vanity chained like a madman in the padded cell of his breast.

LOGAN PEARSALL SMITH
Afterthoughts, 1931

YOUTH

I never felt that there was anything enviable in youth. I cannot recall that any of us, as youths, admired our condition to excess or had a desire to prolong it.

BERNARD BERENSON
Rumor and Reflection, 1952

Today's younger generation is no worse than my own. We were just as ignorant and repulsive as they are, but nobody listened to us.

AL CAPP
Quoted in *Education Digest,*
September 1968

Youth is a disease from which we all recover.

DOROTHY FULDHEIM
A Thousand Friends, 1974

Their intolerance is breathtaking. Do your thing means do their thing.

PAUL GOODMAN
The New Reformation, 1970

It's time to declare war on the mindless Youth Cult that has our time in its grip, demoralizing our people, weakening our system, . . . wasting

297

our experience, betraying our democracy, and blowing out our brains.

GARSON KANIN
*It Takes a Long Time to Become
Young,* 1975

Most young people think they are natural when they are only boorish and rude.

FRANÇOIS, DUC
DE LA ROCHEFOUCAULD
Maxims, 1665

Youth is a wonderful thing. What a crime to waste it on children.

Attributed to
GEORGE BERNARD SHAW

What's more enchanting than the voices of young people, when you can't hear what they say?

LOGAN PEARSALL SMITH
Afterthoughts, 1934

The denunciation of the young is a necessary part of the hygiene of older people, and greatly assists the circulation of the blood.

LOGAN PEARSALL SMITH
All Trivia, 1945

What is youth except a man or woman before it is ready or fit to be seen?

EVELYN WAUGH
A Little Order, 1981

YE SERPENTS, YE GENERATION OF
VIPERS, HOW CAN YE ESCAPE THE
DAMNATION OF HELL?

MATTHEW 23:33

Z

Thou whoreson Zed! thou unnecessary letter!

WILLIAM SHAKESPEARE
King Lear, 1606

ZEAL

The zeal of friends it is that knocks me down, and not the hate of enemies.

JOHANN CHRISTOPH FRIEDRICH VON
SCHILLER
Wallenstein's Death, 1799

Above all, no zeal!

Attributed to
CHARLES-MAURICE DE TALLEYRAND-
PÉRIGORD

ZOLA, ÉMILE

His work is evil, and he is one of those unhappy beings of whom one can say that it would be better had he never been born.

ANATOLE FRANCE
In a review of Zola's
La Terre, 1888

299

Zoo

. . . an idiotic show to gape at on Sunday afternoons . . . that the young
of the species may be instructed in the methods of amour prevailing
among chimpanzees and become privy to the technic employed by jag-
uars, hyenas and polar bears in ridding themselves of lice . . . a form of
idle and witless amusement compared to which a visit to a penitentiary,
or even to a state legislature in session is informing, stimulating and en-
nobling.

H. L. MENCKEN
New York Evening Mail,
February 2, 1918

Nat Shapiro was, over the course of his life, a writer, publisher, record company executive, and a press agent. He produced hundreds of records by such artists as Barbra Streisand, Marlene Dietrich, Nina Simone, Yves Montand, and Michel Legrand, and he was creative godfather to such innovative musicals as *Hair* and *Jacques Brel Is Alive and Well and Living in Paris.* He was editor and publisher of the definitive six-volume *Popular Music: An Annotated Index of American Popular Songs.* He was also coauthor (with Nat Hentoff) of *Hear Me Talkin' to Ya* and *The Jazz Makers,* two standard books on jazz, and compiled *An Encyclopedia of Quotations About Music.* He considered himself a romantic cynic and a conservative anarchist and was a fascinated observer of what he viewed as the "recline and pall of Western civilization."